RATS
Handbook for
Econometric Time Series

WALTER ENDERS

Iowa State University

JOHN WILEY & SONS, INC.

NEW YORK   CHICHESTER   BRISBANE   TORONTO   SINGAPORE

ISBN 0-471-14894-6

Printed in the United States of America

10 9 8 7 6 5 4 3 2 1

Preface

The idea for this handbook was borne shorty after the publication of my *Applied Econometric Time-Series* (New York: John Wiley & Sons) 1995. Many readers contacted me requesting information on how they could perform the estimations covered in the text. In a limited sense, this handbook is intended for those readers. More generally, this manuscript is intended to be a stand-alone workbook for RATS users. Towards this end, each chapter contains an overview of a particular topic in time-series analysis. Next, the chapter discusses those RATS instructions and procedures relevant to the topic. The topic and the appropriate use of the RATS instructions are illustrated with a number of sample programs along with a detailed discussion of the output. The disk included with this handbook provides the data sets necessary to perform the estimations described in the text. In addition, each sample program is contained in a file ending with the suffix *.PRG and the program and the associated output are contained in a file ending with the suffix *.OUT. If you work through the sample programs carefully, you should be able to modify them so as to conduct your own time-series analysis.

The descriptions and programs in this handbook are intended to be compatible with all versions of RATS. If you have RATS 4.0 or later, you should have no trouble running any of the programs as they appear on the data disk. Those with older versions of the program will not be able to estimate the ARCH-type models discussed in Chapter 3. Some RATS procedures can be downloaded from the RATS bulletin board. I have provided instruction for the use of some of the more important of these procedures (especially the JOHANSEN.400 procedure). In addition, there is an Introduction to CATS in RATS.

I would like to thank my wife Linda for typing furiously when the diskette containing Chapter 5 crashed and for putting up with my rantings. Harvey Cutler (Colorado State University) helped me clarify some of the material in Chapter 3. Most of all, I would like to thank the readers of my *Applied Econometric Time-Series* who encouraged me to publish a set of programs that can be used to estimate relatively sophisticated time-series models.

In spite of all my efforts, some errors have undoubtedly crept into the text. Portions of the manuscript that are crystal clear to me, will surely be opaque to others. I plan to keep a list of corrections and clarifications. You can receive a copy (of what I hope is a short list) if you send me an e-mail message at *enders@iastate.edu*.

Contents

Chapter 1: Introduction to RATS   **1**
  Preparing the Data   2
  Linear Regression   10
  Additional Regression Topics   12
  A Model of the U.S. Wholesale Price Index   13
  Additional Exercises   21

Chapter 2: Stationary Time-Series   **23**
  Theoretical Background   23
    1. Stationarity   23
    2. ARIMA processes   24
    3. Autocorrelation and partial autocorrelation functions   25
    4. The Box-Jenkins methodology   30
  RATS Instructions and Procedures   34
    1. BOXJENK   34
    2. CORRELATE   35
    3. FORECAST   36
    4. BJIDENT.SRC   37
    5. BJFORE.SRC   38
    6. AIC and SBC   39
    7. CDF   39
  Sample Programs   40
    1. A model of an AR(1) process   40
    2. A model of an ARMA(1, 1) process   44
    3. A model of the Wholesale Price Index   47
  Additional Exercises   51

Chapter 3: Modeling Volatility   **53**
  Theoretical Background   54
  The ARCH-M Model   59
  Maximum Likelihood Estimation in RATS   62
  RATS Instructions and Procedures   65
    1. MAXIMIZE   65
    2. FRML   67
    3. NLPAR   69
  Sample Programs   69
    1. ARCH errors in a regression model   69

    2. ARCH and GARCH models of the WPI   72
    3. Estimation af an ARCH-M process   78
  Additional Exercises   83

Chapter 4: Tests for Trends and Unit Roots   **85**
  Theoretical Background   85
  Additional Issues in Unit Root Tests   90
  RATS Instructions and Procedures   97
    1. LINREG   97
    2. ADF.SRC   97
    3. DFUNIT.SRC   98
    4. PPUNIT.SRC   99
    5. Others   99
  Sample Programs   100
    1. Dickey-Fuller and Phillips-Perron tests   100
    2. Tests for seasonal unit roots   104
    3. Structural breaks and unit root tests   105
  Additional Exercises   108

Chapter 5: Vector Autoregression Analysis   **109**
  Theoretical Background   109
  Innovation Accounting   113
  Hypothesis Testing   116
  RATS Instructions and Procedures   118
    1. Instructions to estimate a VAR   118
    2. The impulse response functions and variance decompositions   121
    3. Likelihood ratio tests   121
    4. Multivariate AIC and SBC   122
    5. Seemingly Unrelated Regressions (SUR)   123
    6. The Sims-Bernanke decomposition   124
  Sample Programs   126
    1. Hypothesis testing   126
    2. Innovation accounting and forecasting   130
    3. Seemingly Unrelated Regressions   137
    4. The Sims-Bernanke decomposition   140
  Additional Exercises   149

Chapter 6: Cointegration and Error Correction   **151**
  Theoretical Background   151
    1. Cointegrated variables   151
    2. Cointegration and error correction   154
    3. Testing for cointegration: The Engle-Granger methodology   156
  Illustrating the Engle-Granger Methodology   160

Sample Programs   162
   1. The Engle-Granger method for three simulated series   162
   2. Cointegration and the term structure   168
The Johansen Methodology   173
Using the Johansen.400 Procedure   177
   1. Determining the rank of π 180
   2. Testing coefficient restrictions   184
Introduction to CATS in RATS   188
   1. Determining the rank of π 190
   2. Testing coefficient restrictions   192
Additional Exercises   197

Statistical Tables
   A. Empirical Cumulative Distribution of τ 199
   B. Empirical Distribution of Φ 200
   C. Empirical Distribution of the λ_{max} and λ_{trace} Statistics   201

References and Additional Readings   203

Chapter 1   Introduction to RATS

There are many versions of RATS in current use in addition to editions for the Macintosh, Unix, DOS, and Windows platforms. At the time of this writing, the latest PC-based version of RATS is WINRATS 4.20. Nevertheless, the descriptions and programs in this handbook are intended to be compatible with all versions of RATS. If you have RATS 4.0 or later, you should have no trouble running any of the programs as they appear on the data disk. Those with older versions of the program will not be able to estimate the ARCH-type models discussed in Chapter 3. Wherever possible, I have tried to indicate how the instructions may differ between new and older versions of the program. If you have problems with the syntax of a program, you should consult your *RATS User's Manual*. If you have access to a version of RATS with the Dialogue Interface (PC versions 4.0 and later), you can get online help from the HELP pull-down menu.

RATS is a very powerful program capable of performing sophisticated statistical analysis. Although it can conduct a number of regression procedures, its comparative advantage lies in time-series analysis. The aim of this handbook is to illustrate these time-series techniques in a straightforward fashion. This chapter will introduce you to some of the basic instructions and conventions used in RATS. Thereafter, the text differs from the usual computer manual. Each chapter begins with a thorough review of a particular set of topics in time-series analysis. Next, there is a discussion of those RATS instructions and procedures that are relevant to the topic followed by several sample programs utilizing the instructions. The sample programs, output, and data used in the programs are contained on the disk accompanying this handbook. If you work through the sample programs carefully, you should be able to modify them so as to conduct your own time-series analysis. Each chapter concludes with a few supplementary exercises designed to give you additional practice using RATS. This handbook concentrates on the instructions and procedures that most RATS users will incorporate in their programs. As such, you will need to consult the *RATS User's Manual* to perform very specialized tasks.

If your version of RATS uses the Dialogue Interface, simply begin a RATS session and from the FILE MENU, open the program on the data disk entitled: WALKTOUR.PRG. Enter each line and use the discussion below to interpret your output. Be aware that when you begin RATS, there are ACTIVE, OUTPUT, and INPUT windows that may not be identical. If you enter instructions in the ACTIVE window, the output will be displayed in the OUTPUT window. To best learn RATS, you should use the same window for input and output. Simply use the *Window-Use for Input* and the *Window-Use for Output* selections from the WINDOW pull-down menu. If you do not have access to a version of RATS with the Dialogue Interface, use interactive mode but type each of the program statements yourself. In either case, compare your output with that contained in the file WALKTOUR.OUT.

To help you understand the output from the sample programs, several conventions are used concerning typefaces:

Boldface   Within a sample program, a RATS instruction, set of instructions, or a procedure in **boldface** produces the subsequent sample output. Instructions and procedures not in boldface either produce no output or the output is not shown.

Courier 10 point   RATS output is shown in Courier 10 point font. The output is either indented or contained in a highlighted box .

In addition, the Courier 10 point font is sometimes used to separate references to a particular program statement from the remainder of the text.

Italics   Many RATS instructions are used with parameters and options that you need to specify. The fields that you should specify are *italicized*. For example, the ALLOCATE instruction can be used to indicate the terminal date in a data set. Since you need to input the terminal value, the description of the instruction is written as: ALLOCATE *date*.

UPPERCASE   All file names contained on the data disk are in UPPERCASE. In addition, textual references to the proper names of RATS instructions and procedures are all in upper case. RATS itself does not distinguish between UPPERCASE and lowercase characters. Within the sample programs, all names are in lower case.

The best way to introduce RATS is to walk you through a sample program. You can find all of the program statements on the file labeled WALKTOUR.PRG and the program statements and output on the file labeled WALKTOUR.OUT. I suggest that you use this chapter while sitting in front of your computer. Begin RATS, open WALKTOUR.PRG, enter each instruction, and use the discussion below to interpret your output.

Preparing the Data

The first exercise uses exchange rate data found on the file labeled EXRATES.WK1. The file contains quarterly exchange rates for the U.S. dollar against the currencies of the UK, France, Germany, Italy, Canada, and Japan over the sample period 1973:1 through 1990:4. Each observation has been normalized such that the first quarter of 1971 equals 1.00. Here are the first four instructions of the program:

```
calendar 1973 1 4
allocate 1990:4
open data a:\exrates.wk1
data(format=prn,org=obs) /
```

The CALENDAR statement instructs RATS that the data starts with the first period of 1973 and that the data is quarterly. The most commonly used syntax of the CALENDAR instruction is:

calendar *year period frequency*

where: *year*   The year of the first entry in the data set
     period   The period of the first entry in the data set
     frequency   The number of observations per year.

Examples:
For monthly data beginning with February 1973, use `calendar 1973 2 12`.
For semiannual data beginning with July 1973, use `calendar 1973 2 2`.
For annual data it is permissible to use only the starting year. As such, you can omit the period and frequency and use the more compact `calendar 1973` instead of `calendar 1973 1 1`.

Note that you can use only the last two digits for the year. Thus, `calendar 1973 1 4` is equivalent to `calendar 73 1 4`. (Be careful if you have data beginning in the 19th century or once we have reached the year 2000.) Since each RATS instruction can be abbreviated using only the first three letters of the instruction, WALKTOUR.PRG could have used `cal 73 1 4`.

There are other formats for panel data and for daily, weekly, and irregularly spaced data. You should check the *RATS User's Manual* or the Online Help Facility if you need to work with one of these other formats. Do not use a CALENDAR statement for undated data (such as cross-section data).

The second instruction of WALKTOUR.PRG is ALLOCATE. The ALLOCATE instruction tells RATS that the data ends with the fourth quarter of 1990. You will always use ALLOCATE immediately following CALENDAR. If you do not use the CALENDAR instruction, ALLOCATE will be the first statement in your program.

Examples:
For monthly data ending with April 1990 use `allocate 1990:4`.
For monthly data ending with December 1990, use `allocate 1990:12`.
For annual data ending with 1990, use `allocate 1990:1`. The *frequency* (i.e., the number of observations per year) is necessary, even with annual data. You cannot use `allocate 1990`.

For cross-section data, set ALLOCATE equal to the number of observations in your data set. Thus, if you have cross-state data, you can use: `allocate 50`.

The OPEN and DATA statements are used together. The OPEN statement prepares RATS to read the data set named EXRATES.PRN that is on drive a:\. If the disk is in drive b:\, modify this line of the program and use: b:\exrates.prn. The DATA statement describes the characteristics of the data set. In this example, format=wks indicates that the data set is in a Lotus *.WKS format. Depending on your version of RATS, the *.WKS format can be used for any Lotus *.WKS, *.WK1, *.WK3, *.WRK, or *.WR1 file. The other option used is this handbook is the ASCII *.PRN format. All popular word processing programs and spreadsheets can be used to read and edit ASCII files. The *.PRN and *.WKS formats are used here since they are clearly the most popular. You should refer to the *RATS User's Manual* or the Online Help Facility if you have data created using some other format.

The option org=obs indicates that the data is organized by observation (instead of organization by variable). The first five rows of the EXRATES.WK1 file can be used to illustrate the structure of *.WKS and *.PRN files organized by observation. Consider:

UK	FR	GE	IT	CA	JA
0.992291	0.865777	0.822795	0.924480	0.988696	0.783639
0.948830	0.797379	0.747541	0.946576	0.991403	0.736056
0.968126	0.753772	0.654098	0.919008	0.995339	0.736111
1.009192	0.793454	0.696440	0.941104	0.991304	0.763083
. . . . .	. . . . .	. . . . .	. . . . .	. . . . .	. . . . .

Each variable is contained in a column headed by the variable's name. For example, in 1973:1, the pound/dollar and yen/dollar exchange rate indices were 0.992291 and 0.783639 times their respective base period values. In 1973:2, the pound/dollar and yen/dollar exchange rate indices were 0.948830 and 0.736056, respectively. In *.WKS and *.PRN files, it is also permissible to have the first column filled with dates as in:

	UK	FR	GE	IT	CA	JA
1973:1	0.992291	0.865777	0.822795	0.924480	0.988696	0.783639
1973:2	0.948830	0.797379	0.747541	0.946576	0.991403	0.736056
1973:3	0.968126	0.753772	0.654098	0.919008	0.995339	0.736111
1973:4	1.009192	0.793454	0.696440	0.941104	0.991304	0.763083
. . . . .	. . . . .	. . . . .	. . . . .	. . . . .	. . . . .	. . . . .

Notice the slash (/) in the DATA instruction. In RATS, you can set the range explicitly or use a slash to refer to the default range. Here, RATS reads all series over the entire sample period. A more general syntax for this DATA instruction is:

data(format=wks,org=obs) *start end series*
where: *start end* Range of entries to read. The default is the range implied by the
         CALENDAR and ALLOCATE instructions.

series — The list of series to read. If *series* is omitted, all variables in the data set are read into memory.

Examples:

To read only the series *uk* and *ja* over the full sample period, use:

    data(format=wks,org=obs) / uk ja

To read only the series *uk* and *ja* over the sample period 1975:1 to 1989:4, use:

    data(format=wks,org=obs) 75:1 89:4 uk ja

To read all series over the sample period 1975:1 to 1989:4, use:

    data(format=wks,org=obs) 75:1 89:4

The next three instructions of WALKTOUR.PRG are:

    statistics uk
    table / uk ja
    print / uk ja

The STATISTICS and TABLE instructions generate useful information about the data. STATISTICS produces a detailed set of summary statistics on a series you specify. Consider the following output:

statistics uk

```
Statistics on Series UK
Quarterly Data From 1973:01 To 1990:04
Observations    72
Sample Mean     1.35109766667      Variance                  0.069768
Standard Error  0.26413543674      SE of Sample Mean         0.031129
t-Statistic         43.40366       Signif Level  (Mean=0) 0.00000000
Skewness             0.59164       Signif Level  (Sk=0)   0.04477714
Kurtosis             0.19332       Signif Level  (Ku=0)   0.74992335
```

The sample mean and sample variance have straightforward interpretations. The standard error (SE) of the sample mean is the square root of the sample variance divided by the number of observations [i.e., $(0.069768/72)^{0.5} = 0.031129$]. The *t*-statistic for the null hypothesis that the mean equals zero is 43.40366 and the significance level for this value of *t* is too low to report.

TABLE is useful when you want summary statistics on several variables. The simple instruction TABLE produces a table of every variable in the memory (including all data transformations you have made). To prevent the creation of what can be a large amount of output, you typically specify the desired variable names on the TABLE instruction.

```
table / uk ja

Series   Obs      Mean            Std Error        Minimum          Maximum
UK       72    1.35109766667   0.26413543674    0.94883000000    2.15473700000
JA       72    0.61561729167   0.15471136174    0.34800000000    0.84316700000
```

The general syntax of the TABLE instruction is:

table *start end series*

where: *start end*   The range of entries to use in creating the table. A slash (/) defaults to all
                          observations available for each of the series individually.
     series   A list of the series to include in the table.

Examples:
To obtain a table of *uk* and *ja* using only the sample period 1975:1 to 1989:4, use:
     table 75:1 89:4 uk ja

To obtain a table of all variables in memory over the sample period 1975:1 to 1989:4, use:
     table 75:1 89:4

The PRINT instruction has the same syntax as the TABLE instruction. PRINT is a simple way to generate a printout of your data. Consider:

```
print / uk ja

ENTRY            UK              JA
1973:01   0.9922910000000  0.7836390000000
1973:02   0.9488300000000  0.7360560000000
1973:03   0.9681260000000  0.7361110000000
1973:04   1.0091920000000  0.7630830000000
.....       ........        ........
```

Depending on your monitor and printer, RATS can produce high-resolution graphs. The next four lines in WALKTOUR.PRG use the GRAPH instruction to create a plot of the *uk* and *ja* series against time. The syntax is somewhat different from the others we have encountered since GRAPH requires the use of a *supplementary* instruction (or "card") for each series. In RATS, all supplementary cards begin with the pound symbol (#). Also note the use of the dollar sign ($). Although RATS does not have an upper limit on line length, very long lines can be difficult to read. The $ at the end of a line is a continuation character; it indicates that the instruction is continued on the next line below. It is good practice to indent the continuation line so as to maintain the readability of the program. Very long instructions can entail several such continuation lines. Figure 1.1 was created by the statements:

```
graph(Header='UK and Japanese Exchange Rates (1971:1 = 1.00)', $
     key=upleft,patterns) 2
# uk
# ja
```

Figure 1.1: UK and Japanese Exchange Rates (1971:1 = 1.00)

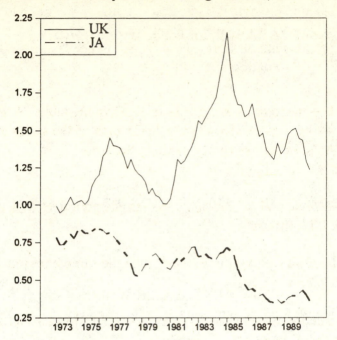

The typical syntax of the GRAPH instruction is:

graph(options) *number*
 # series start end

where: *number* The number of series to graph. Here, the number *2* tells RATS that two series are to be graphed. The names of the series are indicated on the supplementary cards; there is one such card for each series.

    series The name of the series to graph. Remember, there is one supplementary card for each series.

   start end Range to plot. If omitted, RATS uses the current sample range.

The graph created here illustrates only a few of the available options. The commonly used options are:

   HEADER= A string of characters placed in quotes.
   KEY= The location of the KEY. You can use UPLEFT, UPRIGHT, LOLEFT, LORIGHT. The default is none.

NODATES   RATS will label the horizontal axis unless the NODATES option is
            specified.
PATTERNS   If PATTERNS is omitted, RATS uses only colors to distinguish between
            the series. Unless you have a color monitor and printer, you should
            use PATTERNS to instruct RATS to use the default pattern style.
STLYE=   The default style is a line graph. Other popular styles are BAR,
            VERTICAL (as in high-low-close), and STEP. SYMBOLS draws
            symbols at regularly spaced intervals along a line; it is an alternative
            to patterns.

Examples:
To create a bar graph of *uk* without a HEADER or KEY, use:
        graph(style=bar) 1
        # uk

To create a line graph of *uk* over the full sample period and *ja* beginning with 1980:1, use:
        graph 2
        # uk
        # ja 80:1 90:4

The next four instructions in WALKTOUR.PRG illustrate some of the data transformations available in RATS. Each uses the SET instruction to define an entirely new series by transforming one or more of the series already in memory. Consider:

```
set dja 73:2 90:4 = ja(t) - ja(t-1)
set dlja 73:2 90:4 = log(ja(t)) - log(ja(t-1))
set ukja 73:1 90:4 = uk(t)/ja(t)
set time = t
```

The first statement defines *dja* as the first difference of *ja*. The variable *t* in parentheses acts as a time subscript. Thus, for each time period *t* in the interval 1973:2 to 1990:4, *ja(t)* is the value of *ja* in period *t* and *ja(t-1)* is the previous period's value. The first SET instruction directs RATS to subtract *ja(t-1)* from *ja(t)* and call the resultant series *dja*. With this same logic, the second instruction defines *dlja* as the logarithmic change in *ja*, and the third defines *ukja* as the ratio *uk* to *ja* (i.e., the ratio of the pound/dollar exchange rate to the yen/dollar exchange rate). The last statement defines the variable *time*. Internally, RATS sets $t = 1$ for the starting date of calendar, $t = 2$ for the second entry, and so forth. Since ALLOCATE allows for 72 observations, *time* is the sequence of integers from 1 to 72.

The typical syntax you will use for SET is:

set *series start end = function(T)*
where: *series*   The name of the series to create.

start end	The range of the series to set. In newer versions of RATS, a slash (/) or the omission of *start end* both default to the maximum permissible range as indicated on ALLOCATE. If you make a mistake, RATS will create *missing values* instead of an error message whenever possible.
= *function(T)*	The transformation to use. Note that you must use a space before and after the equal sign. RATS accepts addition (+), subtraction (-), multiplication (*), division (/), and exponentiation (**) using the usual order of precedence. ABS(X), EXP(X), LOG(X), and SQRT(X) are used to denote the absolute value, exponential value (i.e., e^x), natural logarithm, and square root of the argument X, respectively. All levels of parentheses ( ) are supported but you cannot use braces { } or brackets [ ] in place of parentheses.

RATS allows you to use braces { } as a shorthand way to represent time subscripts; you can use *series{lag}* in place of *series(t-lag)*. For example, instead of using *ja(t-1)*, you can use *ja{1}*. The number placed in the braces { } indicates the lag number. A negative number in braces indicates a leading value of the variable so that *ja(t+2)* and *ja{-2}* are equivalent ways to write the second lead of *ja*. Also, the notation *{A to B}* can be used to indicate lags *A* through *B* so that *ja{1 to 4}* indicates the first four lags of *ja*. [*Note*: In versions of RATS earlier than 4.0, you must use a time subscript in the definition of *function(T)*.]

Examples:
In newer versions of RATS, the following three SET instructions are equivalent:
   set dja 73:2 90:4 = ja(t) - ja(t-1),
   set dja / = ja - ja(t-1),
   set dja = ja - ja{1}.
To define *jawt* as a declining weighted average of the current and previous three values of
  ja, you can use:
   set / jawt = 0.4*ja + 0.3*ja{1} + 0.2*ja{2} + 0.1*ja(t-3).
A series can be written on to itself. The instruction set ja = log(ja) replaces each
  entry in *ja* by its natural logarithm.

Time-series analysis uses logarithmic transformations and differencing so frequently that RATS contains special instructions for these transformations. The DIFFERENCE and LOG instructions are usually used as follows:

log ja / lja
difference ja / dja

The interpretation of these two instructions is straightforward. The first defines *lja* as the logarithm of *ja*. Thus, log ja / lja is equivalent to set lja 73:1 90:4 = log(ja). The second instruction defines *dja* as the first difference of *ja*. Since you can abbreviate a RATS instruction by its first three letters, `dif ja / dja` is equivalent to `set dja 73:2 90:4 = ja(t) - ja(t-1)`. You must define the *start end* range or use the slash (/) on the DIFFERENCE statement. Unlike the SET statement, if you explicitly define the range, you must allow for the number of lags created.

Linear Regression

Remember that the goal of this chapter is to introduce you to RATS, not to develop time-series analysis. Some of the techniques illustrated below are better conducted using the methodology developed in Chapter 2. However, the LINREG instruction is the backbone of RATS and it is necessary to illustrate its use. As such, suppose you want to estimate the logarithmic change in the yen/dollar exchange rate as the fourth-order autoregressive process:

$$dlja_t = a_0 + a_1 dlja_{t-1} + a_2 dlja_{t-2} + a_3 dlja_{t-3} + a_4 dlja_{t-4} + \epsilon_t$$

where $dlja_i$ is the logarithmic change in the yen/dollar exchange rate in period i, ϵ_t is the error term, and the a_i are regression coefficients. The next two lines in WALKTOUR.PRG estimate the model using ordinary least squares (OLS):

linreg dlja
 # constant dlja{1 to 4}

```
Dependent Variable DLJA - Estimation by Least Squares
Quarterly Data From 1974:02 To 1990:04
Usable Observations       67       Degrees of Freedom      62
Centered R**2      0.143937       R Bar **2      0.088707
Uncentered R**2    0.184401       T x R**2       12.355
Mean of Dependent Variable         -0.011927013
Std Error of Dependent Variable    0.053951264
Standard Error of Estimate         0.051502768
Sum of Squared Residuals           0.1644571750
Regression F(4,62)                        2.6061
Significance Level of F               0.04416018
Durbin-Watson Statistic                1.955968
Q(16-0)                               17.818822
Significance Level of Q               0.33461265


    Variable        Coeff        Std Error       T-Stat      Signif
 ****************************************************************************
 1.  Constant      -0.008597770   0.006515433   -1.31960    0.19182055
 2.  DLJA{1}        0.380057577   0.127409984    2.98295    0.00407824
 3.  DLJA{2}       -0.069354210   0.136191749   -0.50924    0.61239211
 4.  DLJA{3}        0.132964297   0.137935694    0.96396    0.33881154
 5.  DLJA{4}       -0.087810729   0.129181480   -0.67975    0.49919483
```

Notice that the estimation begins in 1974:2; RATS automatically adjusts for the five observations lost due to differencing and the use of four lags. As such, there are 67 usable observations (72 - 5 = 67); given the five parameters estimated, there are 67 - 5 = 62 degrees of freedom. Next, RATS reports four Goodness-of-Fit measures: centered R^2, R-bar square (centered R^2 adjusted for degrees of freedom), uncentered R^2, and TR^2 (number of observations multiplied by the uncentered R^2).[1] The mean and standard error of *dlja* over the 67 observations used in the regression are reported to be -0.011927013 and 0.053951264, respectively. (*Note*: This will differ from the the mean and standard error over all 72 observations.) These are followed by the standard error of the estimate (i.e., the square root of the sum of the squared regression residuals divided by the degrees of freedom) and the sum of squared residuals. You can easily verify that $0.051502768 = (0.1644571750/62)^{0.5}$. The *F*-statistic and its significance level can be used to test the hypothesis that all coefficients in the regression (other than the constant) are zero. Here the *p*-value of the joint test, $a_1 = a_2 = a_3 = a_4 = 0$, is 0.04416018. The Durbin-Watson test for first-order serial correlation in the residuals is 1.955968 (2.0 is the theoretical value of this statistic in the absence of serial correlation). Lastly, the Ljung-Box Q-statistic for the presence of serial correlation among the first 16 residual correlations (approximately 1/4 of the number of usable observations) and the significance level are reported. The Ljung-Box Q-statistic is discussed in detail in the next chapter.

For each right-hand-side variable, the next portion of the output reports the coefficient estimate (Coeff), the standard error of the coefficient (Std Error), the *t*-statistic for the null hypothesis that the coefficient equals zero (T-Stat), and the marginal significance level of the *t*-test (Signif). For example, the coefficient of the first lag of *dlja* is estimated to be 0.380057577 with a standard error of 0.127409984. The associated *t*-test for the null hypothesis $a_1 = 0$ is 0.380057577/0.127409984 = 2.98295. If you use a *t*-table, you can verify that the significance level for this value of *t* is 0.00407824. If you want to use a one-tail test, the appropriate significance level is twice that reported.

This particular regression does not look especially good; the individual *t*-statistics suggest that all but one of the coefficients are insignificant at conventional significance levels. The EXCLUDE, SUMMARIZE, TEST, and RESTRICT instructions allow you to perform hypothesis tests on several coefficients at once. EXCLUDE is followed by a supplementary card listing the variables to exclude from the most recently estimated regression. RATS produces the *F*-statistic and the significance level for the null hypothesis that the coefficients of all excluded variables equal zero. Consider the two exclusion tests used in WALKTOUR.PRG:

```
exclude
# dlja{2 to 4}
      Null Hypothesis : The Following Coefficients Are Zero
      DLJA                Lag(s) 2 to 4
      F(3,62)=        0.37398 with Significance Level 0.77205619
```

---

[1] Let the dependent variable be denoted by y. Uncentered R^2 is 1 - (sum of squared regression residuals)/(sum of squared values of y). Centered R^2 is 1 - (sum of squared regression residuals)/(sum of squared deviations of y from the mean of y). The so-called "usual" R^2 statistic is the centered R^2.

```
exclude
# constant dlja{2 to 4}
      Null Hypothesis : The Following Coefficients Are Zero
      Constant
      DLJA               Lag(s) 2 to 4
      F(4,62)=       0.72028 with Significance Level 0.58133419
```

The first exclusion restriction tests the joint hypothesis $a_2 = a_3 = a_4 = 0$ and the second tests the joint hypothesis $a_0 = a_2 = a_3 = a_4 = 0$. The results support those of the t-tests; neither of these null hypotheses can be rejected at conventional significance levels. SUMMARIZE has the same syntax as EXCLUDE but is used to test the null hypothesis that the sum of the coefficients indicated on the supplementary card is equal to zero. In the following example, the value of t for the null hypothesis $a_1 + a_2 + a_3 + a_4 = 0$ is 1.95386:

```
summarize
# dlja{1 to 4}
      Summary of Linear Combination of Coefficients
      DLJA               Lag(s) 1 to 4
      Value          0.355856934608      t-Statistic              1.95286
      Standard Error 0.182223187842      Signif Level          0.05535352
```

Overall, it would be wise to reestimate this model using only the first lag of *dlja*. As an exercise, you should obtain the final output by entering the following two lines:

```
linreg dlja
# dlja{1}
```

The next section examines some additional topics in regression analysis including the use of the TEST and RESTRICT instructions.

Additional Regression Topics

LINREG has many options that are useful to time-series econometricians. The usual syntax of LINREG is:

linreg(options) *depvar start end residuals*
 # *list*
where: *depvar*   The dependent variable.
     start end   The range to use in the regression. The default is the largest common range of all variables in the regression.
     residuals   Series name for the residuals. Omit if you do not want to save the regression residuals.
     list   The list of explanatory variables.

The most useful options are:

DEFINE=   You can name the equation by setting DEFINE equal to the name you
            choose. Later, you can refer to the equation by its name.
NOPRINT   Do not print the regression output.
VCV   Print the covariance/correlation matrix of the coefficients.

LINREG creates a number of variables that you can use in subsequent computations. A partial list of these variables is:

%BETA   The coefficient vector. The first coefficient estimated is *%BETA(1)*, the
             second *%BETA(2)*, and so on. For example, in the output for *dlja*
             above, the constant is *%BETA(1)*, the coefficient for *dlja{1}* is
             %BETA(2), and so forth.
%NDF   Degrees of freedom.
%NOBS   Number of observations.
%NREG   Number of regressors.
%RSS   Residual sum of squares.
%RSQUARED   Centered R^2 (i.e, the usual measure of R^2)
%SEESQ   Standard error of estimate squared

2. A Model of the U.S. Wholesale Price Index: The file labeled WPI.WK1 contains quarterly values of the U.S. Wholesale Price Index (WPI) over the sample period 1960:1 to 1992:2. We will be analyzing this data in considerable detail in Chapters 2 and 3. For the time being, suppose you want to estimate the inflation rate (i.e., as measured by the logarithmic change in the WPI) as the fourth-order autoregressive process:

$$\pi_t = a_1 \pi_{t-1} + a_2 \pi_{t-2} + a_3 \pi_{t-3} + a_4 \pi_{t-4} + a_5 D_1 + a_6 D_2 + a_7 D_3 + a_8 D_4 + \epsilon_t$$

where π_i is the logarithmic change in the WPI in period i, the D_i are seasonal (quarterly) dummy variables equal to 1 in quarter i and zero in all other quarters, ϵ_t is the error term, and the a_i are regression coefficients. The file labeled WPI_REG.PRG contains all of the program statements discussed below and the file labeled WPI_REG.OUT contains the same statements along with the RATS output. You should use RATS to open WPI_REG.PRG, enter each of the program lines and follow the commentary below. The first six lines of WPI_REG.PRG are:

```
* WPI_REG.PRG.  This program uses LINREG to estimate a simple model of the WPI.
cal 1960 1 4                    ;* Set the calendar from 1960:Q1
all 1992:4                      ;*      to 1992:Q4.
open data a:wpi.wk1             ;* Modify this line if WPI.WK1 is not on drive a:\
data(format=wks,org=obs)
```

```
set dlwpi = log(wpi) - log(wpi{1})    ;* Transforms the data to logarithmic changes.  In older
                                       ;*  versions of RATS, you may need to set the sample
                                       ;*  period explicitly.
```

Notice the asterisk in the first column of the first statement. An asterisk in this position denotes a COMMENT line. Comments allow you to annotate your programs so that you can remember their functions. Several months after writing a program, it is near impossible to remember why you made a particular data transformation or estimated a particular model. You can designate an entire block of comments by using the symbol /* to mark the beginning of the block and */ to mark the end of the block. RATS halts program execution when it encounters the /* symbol as the first nonblank characters in a line. Program execution resumes when the symbol */ occurs as the first nonblank characters in a line. Another useful way to annotate a program is to combine a semicolon with an asterisk (;*). The semicolon can be used to separate two (or more) RATS instructions appearing on the same line. An instruction followed by the symbol ;* allows you to comment on the purpose of the instruction. This handbook makes extensive use all three of these techniques to annotate the text and the sample programs. The commentary for program lines 2 through 6 above is embedded directly in the program.

Next, create a seasonal dummy variable, called *seasons*, using the SEASONAL instruction.

```
seasonal seasons
```

```
/*      The variable seasons contains a value of 1 in the first quarter of every year and a zero in
```
all other quarters. Hence, the first lead of *seasons* leads contains a 1 in the second quarter of each year and a zero in all other quarters. A complete set of quarterly dummy variables can be created using *seasons* and its three leads (or a constant and three leads).[1]

The next two lines use LINREG to estimate the model. Since *start* and *end* values are not specified, the estimation occurs over sample period 61:2 to 92:2. The series name *resids* is the name of the series used to store the regression residuals. Once computed, it is possible to use the *resids* series just as you would use any other series in memory. Here, only the second portion of the output is shown. The complete listing is contained in WPI_REG.OUT.
```
*/
```

```
linreg dlwpi / resids
# dlwpi{1 to 4} seasons{-3 to 0}   ;* Do not include a constant with the four seasonal dummies.
```

---

[1]You can also use lagged values of *seasons* to create the seasonal dummies. The problem is that lagging *seasons*, or any other variable, can result in a loss in number of usable observations.

Coefficient		Estimate	Standard Error	t-statistic	Significance Level
1.	DLWPI{1}	0.405744943	0.091792597	4.42024	0.00002218
2.	DLWPI{2}	0.109399116	0.099030169	1.10470	0.27155411
3.	DLWPI{3}	0.121184136	0.098933762	1.22490	0.22307261
4.	DLWPI{4}	0.144245829	0.092015291	1.56763	0.11966844
5.	SEASONS{-3}	0.005452912	0.002262833	2.40977	0.01752099
6.	SEASONS{-2}	0.001367766	0.002228295	0.61382	0.54052773
7.	SEASONS{-1}	0.002969468	0.002272511	1.30669	0.19388047
8.	SEASONS	-0.000423006	0.002263503	-0.18688	0.85207742

* To obtain the sum of the coefficients on the lagged values of *dlwpi*, use:

summarize
 # dlwpi{1 to 4}

```
Summary of Linear Combination of Coefficients
DLWPI           Lag(s) 1 to 4
Value           0.780574023497      t-Statistic          9.07719
Standard Error  0.085992867413      Signif Level         0.00000000
```

/*   The next part of the program illustrates the use of two instructions that allow RATS to operate like a very powerful calculator. COMPUTE can by used to create a scalar, a matrix, or an element of a series. Note that COMPUTE and SET are quite different in that SET operates on an entire series. DISPLAY is used to print strings of characters enclosed in single quotes (i.e., ' ') and scalars. The next two lines of the program compute and display the Residual Sum of Squares:
*/

compute rss1 = %rss   ;* Recall LINREG creates a variable called %rss
display 'Residual Sum of Squares' rss1
```
       Residual Sum of Squares  0.01503
```

/*   To take another example, recall that the variables %BETA(1) through %BETA(4) contain the four coefficients of dlwpi{1 to 4}. Although it is easier to use the SUMMARIZE instruction, you can obtain the sum of the coefficients on the lagged values of *dlwpi*, using:
*/
compute sum = %beta(1) + %beta(2) + %beta(3) + %beta(4)
display 'SUM OF COEFFICIENTS = ' sum
```
       SUM OF COEFFICIENTS =           0.78057
```

* DISPLAY can do simple arithmetic too. For example, it is perfectly permissible to use:

display 'SUM OF COEFFICIENTS = ' %beta(1) + %beta(2) + %beta(3) + %beta(4)
```
       SUM OF COEFFICIENTS =           0.78057
```

/*   RATS allows you to perform a wide variety of hypothesis tests. Since three of the coefficients of *seasons* are insignificant at conventional values, you might want to determine whether all the seasonals (as a group) are significant. To test the null hypothesis $a_5 = a_6 = a_7 = a_8 = 0$, use:
*/

exclude
 # seasons {- 3 to 0}

```
Null Hypothesis : The Following Coefficients Are Zero
SEASONS            Lag(s) -3 to 0
F(4,117)=          1.76224 with Significance Level 0.14111785
```

* To test whether lags 2 and 3 of *dlwpi* equal zero, use:

exclude
 # dlwpi{2 to 3}

```
Null Hypothesis : The Following Coefficients Are Zero
DLWPI              Lag(s) 2 to 3
F(2,117)=          2.10158 with Significance Level 0.12685549
```

* To test whether lags 2 and 3 of *dlwpi* and all coefficients of *seasons* equal zero, use:

exclude
 # seasons{-3 to 0} dlwpi{2 to 3}

```
Null Hypothesis : The Following Coefficients Are Zero
SEASONS            Lag(s) -3 to 0
DLWPI              Lag(s) 2 to 3
F(6,117)=          2.17096 with Significance Level 0.05060869
```

/*   EXCLUDE can only test whether a group of coefficients is jointly equal to zero. The TEST instruction has a great deal more flexibility; it is able to test joint restrictions on particular values of the coefficients. Suppose you have estimated a model and want to perform a significance test of the joint hypothesis restricting the values of coefficients $a_i, a_j, \ldots$, and a_k to equal $r_i, r_j, \ldots$, and r_k, respectively. Formally:

$$a_i = r_i, \quad a_j = r_j \quad \ldots \quad \text{and} \quad a_k = r_k.$$

To perform the test, you first type TEST followed by two supplementary cards. The first supplementary card lists the coefficients (by their number in the LINREG output list) that you want to restrict and the second lists the restricted value of each. Returning to WPI_REG.PRG, suppose you want to restrict the coefficients of the last three values of *dlwpi* to all be 0.1 (i.e., a_2

= 0.1, a_3 = 0.1, and a_4 = 0.1). To test this restriction, use:
*/

test
 # 2 3 4
 # 0.1 0.1 0.1
```
         F(3,117)= 0.19473 with Significance Level 0.89981002
```

/* The first line instructs RATS to expect the supplementary cards for the TEST procedure. The first supplementary card indicates that coefficients 2, 3, and 4 are to be restricted. Recall that LINREG assigns the number *2* to the second lag of *dlwpi*, the number 3 to the third lag of *dlwpi*, and so on. The second supplementary card lists the value that each coefficient assumes. RATS displays the *F*-value and the significance level of the joint test: a_2 = 0.1, a_3 = 0.1, and a_4 = 0.1. If the restriction is binding, the value of *F* should be high and the significance level should be low. Hence, most econometricians would not reject the restriction as posed here (i.e., they would accept the hypothesis that each equals 0.1). As shown in the examples, TEST is quite flexible.

Examples:
1. To test the restriction that fourth lag of *dlwpi* equals zero, use:
    test
    # 4
    # 0
(Since this is equivalent to a *t*-test, you will get a significance level of 0.11966844.)

2. To test the joint restriction that $a_2 = a_3 = a_4$ = 0.1 and that the coefficients of *seasons{-2 to 0}* all equal zero, use:
    test
    # 2 3 4 6 7 8
    # 0.1 0.1 0.1 0 0 0

      RESTRICT is the most powerful of the hypothesis testing instructions. RESTRICT can test multiple linear restrictions on the coefficients and estimate the restricted model. Although RESTRICT is a bit difficult to use, it can perform the tasks of SUMMARIZE, EXCLUDE, and TEST. Each restriction is entered in the form:

$$\beta_i a_i + \beta_j a_j + \dots + \beta_k a_k = r$$

where: a_i are the coefficients of the estimated model (i.e., each coefficient is referred to by its
          assigned number).
        β_i are weights you assign to each coefficient.
and: *r* represents the restricted value of the sum (which may be zero).

      To implement the test, you type RESTRICT followed by the number of restrictions you want to impose. Each restriction entails the use of two supplementary cards. The first lists the coefficients to be restricted (by their number) and the second lists the values of the β_i and r:

Examples:
1. To test the restriction that the fourth lag of *dlwpi* equals zero, use:

```
restrict 1
# 4
# 1 0
```

The first line instructs RATS to prepare for one linear restriction. The next line is the supplementary card indicating that coefficient number *4* is to be restricted. The last imposes the restriction $1.0*a_4 = 0$.

2. To test the joint restriction that $a_2 + 2a_3 = 0$ (i.e., $1.0*a_2 + 2.0*a_3 = 0$), use:

```
restrict 1
# 2 3
# 1 2 0
```

Again, there is only one restriction. The first supplementary card indicates that coefficients *2* and *3* are to be restricted. The last imposes the restriction $a_2 + 2a_3 = 0$.

The program WPI_REG.PRG tests the restriction that the coefficients of the second and third lags of *dlwpi* are equal (i.e., $a_2 = a_3$ so that $a_2 - a_3 = 0$). Since there is one restriction, the second and third coefficients are involved, and the values of β_2, β_3, and r are 1, -1, and zero, the appropriate program statements are:
```
*/
```
restrict 1
 # 2 3
 # 1 -1 0
```
     F(1,117)= 0.00524 with Significance Level 0.94243658
```

/* If the restriction is binding, the *F*-value should be large and the significance level low. Here, the *F*-statistic is only 0.00525 and the significance level is such that we can accept the restriction (i.e., we do not reject the null hypothesis). As shown below, RESTRICT can be used with the CREATE option to test and estimate the restricted form of the regression. To be a bit more general, suppose you want to test two separate coefficient restrictions and then estimate the restricted model. Let the first restriction be that the sum of the coefficients on the seasonal dummy variables is zero (i.e., $a_5 + a_6 + a_7 + a_8 = 0$). If this were the sole restriction, the SUMMARIZE instruction would suffice. However, suppose you also want to impose the restriction $a_2 = a_3$. Formally, the joint test is $a_5 + a_6 + a_7 + a_8 = 0$ and $a_2 - a_3 = 0$. To illustrate the use of the CREATE option, consider the next five program statements of WPI_REG.PRG. The first prepares RATS for two restrictions (and four supplementary cards) and indicates that the restricted regression is to be estimated. Whenever CREATE is used, you can save the regression residuals simply by providing RATS with the name of the series in which to store the residuals. Here, the regression residuals are stored in the series *resids*. The first two supplementary cards

impose the restriction $a_5 + a_6 + a_7 + a_8 = 0$ and the second two impose the restriction $a_2 - a_3 = 0$.
*/

restrict(create) 2 resids   ;* Do not use CREATE unless you want to estimate the restricted
 # 5 6 7 8   ;*   regression. Note that only the second portion of the
 # 1 1 1 1 0   ;*   output is shown.
 # 2 3
 # 1 -1 0

```
F(2,117)=        1.50339 with Significance Level 0.22663829

Dependent Variable DLWPI - Estimation by Restricted Regression
    Coefficient        Estimate      Standard      t-statistic    Significance
                                     Error                          Level
1.   DLWPI{1}     0.432134391  0.089296727     4.83931      0.00000395
2.   DLWPI{2}     0.136486632  0.055159086     2.47442      0.01475485
3.   DLWPI{3}     0.136486632  0.055159086     2.47442      0.01475485
4.   DLWPI{4}     0.174006541  0.089359927     1.94725      0.05385995
5.   SEASONS{-3}  0.003076851  0.001804666     1.70494      0.09081441
6.   SEASONS{-2} -0.000910348  0.001775471    -0.51274      0.60908645
7.   SEASONS{-1}  0.000577556  0.001768867     0.32651      0.74461071
8.   SEASONS     -0.002744059  0.001797066    -1.52697      0.12942288
```

/*   Note that the joint restriction is not binding at conventional significance levels. Also note that the coefficients of *dlwpi{2}* and *dlwpi{3}* are equal and that the sum of the coefficients on the seasonal dummies is zero.

Now compare the Residual Sum of Squares from the unrestricted regression to that of the restricted regression. Recall that the scalar *rss1* holds the value of the Residual Sum of Squares from the unrestricted regression.
*/
display 'Unrestricted Sum of Squares =' rss1
```
    Unrestricted Sum of Squares =    0.01503
```
display 'Restricted Sum of Squares =' %rss
```
    Restricted Sum of Squares =      0.01541
```

/* Notice that the variables created by LINREG and RESTRICT(CREATE), such as %BETA, %NOBS, and %RSS, are recomputed each time a new estimation occurs. As illustrated here, if you want to compare these variables from one estimation to the next, you must compute and store the original values.

One way to obtain the estimated values of *dlwpi* is to use the SET instruction to subtract the regression residuals from the actual values of *dlwpi*:

set estimated = dlwpi - resids

However, it is a bit easier to use the RATS PRJ instruction. PRJ calculates the estimated values (or projected values) of the dependent variable and stores the result in a series you name. Below PRJ stores the fitted values of *dlwpi*, in the series called *estimated*. Finally, the GRAPH instruction is used to plot the projected and residual values of the estimation.
*/

```
prj estimated
graph(key=upleft,style=symbols,patterns, $
     header='Estimated and Residual Values of the WPI') 2
# estimated
# resids
```

Figure 1.2: Estimated and Residual Values of *dlwpi*

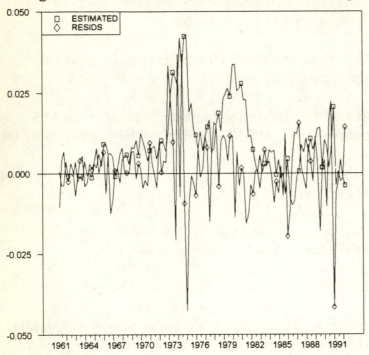

/* The syntax of the PRJ instruction is:

prj *series start end*
where:
series   Name of the series for the fitted values. Note that PRJ always uses the dependent variable from the most recently estimated regression.
start end   Range of entries to project. The default is the range of the most recent regression.

As you can see from Figure 1.2, there are some disturbing features of the residual series. During the early portion of the 1970's, the residuals are very large (in absolute value) and the variance of the residuals appears to be greater in the middle of the sample than in the early and late portions. We have not yet developed the techniques to compare the estimated model to other plausible alternatives. However, these are the concerns of Chapters 2 through 4 of this handbook. An analysis of multivariate time-series methods is contained in Chapters 5 and 6. The point of this chapter has been to introduce you to some of the key features of RATS. To gain further experience using these instructions, you should experiment using the exercises below.

Additional Exercises

1. Perform the following hypothesis tests concerning the model of *dlwpi*:

    (a) Determine whether you can omit the fourth order autoregressive coefficient and all of the seasonal coefficients except that for seasons{-3}. Show that you obtain the identical results using the EXCLUDE, TEST, and RESTRICT instructions. Estimate the resulting model and save the residuals.

    (b) Use the TABLE, STATISTICS, and GRAPH instructions to compare the residual series from your answer to part (a) to those from the unrestricted model.

2. The third column in the data file SIM_2.WK1 contains 100 observations of a series called Y3. The series is undated so that the sample contains observations 1 through 100.

    (a) Modify the first four lines of WALKTOUR.PGM so as to read this series into RATS memory. (*Hint*: Since the series in undated, the CALENDAR instruction is unnecessary. Use `allocate 100`.)

    (b) Generate the sample statistics and plot the series.

    (c) Use the LINREG instruction to estimate the series as an autoregressive process. Use the EXCLUDE instruction to determine the necessary number of lags to use.

    (d) Use PRJ and GRAPH to plot the actual and the projected values of the model.

3. One useful way to create dummy variables is to use the SET instruction in conjunction with logical and relational operators. RATS evaluates these operators and sets those entries for which the expression is true equal to one and those for which the expression is false equal to zero. For example, sample program 3 in Chapter 4 uses:

    set dummy = t>1949:1 to create the series *dummy* with entries equal to zero up to and including 1949:1 and equal to one thereafter

    set pulse = t.eq.1950:1 to create the series *pulse* with entries equal to zero except for the period 1950:1.

    In this exercise, you are to use the model of *dlwpi* to determine whether or not the 1970's were structurally different from the other years in the model. Towards this end, modify WPI_REG.PRG so as to:

(a) Create a dummy variable representing the 1970's using:

set dummy = t>1969:4.and.t<1980:1.

Use the PRINT and GRAPH instructions to guarantee you have properly created the dummy variable.

(b) Estimate the model of *dlwpi* allowing *dummy* to affect the intercept term. Is it appropriate to include *dummy*?

(c) Now use LINREG to obtain the residuals from the model:

$$dlwpi_t = a_0 + a_1 dlwpi_{t-1} + a_2 dlwpi_{t-2} + a_3 dlwpi_{t-3} + a_4 dlwip_{t-4} + \epsilon_t$$

(d) Create the squared residuals series (called *residsq*) using: set residsq = resids**2. Plot the square of the residuals using the GRAPH instruction. Do the squared residuals behave differently during the 1970's?

(e) Use *dummy* to estimate a model of *residsq*.

Chapter 2 — Stationary Time-Series Models

In the last chapter you used the LINREG instruction to estimate some simple autoregressive models of the form:

$$y_t = a_0 + a_1 y_{t-1} + \dots + a_p y_{t-p} + \epsilon_t$$

One aim of this chapter is to develop a wider class of models called Autoregressive Integrated Moving-Average (ARIMA) time-series models. Consider the model ARIMA model:

$$y_t = a_0 + a_1 y_{t-1} + \dots + a_p y_{t-p} + \epsilon_t + \beta_1 \epsilon_{t-1} + \dots + \beta_q \epsilon_{t-q}$$

You cannot use LINREG to estimate such a model since the values of $\epsilon_t, \epsilon_{t-1}, \dots, \epsilon_{t-q}$ must be jointly estimated with the parameters of the model. The first section analyzes the time-series properties of stationary ARIMA models; such models are called ARMA models. In addition, the Box-Jenkins (1976) methodology for identifying, estimating, and forecasting such models is developed. In the second and third sections, the relevant RATS instructions and procedures are explained and illustrated using three sample programs. Especially useful are the BOXJENK, CORRELATE, and FORECAST instructions and the BJIDENT.SRC and BJFORE.SRC procedures.

Theoretical Background

1. Stationarity: A series is said to be **covariance stationary** if its mean and all autocovariances are unaffected by a change of time origin. Formally, a stochastic process having a finite mean and variance is covariance stationary if for all t and t-s:

$$E(y_t) = E(y_{t-s}) = \mu$$

$$E[(y_t - \mu)^2] = E[(y_{t-s} - \mu)^2] = \sigma_y^2 \qquad [\text{Var}(y_t) = \text{Var}(y_{t-s}) = \sigma_y^2]$$

$$E[(y_t - \mu)(y_{t-s} - \mu)] = E[(y_{t-j} - \mu)(y_{t-j-s} - \mu)] = \gamma_s. \qquad [\text{Cov}(y_t, y_{t-s}) = \text{Cov}(y_{t-j}, y_{t-j-s})]$$

where μ, σ_y^2, and γ_s are all constants.

Note that for $s = 0$, γ_0 is equivalent to the variance of y_t. Further, for a covariance stationary series, we can define the **autocorrelation** between y_t and y_{t-s} as:

$$\rho_s = \gamma_s / \gamma_0$$

Since γ_s and γ_0 are time-independent, the autocorrelation coefficients ρ_s are also time-independent.

2. ARIMA processes: A sequence $\{\epsilon_t\}$ is a **white-noise** process if each value in the sequence has a mean of zero, a constant variance, and is distributed independently of all other values in the sequence. Formally, if the notation $E(x)$ denotes the theoretical mean value of x, the sequence $\{\epsilon_t\}$ is a white-noise process if for each time period t:

$$E(\epsilon_t) = E(\epsilon_{t-1}) = ... = 0$$
$$E(\epsilon_t)^2 = E(\epsilon_{t-1})^2 = ... = \sigma^2 \qquad [\text{or } \mathrm{Var}(\epsilon_t) = \mathrm{Var}(\epsilon_{t-1}) = ... = \sigma^2]$$

and for all $s \neq 0$:

$$E(\epsilon_t \, \epsilon_{t-s}) = E(\epsilon_{t-j} \, \epsilon_{t-j-s}) = 0 \text{ for all } j \qquad [\text{or } \mathrm{Cov}(\epsilon_t, \epsilon_{t-s}) = \mathrm{Cov}(\epsilon_{t-j}, \epsilon_{t-j-s}) = 0]$$

In the remainder of this handbook, $\{\epsilon_t\}$ will always refer to a white-noise process and σ^2 will refer to the variance of that process. When it is necessary to refer to two or more white-noise process, symbols such as $\{\epsilon_{1t}\}$ and $\{\epsilon_{2t}\}$ will be used. Now, use a white-noise process to construct the more interesting time series:

$$x_t = \sum_{i=0}^{q} \beta_i \epsilon_{t-i}$$

For each period t, x_t is constructed by taking the values $\epsilon_t, \epsilon_{t-1}, ... , \epsilon_{t-q}$ and multiplying each by the associated value of β_i. A sequence formed in this manner is called a **moving-average** of order q and is denoted by MA(q). It is standard to normalize units such that $\beta_0 = 1$. As indicated below, a MA(q) process may also include an intercept.

Now consider a special type of difference equation called a pth-order linear difference equation with constant coefficients:

$$y_t = a_0 + a_1 y_{t-1} + a_2 y_{t-2} + ... + a_p y_{t-p}$$

The order of the difference equation is given by the value of p. The equation is linear because all values of the dependent variable are raised to the first power. Adding the moving-average component x_t to this equation yields an **autoregressive integrated moving-average** (ARIMA) process:

$$y_t = a_0 + a_1 y_{t-1} + a_2 y_{t-2} + ... + a_p y_{t-p} + \epsilon_t + \beta_1 \epsilon_{t-1} + ... + \beta_q \epsilon_{t-q} \qquad (2.1)$$

If all $\beta_i = 0$, the model is a pth-order autoregression, denoted as AR(p). If all values of a_1 through a_p equal zero, the model is an MA(q) process.

Stationarity and Invertibility of an ARIMA Process: A succinct way to state the necessary and sufficient conditions for the ARIMA process (2.1) to be stationary is:

1. All the values of λ satisfying $\lambda^p - a_1\lambda^{p-1} - a_2\lambda^{p-2} \ldots - a_p = 0$ must lie within the unit circle.

2. Either the sequence must have started infinitely far in the past or the process must always be in equilibrium (so that the effects of any initial conditions vanish).

If one or more of the characteristic roots lie outside the unit circle, the $\{y_t\}$ process is explosive. If exactly d characteristic roots equal unity and the remaining p-d roots lie inside the unit circle, the process is said to be integrated of order d and is denoted by $I(d)$. An ARIMA(p, d, q) process is one with p autoregressive coefficients, d unit roots, and q moving-average coefficients. The dth difference of an $I(d)$ process is always stationary. An $I(0)$ process has all characteristic roots lying inside the unit circle; hence, it is stationary. Such models are referred to as ARMA models.

It is always possible to transform a stationary autoregressive process into an infinite-order moving-average process. Sometimes it is possible to transform a stationary moving-average process (or a mixed autoregressive-moving-average process) into a pure autoregressive process. When this can be done, the process is said to be **invertible**. For example, if $|a_1| < 1$, the first-order autoregressive process $y_t = a_1 y_{t-1} + \epsilon_t$ can be written as:

$$y_t = \sum_{i=0}^{\infty} a_1^i \epsilon_{t-i}$$

However, the moving-average process $y_t = \epsilon_t - \epsilon_{t-1}$ does not have an autoregressive representation. Let L be the lag operator such that $Ly_t = y_{t-1}$ and $L^i y_t = y_{t-i}$. The pure moving-average process $y_t = (1 + \beta_1 L + \beta_2 L^2 + \ldots + \beta_q L^q)\epsilon_t$ is invertible if the values of L satisfying the inverse characteristic equation $1 + \beta_1 L + \beta_2 L^2 + \ldots + \beta_q L^q = 0$ lie outside of the unit circle.

3. Autocorrelation and partial autocorrelation functions: The calculation of the covariances and correlations of a series serves as a useful tool in the Box Jenkins (1976) approach to time-series analysis. Although RATS easily performs these calculations using the CORRELATE instruction, it is useful to illustrate the process by considering four important examples: the AR(1), AR(2), MA(1) and ARMA(1, 1) models. Consider first the AR(2) process:

$$y_t = a_1 y_{t-1} + a_2 y_{t-2} + \epsilon_t$$

We omit an intercept term (a_0) since it has no effect on the autocorrelations. A simple way to derive the autocorrelations is to form the **Yule-Walker** equations. Multiply the second-order difference equation by y_{t-s} for $s = 0$, $s = 1$, $s = 2$, ... and take expectations to form:

$$Ey_t y_t = a_1 Ey_{t-1} y_t + a_2 Ey_{t-2} y_t + E\epsilon_t y_t$$
$$Ey_t y_{t-1} = a_1 Ey_{t-1} y_{t-1} + a_2 Ey_{t-2} y_{t-1} + E\epsilon_t y_{t-1}$$
$$Ey_t y_{t-2} = a_1 Ey_{t-1} y_{t-2} + a_2 Ey_{t-2} y_{t-2} + E\epsilon_t y_{t-2}$$
.
.
$$Ey_t y_{t-s} = a_1 Ey_{t-1} y_{t-s} + a_2 Ey_{t-2} y_{t-s} + E\epsilon_t y_{t-s}$$

By definition, the autocovariances of a stationary series are such that $Ey_t y_{t-s} = Ey_{t-s} y_t = Ey_{t-j} y_{t-j-s} = \gamma_s$. We also know that $E\epsilon_t y_t = \sigma^2$. Since $E\epsilon_t y_{t-s} = 0$, we can use the equations above to form:

$$\gamma_0 = a_1 \gamma_1 + a_2 \gamma_2 + \sigma^2$$
$$\gamma_1 = a_1 \gamma_0 + a_2 \gamma_1$$
$$\gamma_s = a_1 \gamma_{s-1} + a_2 \gamma_{s-2} \text{ for } s \geq 2$$

First consider the special case of an AR(1) process obtained by setting $a_2 = 0$:

$$\gamma_0 = a_1 \gamma_1 + \sigma^2$$
$$\gamma_1 = a_1 \gamma_0 \qquad \text{so that dividing by } \gamma_0 \text{ yields } \rho_1 = a_1$$
$$\gamma_s = a_1 \gamma_{s-1} \qquad \text{so that dividing by } \gamma_0 \text{ yields } \rho_s = a_1 \rho_{s-1}$$

Since ρ_0 necessarily equals unity, we find $\rho_0 = 1$; $\rho_1 = a_1$; $\rho_2 = (a_1)^2$; ...; $\rho_s = (a_1)^s$. For an AR(1) process, a necessary condition for stationarity is for $|a_1| < 1$. Thus, the plot of ρ_s against s-called the autocorrelation function (ACF) or **correlogram**-should converge to zero geometrically if the series is stationary. If a_1 is positive, convergence will be direct and if a_1 is negative, the autocorrelations will follow a dampened oscillatory path around zero. The first two panels on the left-hand side of Figure 2.1 show the theoretical autocorrelation functions for $a_1 = 0.7$ and $a_1 = -0.7$ respectively. Here, ρ_0 is not shown since its value is necessarily unity.

Now return to the more general AR(2) process. Dividing by γ_0 yields:

$$\rho_1 = a_1 \rho_0 + a_2 \rho_1 \qquad\qquad (2.2)$$
$$\rho_s = a_1 \rho_{s-1} + a_2 \rho_{s-2} \text{ for } s \geq 2 \qquad\qquad (2.3)$$

We know that $\rho_0 = 1$, so that from (2.2) $\rho_1 = a_1/(1-a_2)$. Hence, we can find all ρ_s for $s \geq 2$ by solving the difference equation (2.3). For example, for $s = 2$ and $s = 3$:

$$\rho_2 = (a_1)^2/(1-a_2) + a_2$$
$$\rho_3 = a_1[(a_1)^2/(1-a_2) + a_2] + a_2 a_1/(1-a_2)$$

Figure 2.1: Theoretical ACF and PACF Patterns

Autocorrelations   *Partial Autocorrelations*

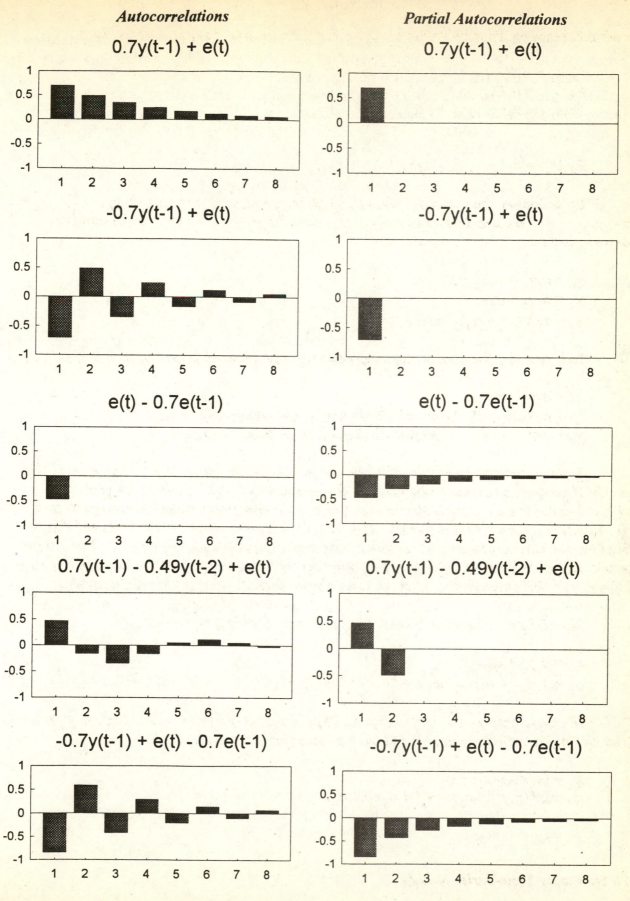

Although the values of the ρ_s are cumbersome to derive, we can easily characterize their properties. Given the solutions for ρ_0 and ρ_1, the remaining ρ_s all satisfy the difference equation (2.3). As in the general case of a second-order difference equation, the solution may be oscillatory or direct. Note that the stationarity condition for y_t necessitates that the $\{\rho_s\}$ sequence must be convergent. The fourth panel on the left-hand side of Figure 2.1 shows the ACF for the process: $y_t = 0.7y_{t-1} - 0.49y_{t-2} + \epsilon_t$. The properties of the various ρ_s follow directly from the equation: $y_t - 0.7y_{t-1} + 0.49y_{t-2} = 0$.

The ACF of an MA(1) Process: Next consider the MA(1) process $y_t = \epsilon_t + \beta\epsilon_{t-1}$. Again, obtain the Yule-Walker equations by multiplying y_t by each y_{t-s} and take expectations:

$$\gamma_0 = \text{Var}(y_t) = Ey_t y_t = E[(\epsilon_t + \beta\epsilon_{t-1})(\epsilon_t + \beta\epsilon_{t-1})] = (1 + \beta^2)\sigma^2.$$
$$\gamma_1 = Ey_t y_{t-1} = E[(\epsilon_t + \beta\epsilon_{t-1})(\epsilon_{t-1} + \beta\epsilon_{t-2})] = \beta\sigma^2$$

and

$$\gamma_s = Ey_t y_{t-s} = E[(\epsilon_t + \beta\epsilon_{t-1})(\epsilon_{t-s} + \beta\epsilon_{t-s-1})] = 0 \quad \text{for all } s > 1$$

Hence, dividing each γ_s by γ_0, it is immediately seen that the ACF is simply $\rho_0 = 1$; $\rho_1 = \beta/(1+\beta^2)$; and $\rho_s = 0$ for all $s > 1$. The third panel on the left-hand side of Figure 2.1 shows the ACF for the MA(1) process $y_t = \epsilon_t - 0.7\epsilon_{t-1}$.

The Autocorrelation Function of an ARMA(1, 1) Process: Lastly, let $y_t = a_1 y_{t-1} + \epsilon_t + \beta_1\epsilon_{t-1}$. If you use the now familiar procedure, the Yule-Walker equations are:

$$Ey_t y_t = a_1 Ey_{t-1}y_t + E\epsilon_t y_t + \beta_1 E\epsilon_{t-1}y_t \quad \Rightarrow \quad \gamma_0 = a_1\gamma_1 + \sigma^2 + \beta_1(a_1+\beta_1)\sigma^2 \tag{2.4}$$
$$Ey_t y_{t-1} = a_1 Ey_{t-1}y_{t-1} + E\epsilon_t y_{t-1} + \beta_1 E\epsilon_{t-1}y_{t-1} \Rightarrow \gamma_1 = a_1\gamma_0 + \beta_1\sigma^2 \tag{2.5}$$
$$Ey_t y_{t-2} = a_1 Ey_{t-1}y_{t-2} + E\epsilon_t y_{t-2} + \beta_1 E\epsilon_{t-1}y_{t-2} \Rightarrow \gamma_2 = a_1\gamma_1 \tag{2.6}$$

.
.

$$Ey_t y_{t-s} = a_1 Ey_{t-1}y_{t-s} + E\epsilon_t y_{t-s} + \beta_1 E\epsilon_{t-1}y_{t-s} \quad \Rightarrow \quad \gamma_s = a_1\gamma_{s-1} \tag{2.7}$$

Solving (2.4) and (2.5) simultaneously for γ_0 and γ_1 and forming $\rho_1 = \gamma_1/\gamma_0$, you can verify that:

$$\rho_1 = \frac{(1 + a_1\beta_1)(a_1 + \beta_1)}{(1 + \beta_1^2 + 2a_1\beta_1)}$$

From (2.7) $\rho_s = a_1\rho_{s-1}$ for all $s \geq 2$.

Thus, the ACF for an ARMA(1, 1) process is such that the magnitude of ρ_1 depends on both a_1 and β_1. Beginning with this value of ρ_1, the ACF of an ARMA(1, 1) process looks like that of the AR(1) process. If $0 < a_1 < 1$, convergence will be direct and if $-1 < a_1 < 0$, the autocorrelations will oscillate. The ACF for the function $y_t = -0.7y_{t-1} + \epsilon_t - 0.7\epsilon_{t-1}$ is shown as the last panel on the left-hand-side of Figure 2.1.

The Partial Autocorrelation Function: In an AR(1) process, y_t and y_{t-2} are correlated even though y_{t-2} does not directly appear in the model. The correlation between y_t and y_{t-2} (i.e., ρ_2) is equal to the correlation between y_t and y_{t-1} (i.e., ρ_1) multiplied by the correlation between y_{t-1} and y_{t-2} (i.e., ρ_1 again) so that $\rho_2 = (\rho_1)^2$. It is important to note that all such "indirect" correlations are present in the ACF of any autoregressive process. In contrast, the **partial autocorrelation** between y_t and y_{t-s} eliminates the effects of the intervening values y_{t-1} through y_{t-s+1}. As such, in an AR(1) process the partial autocorrelation between y_t and y_{t-2} is equal to zero. The most direct way to find the partial autocorrelation function is to first form the series $\{y_t^*\}$ by subtracting the mean of y (μ) from each observation: $y_t^* \equiv y_t - \mu$. Next, form the first-order autoregression equation:

$$y_t^* = \phi_{11} y_{t-1}^* + e_t$$

where e_t is an error term. Here the symbol $\{e_t\}$ is used since this error process may not be white-noise.

Since there are no intervening values, ϕ_{11} is both the autocorrelation and the partial autocorrelation between y_t and y_{t-1}. Now form the second-order autoregression equation:

$$y_t^* = \phi_{21} y_{t-1}^* + \phi_{22} y_{t-2}^* + e_t$$

Here ϕ_{22} is the partial autocorrelation coefficient between y_t and y_{t-2}. In other words, ϕ_{22} is the correlation between y_t and y_{t-2} controlling for (i.e., "netting out") the effect of y_{t-1}. Repeating this process for all additional lags s yields the partial autocorrelation function (PACF). In practice, with sample size T, only $T/4$ lags are used in obtaining the sample PACF.

For an AR(p) process, there is no direct correlation between y_t and y_{t-s} for $s > p$. Hence, all values of ϕ_{ss} for $s > p$ will be zero and the PACF for a pure AR(p) process should cut to zero for all lags greater than p. This is a useful feature of the PACF that can aid in the identification of an AR(p) model. In contrast, consider the PACF for the MA(1) process: $y_t = \epsilon_t + \beta\epsilon_{t-1}$. If the series is invertible, it has the infinite-order autoregressive representation $y_t / (1 + \beta L) = \epsilon_t$ or:

$$y_t - \beta y_{t-1} + \beta^2 y_{t-2} - \beta^3 y_{t-3} + \dots = \epsilon_t.$$

As such, the PACF will <u>not</u> jump to zero since y_t will be correlated with all of its own lags. Instead, the PACF coefficients exhibit a geometrically decaying pattern. If $\beta < 0$, decay is direct and if $\beta > 0$, the PACF coefficients oscillate.

More generally, the PACF of a stationary ARMA(p, q) process must ultimately decay towards zero. The decay pattern depends on the coefficients of the polynomial $(1 + \beta_1 L + \beta_2 L^2 +$

$... + \beta_q L^q)$. The right-hand-side panels of Figure 2.1 show the partial autocorrelation functions of the five indicated processes. For stationary processes, the key points to note are:

1. The ACF of an ARMA(p, q) process will begin to decay at lag q. Beginning at lag q, the coefficients of the ACF (i.e., the ρ_i) will satisfy the difference equation ($\rho_i = a_1 \rho_{i-1} + a_2 \rho_{i-2} + ... + a_p \rho_{i-p}$). Since the characteristic roots are inside the unit circle, the autocorrelations will decay beginning at lag q. Moreover, the pattern of the autocorrelation coefficients will mimic that suggested by the characteristic roots.

2. The PACF of an ARMA(p, q) process will begin to decay at lag p. Beginning at lag p, the coefficients of the PACF (i.e., the ϕ_{ii}) will mimic the ACF coefficients from the model: $y_t / (1 + \beta_1 L + \beta_2 L^2 + ... + \beta_q L^q)$.

We can illustrate the usefulness of the ACF and PACF functions using the model $y_t = a_0 + 0.7 y_{t-1} + \epsilon_t$. If we compare the top two panels in Figure 2.1, the ACF shows the monotonic decay of the autocorrelations while the PACF exhibits the single spike at lag 1. Suppose you instruct RATS to construct the ACF and PACF for a data series. If the actual patterns compare favorably to the theoretical patterns, you might try to estimate data using an AR(1) model. Correspondingly, if the ACF exhibited a single spike and the PACF exhibited monotonic decay (see the third panel for the model $y_t = \epsilon_t - 0.7 \epsilon_{t-1}$), you might try an MA(1) model.

4. The Box-Jenkins methodology: Box and Jenkins (1976) popularized a three-stage method aimed at selecting an appropriate model for the purpose of estimating and forecasting a univariate time series.

In the **Identification Stage**, use the GRAPH instruction to visually examine the time plot of the series. Plotting each observation of the $\{y_t\}$ sequence against t, provides useful information concerning outliers, missing values, and structural breaks in the data. Nonstationary variables may have a pronounced trend or appear to meander without a constant long-run mean or variance. Missing values and outliers can be corrected at this point. At one time, the standard practice was to first-difference any series deemed to be nonstationary. Currently, a large literature is evolving that develops formal procedures to check for nonstationarity. We defer this discussion until Chapter 4 and assume that we are working with stationary data.

Next, the sample ACF and PACF can be constructed using the RATS CORRELATE instruction. These sample autocorrelations can be compared to various theoretical functions to help identify the actual nature of the data-generating process. Let r_s be the sample autocorrelation between y_t and y_{t-s}. Box and Jenkins (1976) discuss the distribution of the sample values of r_s under the null that y_t is stationary with normally distributed errors. In a sample with T usable observations, if the true value of $r_s = 0$ [i.e., if the true data generating process is an MA(s-1) process], the sampling variance of r_s is such that:

$$Var[r_s] = T^{-1} \qquad\qquad \text{for } s = 1$$

$$= [1 + 2\sum_{j=1}^{s-1} r_j^2]T^{-1} \quad \text{for } s > 1$$

Moreover, in large samples (i.e., for large values of T), r_s will be normally distributed with a mean equal to zero. For the PACF coefficients, under the null hypothesis of an AR(p) model (i.e, under the null that all $\phi_{p+i,p+i}$ are zero) the variance of the $\phi_{p+i,p+i}$ is approximately T^{-1}.

In practice, we can use these sample values to form the sample autocorrelation and partial autocorrelation functions and test their significance. For example, if we use a 95% confidence interval (i.e., two standard deviations), and the calculated value of r_1 exceeds $2T^{-1/2}$, it is possible to reject the null hypothesis that the first-order autocorrelation is not statistically different from zero. Rejecting this hypothesis means rejecting an MA(s-1) = MA(0) process and accepting the alternative $q > 0$. Next, try $s = 2$; Var(r_2) is: $(1+2r_1^2)/T$. If r_1 is 0.5 and T is 100, the variance of r_2 is 0.015 and the standard deviation is about 0.123. Thus, if the calculated value of r_2 exceeds 2(0.123), it is possible to reject the hypothesis $r_2 = 0$. Here, rejecting the null means accepting the alternative that $q > 1$. In practice, the maximum number of sample autocorrelations and partial autocorrelations to use is $T/4$.

If you construct a large number of autocorrelations, some will exceed two standard deviations as a result of pure chance even though the true values in the data-generating process are zero. The Q-statistic can be used to test whether a group of autocorrelations is significantly different from zero. Ljung and Box (1978) used the sample autocorrelations to form the statistic:

$$Q = T(T + 2)\sum_{k=1}^{s} r_k^2/(T-k)$$

If the sample value of Q exceeds the critical value of χ^2 with s degrees of freedom, then *at least* one value of r_k is statistically different from zero at the specified significance level. The intuition behind the use of the statistic is that high sample autocorrelations lead to large values of Q. Certainly, a white-noise process (in which all autocorrleations should be zero) would have a Q value of zero. If the calculated value of Q exceeds the appropriate value in a chi-square table, we can reject the null of no significant autocorrelations. Note that rejecting the null means accepting an alternative that at least one autocorrelation is not zero. You can use the RATS CORRELATE instruction to generate these Q-statistics and their significance levels.

A comparison of the sample ACF and PACF to those of various theoretical ARMA processes may suggest several plausible models. In the **Estimation Stage**, each of the tentative models is fit and the various a_i and β_i coefficients are examined. In this second stage, the estimated models are compared using the criteria listed below.

Parsimony: A fundamental idea in the Box-Jenkins approach is the *Principle of*

Parsimony. Parsimony (meaning sparseness or stinginess) should come as second nature to economists. Incorporating additional coefficients will necessarily increase fit (e.g., the value of R^2 will increase) at a cost of reducing degrees of freedom. Box and Jenkins argue that parsimonious models produce better forecasts than overparameterized models. A parsimonious model fits the data well without incorporating any needless coefficients. The aim is to approximate the true data-generating process but not to pin down the exact process.

Stationarity and Invertibility: The distribution theory underlying the use of the sample ACF and PACF as approximations to those of the true data-generating process assumes that the $\{y_t\}$ sequence is stationary. Moreover, t-statistics and Q-statistics also presume that the data is stationary. The estimated autoregressive coefficients should be consistent with this underlying assumption. Hence, we should be suspicious of an AR(1) model if the estimated value of a_1 is close to unity.

The Box-Jenkins approach also necessitates that the model be **invertible**. Invertibility is important because the use of the ACF and PACF implicitly assumes that the $\{y_t\}$ sequence can be well approximated by an autoregressive model. Values of β_i that suggest noninvertibility usually result from a poorly formulated model.

Goodness of Fit: A good model will fit the data well. Obviously, R^2 and the average of the residual sum of squares are common "goodness-of-fit" measures in ordinary least squares. The problem with these measures is that the "fit" necessarily improves as more parameters are included in the model. There exist various model selection criteria that tradeoff a reduction in the residual sum of squares for a more **parsimonious** model. The two most commonly used model selection criteria are the Akaike Information Criterion (AIC) and the Schwartz Bayesian Criterion (SBC) that can be calculated as:[1]

AIC $= T \ln(\text{residual sum of squares}) + 2n$
SBC $= T \ln(\text{residual sum of squares}) + n \ln(T)$

where n = number of parameters estimated ($p + q$ + possible constant term) and T = number of usable observations.

Typically in creating lagged variables, some observations are lost. To adequately compare the alternative models, T should be kept fixed. For example, with 100 data points, estimate an AR(1) and an AR(2) using only the last 98 observations in each estimation. Compare the two models using $T = 98$.

Ideally, the AIC and SBC will be as small as possible (*Note*: both can be negative). We can use these criteria to aid in selecting the most appropriate model; model A is said to fit better

---

[1] The formulas reported here and in the *RATS User's Manual* are easily computable monotonic transformations of the AIC and SBC. They will select the same model as the actual AIC and/or SBC.

than model B if the the AIC (or SBC) for A is smaller than for model B. In using the criteria to compare alternative models, we must estimate over the same sample period. For each, increasing the number of regressors increases n but should have the effect of reducing the residual sum of squares. Thus, if a regressor has no explanatory power, adding it to the model will cause both the AIC and SBC to increase. Since $\ln(T)$ will be greater than 2, the SBC will always select a more parsimonious model than the AIC. RATS does not generate the AIC or SBC internally. However, you can use the formulas presented in the next section to calculate and display both.

The third stage in the Box-Jenkins methodology involves **Diagnostic Checking**. The standard practice is to plot the residuals to look for outliers and for periods in which the model does not fit the data well. The STATISTICS and GRAPH instructions are especially helpful. Any evidence of serial correlation implies a systematic movement in the $\{y_t\}$ sequence that is not accounted for by the ARMA coefficients included in the model. Hence, any of the tentative models yielding nonrandom residuals should be eliminated from consideration. To check for correlation in the residuals, construct the ACF and the PACF of the *residuals* of the estimated model. You can then use the Ljung-Box Q-statistic to determine whether any or all of the residual autocorrelations or partial autocorrelations are statistically significant. Note that when forming the s correlations from an estimated ARMA(p, q) model, the degrees of freedom are reduced by the number of estimated coefficients. Hence, if we use the residuals of an ARMA(p, q) model, Q has a χ^2 with $s-p-q$ degrees of freedom (if a constant is included, the degrees of freedom are $s-p-q-1$). As discussed in the next section, RATS allows you to adjust for this loss in degrees of freedom by using the DFC (degrees of freedom correction) option in the CORRELATE instruction.

If there are sufficient observations, fitting the same ARMA model to each of two subsamples can provide useful information concerning the assumption that the data-generating process is unchanging. Divide the number of usable observations (T = %nobs) into two subsamples with m observations in the first and $n = T - m$ in the second. Denote the residual sum of squares as RSS and let $a_i(k)$ and $\beta_i(k)$ be the coefficients a_i and β_i estimated in subsample k. You can use each subsample to estimate the two models:

$$y_t = a_0(1) + a_1(1)y_{t-1} + \ldots + a_p(1)y_{t-p} + \epsilon_t + \beta_1(1)\epsilon_{t-1} + \ldots + \beta_q(1)\epsilon_{t-q} \quad \text{using } 1, \ldots m$$
$$y_t = a_0(2) + a_1(2)y_{t-1} + \ldots + a_p(2)y_{t-p} + \epsilon_t + \beta_1(2)\epsilon_{t-1} + \ldots + \beta_q(2)\epsilon_{t-q} \quad \text{using } m+1, \ldots T$$

Let the residual sum of the squares from each model be RSS_1 and RSS_2, respectively. To test the restriction that all coefficients are equal [i.e., $a_0(1) = a_0(2)$ and $a_1(1) = a_1(2)$ and ... $a_p(1) = a_p(2)$ and $\beta_1(1) = \beta_1(2)$ and ... $\beta_q(1) = \beta_q(2)$] use an F-test and form:

$$F = \frac{(RSS - RSS_1 - RSS_2)/(n)}{(RSS_1 + RSS_2)/(T - 2n)}$$

where n = number of parameters estimated ($n = p + q + 1$ if an intercept is included and $p + q$

otherwise), and the number of degrees of freedom are $(n, T - 2n)$.

Intuitively, if the restriction is not binding, the total from the two models (i.e., $RSS_1 + RSS_2$) should equal the sum of the squared residuals from the entire sample estimation. Hence, F should equal zero. The larger the calculated value of F, the more restrictive is the assumption that the two sets of coefficients are equal.

Finally, you can use the model to **Forecast**. The RATS FORECAST instruction can be used to make two types of conditional forecasts. As shown in sample program 2, you can use your ARMA model to form the conditional forecasts from the perspective of time period T (i.e., the last time period in your sample) of the values of $y_{T+1}, y_{T+2}, \ldots$. A properly estimated model will provide good short-term forecasts of $E_T y_{T+j}$. Also, as shown in sample program 3 you can use so-called out-of-sample forecasting as a useful way to compare alternative models.

RATS Instructions and Procedures

RATS contains several instructions and procedures that allow you to fully implement the Box-Jenkins methodology. The most useful are listed below:

1. BOXJENK: Estimates ARMA, transfer function, and intervention models. Consult the *RATS User's Manual* for details concerning transfer functions and intervention models. BOXJENK creates the same variables as the LINREG instruction (such as %BETA and %RSS). In addition, you can use TEST and RESTRICT to test hypotheses on the coefficients. The coefficients are numbered as in LINREG. The syntax and principal options of BOXJENK are:

boxjenk(options) *depvar start end residuals*
where: *depvar*   The dependent variable
        start end   The range to use in the estimation. The default is the maximum range over which it is possible to estimate the model. If you set start, be sure to allow for AR lags and the effect of differencing. You do not have to allow for MA lags.
        residuals   The name of the series to call the residuals. Omit if you do not want to save the residuals. Note that you must save the residuals if you want to forecast.

The important options for our purposes are:

CONSTANT   You must specify *constant* if you want to include an intercept.
DIFFS=   Number of regular differences. [Default = 0]

AR=	List of autoregressive coefficients. [Default = 0]
MA=	List of moving-average coefficients. [Default = 0]

Note: The options ar $= p$ and ma $= q$ include AR coefficients 1 through p and MA coefficients 1 through q. In newer versions of RATS, ar $= \| \text{ } list \text{ } \|$ and ma $= \| \text{ } list \text{ } \|$ include only those coefficients enumerated in *list*. For example, ar $= 4$ calls for the inclusion of autoregressive coefficients a_1, a_2, a_3, and a_4. Instead, ar $= \|1, 4\|$ calls for the inclusion of autoregressive coefficients a_1 and a_4 but not a_2 or a_3.

SAR=	List of seasonal autoregressive coefficients. [Default = 0]
SMA=	List of seasonal moving-average coefficients. [Default = 0]
DFC=	Degrees of freedom correction. Corrects for degrees of freedom lost due to parameter estimation. When you use residuals from one model as the dependent variable in a second estimation, degrees of freedom are lost as a result of the first round of parameter estimation. Set DFC= *number of parameters estimated in the first equation minus the number of repeated parameters in the second.*
DEFINE=	If you want to use FORECAST, you must specify the equation number or name for later use.

Examples:

1. boxjenk(define=model_1,constant,ar=2,ma=2) y 3 100 resids

    This statement estimates the model $y_t = a_0 + a_1 y_{t-1} + a_2 y_{t-2} + \epsilon_t + \beta_1 \epsilon_{t-1} + \beta_2 \epsilon_{t-2}$ over the sample period 3 through 100 (since two observations are lost due to the 2 ar coefficients) and saves the residuals in a series called *resids*. This model is defined as *model_1* to be used with FORECAST.

2. boxjenk(ar=2,ma=||2||) y /

    This statement estimates the model $y_t = a_1 y_{t-1} + a_2 y_{t-2} + \epsilon_t + \beta_2 \epsilon_{t-2}$ over the sample period 3 through T (since two observations are lost due to the 2 ar coefficients). Note the absence of a constant. Early versions of RATS do not allow you to use the ar $= \|list\|$ or ma $= \|list\|$ feature.

3. boxjenk(ar=2,diffs=1) y /

    This statement estimates the model $\Delta y_t = a_1 \Delta y_{t-1} + a_2 \Delta y_{t-2} + \epsilon_t$ over the sample period 4 through T (since one observation is lost due to differencing and two additional observations are lost due to the 2 autoregressive coefficients).

2. CORRELATE: Calculates the autocorrelations (and the partial autocorrelations) of a specified series. The syntax and principal options are:

correlate(options) *series start end*

where: *series*	The series used to compute the correlations.
start end	The range of entries to use. The default is the entire series.

The principal options are:

NUMBER=   The number of autocorrelations to compute. The default is the integer value of one-fourth the total number of observations.

PARTIAL=   Series for the partial autocorrelations. If you omit this option, the PACF will not be calculated.

QSTATS   Use this option if you want the Ljung-Box Q-statistics.

DFC=   Degrees of freedom correction. Use this option if you want the Q-statistics of the residuals from an estimated ARMA model. Set DFC=*number of parameters in the estimated model* to account for the associated loss in degrees of freedom.

SPAN=   Use with *qstats* to set the width of the intervals tested. For example, with quarterly data, you can set *span = 4*, to obtain $Q(4)$, $Q(8)$, $Q(12)$, and so forth.

Examples:

1. cor(partial=pacf) y

In the first sample program below, the *y* series contains 100 observations. This instruction produces 24 autocorrelations and partial correlations.

2. cor(partial=pacf,qstats,number=24,span=8,dfc=%nreg) resids

This syntax is appropriate to analyze the residuals of a previously estimated model. Since NUMBER=24, the statement produces the first 24 autocorrelations and partial autocorrelations of the *resids* series. Since SPAN=8, the Q-statistics for the first 8, 16, and 24 of the autocorrelations are generated. The option dfc=%nreg sets the degrees of freedom correction equal to the numbers of regressors in the model generating *resids*.

3. FORECAST: Creates dynamic forecasts of a previously defined equation. (*NOTE*: The residuals from the estimated model must be saved.) FORECAST uses a supplementary card for each equation in the system. In univariate forecasting, the typical syntax for FORECAST is:

forecast(print) *number steps start*
 # equation forecasts

where: *number*   The number of equations in the system. In univariate forecasting, number is necessarily equal to 1.

    steps   The number of forecasts to create.

    start   The starting period of the forecasts.

    equation   The name of the previously defined equation.

    forecasts   The name of the series in which you want to save the forecasts. This field is optional.

Example:
The following three statements (taken from the sample program ARMA.PRG below) are typical of the use of FORECAST. The first estimates the series *y* as an ARMA(1, 1) process and saves the residuals in the series *resids*. This equation is defined as *eq1*. The second indicates that this is a univariate model (since *number* is set to 1) and instructs RATS to generate five forecasts beginning with the forecast of observation 101. The supplementary card indicates the name of the equation to use for forecasting (i.e., *eq1*):

```
boxjenk(define=eq1,ar=1,ma=1) y / resids
forecast(print) 1 5 101
# eq1
```

4. BJIDENT.SRC: Creates a high-resolution graph the ACF and PACF of a specified series. BJIDENT is the first of the RATS' procedures discussed in this handbook. A procedure is similar to an instruction with the important exception procedures must be compiled before use.[1] As discussed below, BJIDENT.SRC can be compiled using the instruction `source(noecho)` `c:\`*directory*`\bjident.src`. After compiling, BJIDENT.SRC is used as:

@bjident(options) *series start end*
where: *series*   Series used to compute the correlations.
    start end   Range of entries to use. The default is the entire series.

The principal options are:

DIFF=	The number of regular differences. The default is zero.
SDIFFS=	The number of seasonal differences. The default is zero.
TRANS=	Set TRANS=LOG if you want the ACF of log(*series*) and set TRANS=ROOT if you want the ACF of *series***0.5.

Examples:
1. The SOURCE instruction compiles the BJIDENT.SRC procedure. Here is is assumed that BJIDENT.SRC resides on drive c:\rats. The NOECHO option directs RATS not to display the compiled program on the screen. The second statement displays a graph of the ACF and PACF of the series *y*; since *start end* is left unspecified, the entire sample period is used:

```
source(noecho) c:\rats\bjident.src
@bjident y
```

---

[1] Instructions are built into the RATS computer code. Procedures allow RATS to take up a relatively small amount of your computer's memory since you compile only those procedures needed for a particular task. All procedures packaged with RATS end with *.SRC.

2. Within any program, a procedure needs to be compiled only once. After compilation, the following statement graphs the ACF and PACF of *y* and the first difference of *y* for observations 51 through 100:

@bjident(diff=1) y 51 100.

5. BJFORE.SRC: Estimates a specified model and computes forecasts. Before it can be used, BJFORE.SRC must be compiled using the SOURCE instruction. (See the discussion of BJIDENT.SRC for the syntax of SOURCE.) After compiling the procedure is used as:

@bjfore(options) *series start end forecasts*
where: *series*   Series to be forecast
      start end   Range of entries to forecast. The default is the range of *series*.
      forecasts   Series for computed forecasts

The principal options are:

DIFFS=	Number of regular differences. The default is zero.
SDIFFS=	Number of seasonal differences. The default is zero.
ARS=	Number of autoregressive coefficients. The default is zero.
MAS=	Number of moving-average coefficients. The default is zero.
SAS=	Number of seasonal autoregressive coefficients.
SMA=	Number of seasonal moving-average coefficients. The default is zero.
SPAN=	Seasonal span.
TRANS=	Used to transform the raw series as in BJIDENT.SRC.
NOCONSTANT	In BJFORE.SRC, *constant* is the default. Use *noconstant* if you do not want a constant.

Example:
1. The first statement compiles the procedure (assumed to reside on drive c:\rats). Since the NOECHO option is not specified, the source code of BJFORE.SRC is displayed on the screen. The next statement uses BJFORE.SRC to estimate an ARMA(1, 1) model without a constant. The estimation runs over the entire sample period. Forecasts are specified for periods 101 through 105 and are stored as entries 101 through 106 in the series *fores*. The PRINT instruction displays the forecasts:

source c:\rats\bjfore.src
@bjfore(ars=1,mas=1,noconstant) y 101 105 fores
print / fores

2. To estimate an ARMA(1, 1) model with a constant and to generate forecasts over periods 80 to 100, use:

```
@bjfore(ars=1,mas=1) y 80 100 fores
print / fores
```

6. AIC and SBC: RATS does not automatically calculate the AIC of the SBC. However, as illustrated in sample programs 1 through 3, it is straightforward to compute and display these criteria. For example, after estimating an AR(1) model of dlwpi, you can compute the AIC and SBC as as reported on page 32 as:

```
boxjenk(constant,ar=1) dlwpi / resid
compute sbc = %nobs*log(%rss) + %nreg*log(%nobs)
compute aic = %nobs*log(%rss) + 2*%nreg
display 'AIC' aic 'SBC' sbc
```

In this example:

%nobs	The number of usable observations in the previously estimated model
%rss	The residual sum of squares in the previously estimated model
%nreg	The number of regressors (including the constant) in the previously estimated model

7. CDF: Computes the marginal significance level of a statistic using the F, t, χ^2, or Normal distribution. For the t-test and Normal distributions, divide the marginal significance level by two for a 1-tailed test. The syntax for CDF is:

cdf *distribution statistic degree1 degree2*

where:	*distribution*	You can specify either FTEST, TTEST, CHI, or NORMAL.
	statistic	The test statistic in the form of a number, variable, or expression.
	degree1	The degrees of freedom for the t-test and χ^2-test. The numerator degrees of freedom for the F-test.
	degree2	The denominator degrees of freedom for the F-test. Otherwise leave blank.

Example:
Sample program 3 performs an F-test for structural change. The number of observations is *nobs*, the number of regressors is *%nreg*, the residual sum of squares from the full model is *rssall*, and the residual sums of squares from the two subsamples are *rss1* and *rss2*. The first statement computes the test statistic F and the second computes the marginal significance level. The numerator degrees of freedom are *%nreg* and the denominator degrees of freedom are *nobs-2*%nreg*.

```
compute F = ((rssall-rss1-rss2)/%nreg)/((rss1+rss2)/(nobs-2*%nreg))
cdf ftest F %nreg nobs-2*%nreg
```

Sample Programs

1. A model of an AR(1) process. The first column of the file entitled SIM_2.PRN contains 100 values of a simulated AR(1) process. The series is called $y1$. The following program will identify and estimate the AR(1) process. You can find the entire program on the file labeled AR1.PRG and the program and output of the file labeled AR1.OUT. The first five lines of the program are:

```
all 100
open data a:sim_2.prn          ;* Modify this line if the data disk is not in drive a:\.
data(format=prn,org=obs) / y1
set y = y1
statistics y
```

```
Statistics on Series Y
Observations    100
Sample Mean     -0.5707421000        Variance                    1.939986
Standard Error   1.3928337567        SE of Sample Mean           0.139283
t-Statistic     -4.09770             Signif Level (Mean=0) 0.00008548
Skewness        -0.31011             Signif Level (Sk=0)   0.21239389
Kurtosis        -0.34771             Signif Level (Ku=0)   0.49326147
```

```
/* The first line allocates space for 100 observations. Note that the CALENDAR instruction is
not needed since the series is not dated. Setting y1 = y allows all of the statements below to be
copied for your use in other programs; simply rename your series y. In your own programs, the
STATISTICS and the GRAPH instructions should always be used. Together, they can indicate
missing values, outliers, and possibly suggest appropriate transformations. You can create a
graph of the y series using:
*/
```

```
graph 1               ;* The graph is not shown.
# y
```

```
/* The first step in the Box-Jenkins methodology is to examine the ACF and PACF. To obtain a
printout of the ACF and PACF, use the CORRELATE instruction. You can obtain a high-
resolution graph of the ACF and PACF using the BJIDENT.SRC procedure. RATS calculates
approximately T/4 correlations; below, correlations 13 through 24 are omitted in order to save
space. Note that the decay in the ACF and the single spike in the PACF suggest an AR(1) model.
*/
```

cor(partial=pacf) y

```
Correlations of Series Y
Autocorrelations
1:  0.7394471   0.5842742   0.4711052   0.3885974   0.3443781   0.3350914
7:  0.2972265   0.3251536   0.2689485   0.2007991   0.1886648   0.0824284

Partial Autocorrelations
1:  0.7394471   0.0827245   0.0302927   0.0255939   0.0601121   0.0889353
7: -0.0165335   0.1438633  -0.1002338  -0.0653562   0.0699026  -0.2040191
```

* To use BJIDENT.SRC, first compile the procedure using the SOURCE instruction followed by
*   the name of the procedure.

source(noecho) c:\rats\bjident.src ;* Modify this line if BJIDENT.SRC is not on drive c:\rats
@bjident y

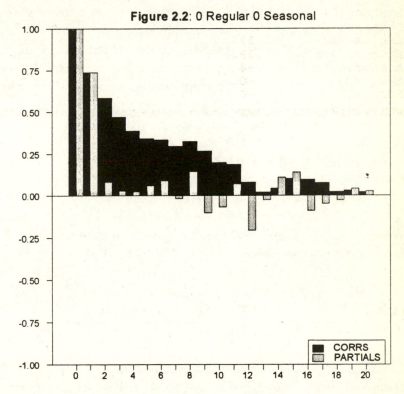

Figure 2.2: 0 Regular 0 Seasonal

/*The default heading of the graph indicates the number of differences and the number of seasonal differences entered as options for BJIDENT.SRC. Since the options DIFFS= and SDIFFS= were not specified, the default values of zero are indicated. The PACF shows a single significant spike at lag 1 (approximately equal to 0.739) and the decline in the ACF approximates the decay pattern of $\rho_s = (0.739)^s$. The only ambiguous issue is the relatively large PACF coefficient at lag 12.

The next line of AR1.PRG instructs RATS to estimate an AR(1) model including a constant over the full sample period and to save the residuals in the series *resids*.
*/

boxjenk(constant,ar=1) y / resids

```
Dependent Variable Y - Estimation by Box-Jenkins
Iterations Taken    3
Usable Observations       99      Degrees of Freedom     97
Centered R**2       0.561907      R Bar **2   0.557391
Uncentered R**2     0.627560      T x R**2      62.128
Mean of Dependent Variable       -0.582649091
Std Error of Dependent Variable   1.394797238
Standard Error of Estimate        0.927943146
Sum of Squared Residuals         83.524612752
Durbin-Watson Statistic              2.112719

Coefficient      Estimate      Standard      t-statistic    Significance
                               Error                        Level
1.   CONSTANT -0.558596416   0.379943061    -1.47021        0.14474097
2.   AR{1}     0.754471837   0.067640691    11.15411        0.00000000
```

/* Notice that the BOXJENK instruction displays many of the same statistics as LINREG. An important difference is that BOXJENK uses a nonlinear search procedure to find estimates of the ARMA coefficients. Here, the process converged in three iterations. If the RATS search procedure does not converge within the default number of 20, you can use the ITERATIONS= option. Be aware that a large number of required iterations can indicate a poorly specified model or a model with a flat likelihood surface (so that the coefficient estimates lack precision). The next three lines compute and display the AIC and SBC:
*/

compute aic = %nobs*log(%rss) + 2*%nreg
compute sbc = %nobs*log(%rss) + %nreg*log(%nobs)
display 'aic = ' AIC 'sbc = ' sbc
```
     aic = 442.08899    sbc = 447.27923
```

* Since the constant does not appear to be significant, reestimate the model without the constant:

boxjenk(ar=1) y / resids

Coefficient	Estimate	Standard Error	t-statistic	Significance Level
AR{1}	0.7904697094	0.0624405894	12.65955	0.00000000

* Again, compute and display the AIC and SBC:

compute aic = %nobs*log(%rss) + 2*%nreg
compute sbc = %nobs*log(%rss) + %nreg*log(%nobs)
display 'aic = ' AIC 'sbc = ' sbc
```
     aic = 441.93682    sbc = 444.53194
```

/* Note that the AIC and SBC both select the model without the constant. Now perform some diagnostic checking of the residuals by using the CORRELATE instruction. The number of Q-statistics is approximately 1/4 the number of observations. Span = 8 yields $Q(8)$, $Q(16)$, and

Q(24). Note that dfc = %nreg sets DFC equal to the number of parameters estimated.
*/

cor(partial=pacf,qstats,number=24,span=8,dfc=%nreg) resids

```
Correlations of Series RESIDS
Autocorrelations
      1: -0.0972263  0.0044385  0.0057530 -0.0445299 -0.0461781  0.0911488
      7: -0.0862466  0.1661004  0.0664142 -0.0299726  0.1805000 -0.0341879

Partial Autocorrelations
      1: -0.0972263 -0.0050623  0.0057490 -0.0438056 -0.0553876  0.0823474
      7: -0.0705301  0.1535279  0.0929978 -0.0094311  0.1892035 -0.0022467

Ljung-Box Q-Statistics
Q(8)  =           6.1387.  Significance Level 0.52365083
Q(16) =          15.7430.  Significance Level 0.39933690
Q(24) =          21.0243.  Significance Level 0.57960138
```

/* Since there does not appear to be any serial correlation in the residuals, we could stop at this point. However, suppose you wanted to capture the effect of the PACF coefficient at lag 11. You might try to estimate the model with a MA term at lag 11 using:
*/

boxjenk(ar=1,ma=∥11∥) y / resids

Coefficient	Estimate	Standard Error	t-statistic	Significance Level
AR{1}	0.7748256694	0.0649680179	11.92626	0.00000000
MA{11}	0.2205957837	0.1048030512	2.10486	0.03788792

/* The MA(11) is significant at the 5% level. The next three lines compute and display the AIC and SBC. Note that the sample period is equivalent to that of the AR(1) model since no observations are lost due to moving-average terms:
*/

compute aic = %nobs*log(%rss) + 2*%nreg
compute sbc = %nobs*log(%rss) + %nreg*log(%nobs)
display 'aic = ' AIC 'sbc = ' sbc
```
        aic = 439.42397    sbc = 444.61420
```

/* The AIC selects the model with the MA(11) term while the more parsiminous SBC selects the model without the MA(11) term. To clarify the issue, you could perform other diagnostic checks to distinguish between the AR(1) and the ARMA(1, ∥11∥) models. As shown below, these include splitting the sample period and using within-sample forecasting. As an exercise, estimate y as an AR(2) and as an ARMA(1, 1). Show that neither of these models is superior to the AR(1):

boxjenk(ar=2) y / resids   ;* Estimates the AR(2) model.
boxjenk(ar=1,ma=1) y / resids   ;* Estimates an ARMA(1, 1) model.

2. A model of an ARMA(1, 1) process: The second column in the file entitled SIM_2.WK1 contains the 100 values of a simulated ARMA(1, 1) process. This series is called *y2*. The following program will identify and estimate the process and perform out-of-sample forecasts. You can find the entire program on the file labeled ARMA.PRG and the program and output on the file labeled ARMA.OUT.

```
all 100                      ;* Allocates space for 100 observations.
open data a:sim_2.wk1        ;* Modify this line if SIM_2.WK1 is not on drive a:\ .
data(format=wks,org=obs) / y2
set y = y2                   ;* Instead of retyping the statements used in sample
                             ;*  program 1, you can define y = y2 and copy the program.
cor(partial=pacf) y    ;* Calculates the ACF and PACF.  RATS actually displays 25 correlations.
```

```
Autocorrelations
1: -0.8343832   0.5965290 -0.4399660   0.3497725 -0.3187445   0.3316348
7: -0.3371782   0.3166056 -0.2761497   0.1789269 -0.0839172   0.0375969

Partial Autocorrelations
1: -0.8343832 -0.3280607 -0.1942903 -0.0145160 -0.1398293   0.0891766
7:  0.0004337   0.0143662   0.0166776 -0.1987821 -0.0462206 -0.0212410
```

* The ACF and PACF suggest an ARMA(1, 1) or possibly an AR(2) model. First, estimate the
*   AR(2) using:

```
boxjenk(ar=2) y / resids        ;* As an exercise, show that a constant is not necessary.
```

Coefficient	Estimate	Standard Error	t-statistic	Significance Level
AR{1}	-1.167961923	0.093965958	-12.42963	0.00000000
AR{2}	-0.378168657	0.092658981	-4.08130	0.00009263

* The estimated coefficients are highly significant. Now obtain the ACF and PACF of the
* residuals using the CORRELATE instruction:

```
cor(partial=pacf,qstats,number=24,span=8,dfc=%nreg) resids
```

```
Correlations of Series RESIDS
Autocorrelations
1: -0.1058752 -0.2105054 -0.0940192 -0.0330828   0.0545117   0.1541513
7: -0.1257205 -0.0300117 -0.1509400   0.0459215   0.0913653 -0.0850088

Partial Autocorrelations
1: -0.1058752 -0.2242285 -0.1544542 -0.1268651 -0.0308003   0.1183770
7: -0.0977745   0.0026778 -0.1916767 -0.0286644 -0.0130383 -0.1411953

Ljung-Box Q-Statistics
Q(8)  =   11.4352.  Significance Level 0.07582148
Q(16) =   18.3056.  Significance Level 0.19321646
Q(24) =   22.5851.  Significance Level 0.42546527
```

/*   Note that the number of Q-statistics is approximately 1/4 the number of observations. Span = 8 yields the $Q(8)$, $Q(16)$, and $Q(24)$ statistics. Note that dfc=%nreg automatically sets DFC equal to the number of parameters estimated. Here, %nreg = 2. There is strong evidence of serial correlation in the residuals; r_2 = -0.2105 and $Q(8)$ has a significance level of 0.07582148. After displaying the AIC and SBC, alternative models should be explored:
*/

```
compute aic = %nobs*log(%rss) + 2*%nreg
compute sbc = %nobs*log(%rss) + %nreg*log(%nobs)
display 'aic = ' AIC 'sbc = ' sbc
        aic =   482.77291   sbc = 487.94285
```

/*   You can verify that AR(1) and MA(1) models are inadequate. The next four program statements estimate an ARMA(1, 1) model and compute and display the AIC and SBC. To ensure that the AIC and SBC are comparable to that of the AR(2) model, specify the *start end* values as 3 and 100. At this point, we are not interested in the coefficient estimates so that the NOPRINT option can be used.
*/

```
boxjenk(noprint,ar=1,ma=1) y 3 100          ;* Do not use the default sample period.
compute aic = %nobs*log(%rss) + 2*%nreg
compute sbc = %nobs*log(%rss) + %nreg*log(%nobs)
display 'aic = ' AIC 'sbc = ' sbc
        aic = 471.04957 sbc = 476.21950
```

/* Both the AIC and SBC select the ARMA(1, 1) model. Next, estimate the ARMA(1, 1) model over the entire sample period. The DEFINE= option is necessary since forecasts are desired; the equation name is *eq1*. It is also necessary to save the residuals for the FORECAST instruction.
*/

boxjenk(define=eq1,ar=1,ma=1) y / resids

Coefficient	Estimate	Standard Error	t-statistic	Significance Level
AR{1}	-0.678933302	0.075530960	-8.98881	0.00000000
MA{1}	-0.676102671	0.080563072	-8.39222	0.00000000

/* The coefficients are highly significant. Notice that the point estimates imply a stationary and invertible process. Next, obtain the ACF, PACF, and Q-statistics of the residuals using the CORRELATE instruction. The option dfc=%nreg corrects for the fact that *resids* is estimated from a model with two regressors. In the output reported below, you can see that there does not appear to be any serial correlation in the residual series:
*/

```
cor(partial=pacf,qstats,number=24,span=8,dfc=%nreg) resids
```

```
Correlations of Series RESIDS
Autocorrelations
1:   0.0102828   0.0147699  -0.0102395  -0.0525937   0.0536500   0.0877636
7:  -0.1401794  -0.0483144  -0.1823489  -0.0319496   0.0227910  -0.1267464

Partial Autocorrelations
1:   0.0102828   0.0146657  -0.0105433  -0.0526209   0.0551864   0.0885914
7:  -0.1468255  -0.0509429  -0.1725135  -0.0247100   0.0037079  -0.1358980

Ljung-Box Q-Statistics
Q(8)   =    3.8618.   Significance Level 0.69536951
Q(16)  =   10.7422.   Significance Level 0.70616013
Q(24)  =   14.2357.   Significance Level 0.89290305
```

/* Next, the estimated model can be used to obtain out-of-sample forecasts. The following two statements produce five forecasts beginning with period 101. The supplementary card for FORECAST specifies the previously defined equation *eq1*:
*/

forecast(print) 1 5 101
 # eq1

```
        Entry           Y
          101   -0.984745381851
          102    0.668576433734
          103   -0.453918805797
          104    0.308180593662
          105   -0.209234068068
```

/*   Given the value of y_{100} and the estimated value of ϵ_{100}, these five forecasts are the values $E_{100}y_{101}$, $E_{100}y_{102}$, and so on. Alternatively, the RATS BJFORE.SRC procedure could have been used to estimate the identical ARMA(1, 1) model and obtain the same out-of-sample forecasts. The next three lines of ARMA.PRG illustrate the general method. First, compile the procedure. Next, use BJFORE.SRC to estimate an ARMA(1, 1) model without a constant (the estimation runs from period 2 through 100). Forecasts are specified for periods 101 through 105 and are stored as entries 101 through 105 in the series *fores*. Use the PRINT instruction to display the forecasts. Note that BJFORE.SRC will display the results of the estimated model in precisely the same format as that shown above.
*/

source(noecho) c:\rats\bjfore.src   ;* Alter this line if BJFORE.SRC is not in c:\rats.
@bjfore(ars=1,mas=1,noconstant) y 101 105 fores
print / fores

```
        ENTRY          FORES
          101       -0.9847454
          102        0.6685764
          103       -0.4539188
          104        0.3081806
          105       -0.2092341
```

3. A model of the Wholesale Price Index: The file entitled WPI.WK1 contains quarterly U.S. Wholesale Price Index data from 1960:1 to 1992:2. In the previous chapter, you used the LINREG instruction to estimate this series as an AR(4) process with seasonal dummy variables. This exercise illustrates how to use the Box-Jenkins methodology to estimate the same series as a more parsimonious ARMA process. You can find the entire program on the file labeled WPI.PRG and the program and output of the file labeled WPI.OUT. The first five lines are identical to those in WPI_REG.PRG; the sixth line is used to compile BJIDENT.SRC:

```
cal 1960 1 4                    ;* Set the calendar from 1960:1
all 1992:4                      ;*      to 1992:4.
open data a:wpi.wk1             ;* Opens data set wpi.wk1 assumed to be on drive a:\ .
data(format=wks,org=obs)
set dlwpi = log(wpi) - log(wpi{1})
source(noecho) c:\rats\bjident.src   ;* Modify this line if BJIDENT.SRC is not on drive c:\rats.
```

* The next two instructions help to identify *dlwpi*. As an exercise, verify that the WPI
*   itself does not have the characteristics of a stationary series:

cor(partial=pacf) dlwpi

```
Autocorrelations
1:   0.5878711   0.4993113   0.4584863   0.4719989   0.3327979   0.3454482
7:   0.2051063   0.1435376   0.1000362   0.1188517   0.0485385   0.0715192

Partial Autocorrelations
1:   0.5878711   0.2348977   0.1549665   0.1804368  -0.0983210   0.0855705
7:  -0.1697844  -0.0897234  -0.0188172   0.0372592   0.0012882   0.0705760
```

@bjident dlpi /

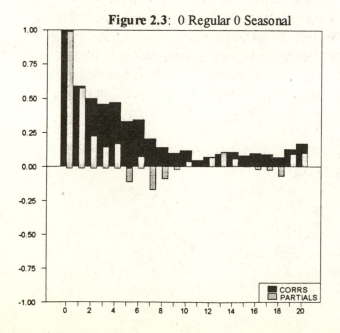

Figure 2.3: 0 Regular 0 Seasonal

/* The ambiguous ACF and PACF are not suggestive of a simple AR(p) or MA(q) process. There are several large spikes in the ACF and in the PACF. It is likely that the logarithmic change in the Wholesale Price Index is an ARMA(p, q) process. Begin by estimating an ARMA(1, 1) model.

To estimate an ARMA(1, 1) model with an intercept and to save the residuals, use:
*/

boxjenk(constant,ar=1,ma=1) dlwpi / resids

Coefficient	Estimate	Standard Error	t-statistic	Significance Level
CONSTANT	0.010484902	0.004405769	2.37981	0.01883337
AR{1}	0.889069641	0.059263358	15.00201	0.00000000
MA{1}	-0.514522826	0.111683147	-4.60699	0.00000992

/* The coefficients are significant at conventional levels. Now, check the residuals for serial correlation. SPAN = 8 produces the Q-statistics for intervals of eight periods. Here, the DFC= option is used since *resids* has been estimated:
*/

cor(partial=pacf,qstats,span=8,dfc=%nreg) resids

```
Autocorrelations
1:   0.0074000 -0.0485621 -0.0120277   0.1585506 -0.0483299   0.1502811
7:  -0.0709830 -0.0954604 -0.1005335   0.0133654 -0.1225670 -0.0374033

Partial Autocorrelations
1:   0.0074000 -0.0486195 -0.0113184   0.1567634 -0.0534576   0.1706623
7:  -0.0832060 -0.1059913 -0.0898829 -0.0540433 -0.1009550 -0.0392973

Ljung-Box Q-Statistics
Q(8)  =    9.0642.  Significance Level 0.10653191
Q(16) =   13.2492.  Significance Level 0.42875481
Q(24) =   18.5435.  Significance Level 0.61439740
Q(32) =   30.7083.  Significance Level 0.37930107
```

* The next three lines compute the AIC and SBC:

compute sbc = %nobs*log(%rss) + %nreg*log(%nobs)
compute aic = %nobs*log(%rss) + 2*%nreg
display 'AIC' aic 'SBC' sbc
```
        AIC -523.39339    SBC -514.83730
```

* Use the next three lines to graph the residuals and plot the residual ACF and PACF:

graph 1
resids
@bjident resids

/* The output from these three statements is not shown; you can construct the graphs by entering these lines in the file labeled WPI.OUT. Many would be content with the performance of the ARMA(1, 1) model. However, further experimentation suggests the possibility of a moving-average coefficient at lag 4 (possibly due to seasonality). To illustrate the techniques involved,

estimate the ARMA(1, ||1,4||) model:
*/

boxjenk(constant,ar=1,ma=||1,4||) dlwpi / resids

Coefficient	Estimate	Standard Error	t-statistic	Significance Level
CONSTANT	0.010068060	0.003924889	2.56518	0.01150351
AR{1}	0.787459940	0.086482981	9.10537	0.00000000
MA{1}	-0.437369411	0.112668222	-3.88192	0.00016746
MA{4}	0.295697878	0.090426056	3.27005	0.00139221

* The MA(4) term is highly significant. You can check the residuals using:

cor(partial=pacf,qstats,span=8,dfc=%nreg) resids ;* See WPI.OUT for the output.

/* Since the inclusion of an MA(4) term does not alter the estimation period, you can construct the AIC and SBC as:
*/
compute sbc = %nobs*log(%rss) + %nreg*log(%nobs)
compute aic = %nobs*log(%rss) + 2*%nreg
display 'AIC' aic 'SBC' sbc
      AIC -527.39070   SBC -515.98258

/* Both the AIC and SBC select the model with the MA(4) term. In addition to plotting the residuals and the ACF and PACF of the residuals, it is desirable to test the stability of the coefficients using an F-test. First compute the residual sum of squares of the overall model.
*/

compute rssall = %rss ; compute nobs = %nobs

* Next, split the sample and estimate the ARMA(1,||1,4||) model over the first period:

boxjenk(noprint,constant,ar=1,ma=||1,4||) dlwpi 1960:3 1971:4

* Compute the residual sum of squares of the first period:

compute rss1 = %rss

* Estimate the model over the second period and compute the residual sum of squares:

boxjenk(noprint,constant,ar=1,ma=||1,4||) dlwpi 1972:1 1992:2
compute rss2 = %rss

* Now compute and display the *F*-statistic:

```
compute F = ((rssall-rss1-rss2)/%nreg)/((rss1+rss2)/(nobs-2*%nreg))
```
display F
```
        0.53825
```

* Alternatively, use the RATS CDF instruction for an F-test to obtain the value of F and its
* significance level:

cdf ftest F %nreg nobs-2*%nreg   ;* Calculate the significance level of F = 0.53825.
```
     F(4,120)=        0.53825 with Significance Level 0.70789873
```

* Another way to obtain the same result is to use:
display %ftest(F,%nreg,nobs-2*%nreg)
```
        0.70790
```

* Conclude there is no evidence of structural change. As another diagnostic check, compare the
*   out-of-sample forecasts of the ARMA(1, 1) and ARMA(1, ||1,4||) models. Shorten the sample
*   period to 1990:4 and estimate each model over the shorter period. Compare the forecasts
*   of the two models with the last six of the actual observations. Note that it is necessary to
*   include the *define=* option and to save the residuals in order to forecast:

boxjenk(noprint,define=eq1,constant,ar=1,ma=||1,4||) dlwpi 60:3 90:4 resids

forecast(print) 1 6 1991:1 ;* Produce six forecasts using *eq1* beginning with 1991:1.
 # eq1 fore1   ;* *fore1* is the name of the series containing the forecasts.

```
        Entry        DLWPI
        1991:01  0.0188847938082
        1991:02  0.0125375481187
        1991:03  0.0174885621627
        1991:04  0.0225979697379
        1992:01  0.0202683832426
        1992:02  0.0184263689702
```

* Repeat the process using the ARMA(1, 1) model:

boxjenk(noprint,define=eq2,constant,ar=1,ma=1) dlwpi 60:3 90:4 resids
forecast(print) 1 6 1991:1
 # eq2 fore2
```
        Entry        DLWPI
        1991:01  0.0188094779885
        1991:02  0.0180561216989
        1991:03  0.0173876265086
        1991:04  0.0167944333202
        1992:01  0.0162680598116
        1992:02  0.0158009791438
```

* Next calculate the squared forecast errors and produce the summary statistics with the TABLE
*   instruction:

```
set error1 91:1 92:2 = (dlwpi - fore1)**2
set error2 91:1 92:2 = (dlwpi - fore2)**2
```
table / error1 error2

Series	Obs	Mean	Standard Error	Minimum	Maximum
ERROR1	6	0.00057785770	0.00051875480	0.00006094613	0.00158046929
ERROR2	6	0.00055395699	0.00055631156	0.00002684701	0.00157448658

/* Conclude that the ARMA(1, 1) model produces better out-of-sample forecasts than the ARMA(1, ||1,4||) model. The mean of the squared errors is lower, as are the minimum and maximum squared errors.
*/

Additional Exercises

1. The third column in SIM_2.WK1 contains the 100 values of an AR(2) process; this series is called *y3*. Modify sample program 3 to show that an AR(2) model of *y3* is preferable to ARMA(1, 1) and MA(2) models.

2. In the previous chapter, you used the LINREG instruction to estimate *dlwpi* as an AR(4) process with four seasonal dummy variables. In addition, you were asked to show that you can omit the fourth-order autoregressive coefficient and all the seasonal coefficients except seasons{-3}. Compare these two models to the ARMA(1, ||1,4||) model of *dlwpi*.

3. The file entitled US.PRN contains quarterly value of the U.S. money supply (M1) from 60:1 to 91:4.

   (a) Plot the sequence against time and obtain the ACF, PACF, and Q-statistics. Does the series appear to be stationary?

   (b) Detrend the data by estimating the regression: $\Delta \log(M1)_t = a_0 + b(time) + e_t$.

   Plot the residuals (i.e., the $\{e_t\}$ sequence) against time and obtain the ACF, PACF, and Q-statistics. Does detrending seem to render the sequence stationary?

   (c) Calculate the ACF and PACF of the first-difference of $\log(M1)$. Does differencing seem to render the sequence stationary?

   (d) Seasonally difference the money supply as: $\Delta_4 \log(M1)_t = \log(M1)_t - \log(M1)_{t-4}$. Use BJIDENT.SRC to plot the ACF and PACF.

(e) For convenience, let $m4_t$ denote $\Delta_4 \log(M1)_t$. Use BOXJENK to estimate the seasonally differenced log of the money supply as the AR(1) process:

$$m4_t = a_0 + a_1 m4_{t-1} + \epsilon_t$$

Examine the diagnostic statistics to show that this model is inappropriate.

(f) Now, define $\Delta m4\_1_t = m4_t - m4_{t-1}$ so that $\Delta m4\_1_t$ is the first difference of the seasonal difference of the money supply. Estimate $\Delta m4\_1_t$ as:

$$\Delta m4\_1_t = (1 + \beta_4 L^4)\epsilon_t$$

Examine the diagnostic statistics. Explain why the model appears to be satisfactory.

(g) Obtain the money supply forecasts for 92:1 through 92:4.

4. Modify sample program 1 so as to estimate the $\{y_t\}$ series as an AR(2) and as an ARMA(1, 1) process. Use the appropriate diagnostic tests to show that neither of these models is superior to the AR(1).

5. Modify sample program 2 so as to estimate the $\{y_t\}$ series as an MA(2) process. Use the appropriate diagnostic tests to show that neither of these models is superior to the AR(1).

Chapter 3 — Modeling Volatility

Many economic time series exhibit phases of relative tranquility followed by periods of high volatility. A stochastic variable with a constant variance is called *homoskedastic* as opposed to *heteroskedastic*. For series exhibiting volatility, the unconditional variance may be constant even though the variance during some periods is unusually large. This chapter will extend the tools developed in Chapter 2 to model such conditional heteroskedasticity.

Figure 3.1 illustrates the behavior of the U.S. inflation rate as measured by the GNP deflator and the Producer Price Index. Casual inspection does have its perils and formal testing is necessary to substantiate any first impressions, yet the strong visual pattern is that of heteroskedasticity. During the 1970's, U.S. producer prices fluctuated wildly as compared with the 1960's and 1980's. If the variance is not constant, a series is not stationary. However, it may be the case that a series is stationary in that the unconditional (or long-run) variance is constant but there are periods in which the conditional variance fluctuates. If, for example, the conditional variance follows a stationary AR(1) process, the long-run variance is constant but the variance at t is dependent on the

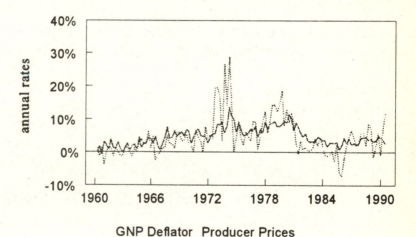

Figure 3.1: U.S. Price Indices (Percent Change)

GNP Deflator   Producer Prices

variance in $t\text{-}1$. Such series are known as *conditionally heteroskedastic*. This chapter will demonstrate how to use the tools developed in Chapter 2 to identify and estimate conditionally heteroskedastic series.

It is easy to imagine instances in which you might want to forecast the conditional variance of a series. As an asset holder, you would be interested in forecasts of the rate of return *and* its variance over the holding period. The unconditional variance (i.e., the long-run value of the variance) would be unimportant if you plan to buy the asset at t and sell at $t+1$.

Theoretical Background

Engle (1982) shows that it is possible to simultaneously model the mean *and* the variance of a series. For example, let $\{\hat{\epsilon}_t\}$ denote the estimated residuals from the model:

$$y_t = a_0 + a_1 y_{t-1} + \epsilon_t$$

so that the conditional variance of y_t is:

$$\begin{aligned} \text{Var}(y_t|y_{t-1}) &= E_{t-1}[(y_t - a_0 - a_1 y_{t-1})^2] \\ &= E_{t-1}\epsilon_t^2 \end{aligned}$$

Standard Box-Jenkins methods assume this variance is equal to the unconditional variance σ^2. Instead, suppose that the conditional variance is not constant. One simple strategy to model the conditional variance would be to estimate an $AR(q)$ process using the *squares* of the estimated residuals:

$$\hat{\epsilon}_t^2 = \alpha_0 + \alpha_1 \hat{\epsilon}_{t-1}^2 + \alpha_2 \hat{\epsilon}_{t-2}^2 + \ldots + \alpha_q \hat{\epsilon}_{t-q}^2 + v_t \tag{3.1}$$

where v_t is a white-noise process.

If the values of $\alpha_1, \alpha_2, \ldots, \alpha_q$ all equal zero, the estimated variance is simply the constant α_0. Otherwise, the conditional variance of y_t evolves according to the autoregressive process given by (3.1). As such, you can use (3.1) to forecast the conditional variance at $t+1$ as:

$$E_t \hat{\epsilon}_{t+1}^2 = \alpha_0 + \alpha_1 \hat{\epsilon}_t^2 + \alpha_2 \hat{\epsilon}_{t-1}^2 + \ldots + \alpha_q \hat{\epsilon}_{t+1-q}^2.$$

For this reason, an equation like (3.1) is called an <u>A</u>uto-<u>R</u>egressive <u>C</u>onditional <u>H</u>eteroskedastic (ARCH) model. The are many possible applications for ARCH models since the residuals in (3.1) can come from an autoregression, an ARMA model, or a standard regression model.

In actuality, the linear specification of (3.1) is not the most convenient. The reason is that the model for $\{y_t\}$ and the conditional variance are best estimated simultaneously using maximum likelihood techniques. Since this estimation technique uses the logarithm of the variance, it is more tractable to specify v_t as a multiplicative disturbance. The simplest example from the class of multiplicative conditionally heteroskedastic models proposed by Engle (1982) is:

$$\epsilon_t = v_t \sqrt{\alpha_0 + \alpha_1 \epsilon_{t-1}^2} \tag{3.2}$$

where v_t = white-noise process such that $\sigma_v^2 = 1$, v_t and ϵ_{t-1} are independent of each other; and α_0 and α_1 are constants such that $\alpha_0 > 0$ and $0 < \alpha_1 < 1$.

Since v_t is white noise and is independent of ϵ_{t-1}, it is easy to show that the elements of the $\{\epsilon_t\}$ sequence have a mean of zero and are uncorrelated. Since $\sigma_v^2 = 1$ and the unconditional variance of ϵ_t is identical to that of ϵ_{t-1} (i.e., $E\epsilon_t^2 = E\epsilon_{t-1}^2$), the unconditional variance is:

$$E\epsilon_t^2 = \alpha_0 / (1 - \alpha_1)$$

Thus, the unconditional mean and variance are unaffected by the presence of the error process given by (3.2). Similarly, it is easy to show that the conditional mean of ϵ_t is equal to zero. Given that v_t and ϵ_{t-1} are independent and that $Ev_t = 0$, the conditional mean of ϵ_t is:

$$E(\epsilon_t | \epsilon_{t-1}, \epsilon_{t-2}, ...) = Ev_t E(\alpha_0 + \alpha_1 \epsilon_{t-1}^2)^{0.5} = 0$$

At this point, you might be thinking that the properties of the $\{\epsilon_t\}$ sequence are not affected by (3.2) since the mean is zero, the variance is constant, and all autocovariances are zero. However, the influence of (3.2) falls entirely on the conditional variance. Since $\sigma_v^2 = 1$, the variance of ϵ_t conditioned on the past history of $\epsilon_{t-1}, \epsilon_{t-2}, ...$ is:

$$E(\epsilon_t^2 | \epsilon_{t-1}, \epsilon_{t-2} ...) = \alpha_0 + \alpha_1 \epsilon_{t-1}^2 \qquad (3.3)$$

In (3.3), the conditional variance of ϵ_t is dependent on the realized value of ϵ_{t-1}^2. If the realized value of ϵ_{t-1}^2 is large, $E_{t-1}\epsilon_t^2$ will be large as well. In (3.3), the conditional variance follows a first-order autoregressive process denoted by ARCH(1). As opposed to a usual autoregression, the coefficients α_0 and α_1 have to be restricted. In order to ensure that the conditional variance is always positive, it is necessary to assume that both α_0 and α_1 are positive. After all, if α_0 is negative, a sufficiently small realization of ϵ_{t-1} will mean that (3.3) is negative. Similarly, if α_1 is negative, a sufficiently large realization of ϵ_{t-1} can render a negative value for the conditional variance. Moreover, to ensure the stability of the autoregressive process, it is necessary to restrict α_1 such that $0 < \alpha_1 < 1$.

This discussion illustrates the essential features of any ARCH process. In an ARCH model, the error structure is such that the conditional and unconditional means are equal to zero. Moreover, the $\{\epsilon_t\}$ sequence is serially uncorrelated since for all $s \neq 0$, $E\epsilon_t\epsilon_{t-s} = 0$. The key point is that the errors are <u>not</u> independent since they are related through their second moment (recall that correlation is a linear relationship). The conditional variance itself is an autoregressive process resulting in conditionally heteroskedastic errors. When the realized value of ϵ_{t-1} is far from zero-so that $\alpha_1(\epsilon_{t-1})^2$ is relatively large-the variance of ϵ_t will tend to be large.

To formally examine the relationship between conditional heteroskedasticity and the properties of the $\{y_t\}$ sequence, the conditional mean and variance of y_t are given by:

$$E_{t-1}y_t = a_0 + a_1 y_{t-1}$$

and

$$\mathrm{Var}(y_t | y_{t-1}, y_{t-2}, \ldots) = E_{t-1}(y_t - a_0 - a_1 y_{t-1})^2$$
$$= E_{t-1}\epsilon_t^2$$
$$= \alpha_0 + \alpha_1(\epsilon_{t-1})^2$$

Since α_1 and ϵ_{t-1}^2 cannot be negative, the minimum value for the conditional variance is α_0. For any nonzero realization of ϵ_{t-1}, the conditional variance of y_t is positively related to α_1. It can also be shown that the unconditional variance of y_t is:

$$\mathrm{Var}(y_t) = \left(\frac{\alpha_0}{1 - \alpha_1} \right) \left(\frac{1}{1 - a_1^2} \right)$$

Hence, the variance of the $\{y_t\}$ sequence is increasing in both α_1 and the absolute value of a_1. The ARCH process given by (3.2) has been extended in several interesting ways. Engle's (1982) original contribution considered the entire class of higher-order ARCH(q) processes:

$$\epsilon_t = v_t \sqrt{\alpha_0 + \sum_{i=1}^{q} \alpha_i \epsilon_{t-i}^2} \tag{3.4}$$

In (3.4), all shocks from ϵ_{t-1} to ϵ_{t-q} have a direct effect on ϵ_t so that the conditional variance acts like an autoregressive process of order q.

The GARCH Model: Bollerslev (1986) extended Engle's original work by developing a technique that allows the conditional variance to be an ARMA process. Now let the error process be such that:

$$\epsilon_t = v_t \sqrt{h_t} \quad \text{where } \sigma_v^2 = 1$$

and

$$h_t = \alpha_0 + \sum_{i=1}^{q} \alpha_i \epsilon_{t-i}^2 + \sum_{i=1}^{p} \beta_i h_{t-i} \tag{3.5}$$

Since $\{v_t\}$ is a white-noise process, the conditional and unconditional means of ϵ_t are equal to zero. If you take the expected value of ϵ_t, it is easy to verify that:

$$E\epsilon_t = Ev_t \sqrt{h_t} = 0$$

The important point is that the conditional variance of ϵ_t is given by $E_{t-1}\epsilon_t^2 = h_t$. Thus, the conditional variance of ϵ_t is the ARMA process given by the expression h_t in (3.5).

This Generalized ARCH(*p, q*) model-called GARCH*(p, q)*-allows for both autoregressive and moving-average components in the heteroskedastic variance. If you set $p = 0$ and $q = 1$, it is clear that the first-order ARCH model given by (3.2) is simply a GARCH(0, 1) model. If all the β_i equal zero, the GARCH (p, q) model is equivalent to an ARCH(q) model. The benefits of the GARCH model should be clear; a high-order ARCH model may have a more parsimonious GARCH representation that is much easier to identify and estimate. This is particularly important since all coefficients in (3.5) must be positive. Moreover, to ensure that the conditional variance is finite, all characteristic roots of (3.5) must imply convergence. Clearly, the more parsimonious model will entail fewer coefficient restrictions.

The key feature of GARCH models is that the conditional variance of the *disturbances* of the $\{y_t\}$ sequence constitutes an ARMA process. Hence, it is to be expected that the residuals from a fitted model should display this characteristic pattern. To explain, suppose you estimate a model of the $\{y_t\}$ process. If your model of $\{y_t\}$ is adequate, the ACF and PACF of the residuals should be indicative of a white-noise process. However, the ACF of the *squared* residuals can help identify the order of the GARCH process. Since $E_{t-1}\epsilon_t^2 = h_t$, we can rewrite (3.5) as:

$$E_{t-1}\epsilon_t^2 = \alpha_0 + \sum_{i=1}^{q} \alpha_i \epsilon_{t-i}^2 + \sum_{i=1}^{p} \beta_i h_{t-i} \tag{3.6}$$

Equation (3.6) looks very much like an ARMA(q, p) process in the $\{\epsilon_t^2\}$ sequence. If there is conditional heteroskedasticity, the correlogram should be suggestive of such a process. The technique to construct the correlogram of the squared residuals is as follows:

Step 1: Estimate the $\{y_t\}$ sequence using the "best fitting" ARMA model (or regression model) and obtain the squares of the fitted errors $\hat{\epsilon}_t^2$. Also calculate the sample variance of the residuals ($\hat{\sigma}^2$) defined as:

$$\hat{\sigma}^2 = \sum_{t=1}^{T} \hat{\epsilon}_t^2 / T$$

where T = number of residuals.

Step 2: Calculate and plot the sample autocorrelations:

$$\rho(i) = \frac{\sum\limits_{t=i+1}^{T} (\hat{\epsilon}_t^2 - \hat{\sigma}^2)(\hat{\epsilon}_{t-i}^2 - \hat{\sigma}^2)}{\sum\limits_{t=1}^{T} (\hat{\epsilon}_t^2 - \hat{\sigma}^2)^2}$$

Step 3: In large samples, the standard deviation of $\rho(i)$ can be approximated by $T^{-1/2}$. Individual values of $\rho(i)$ that are significantly different from zero are indicative of GARCH errors. As in Chapter 2, the Ljung-Box Q-statistic is:

$$Q = T(T+2) \sum_{i=1}^{n} \rho(i)/(T-i)$$

Q has an asymptotic χ^2 distribution with n degrees of freedom if the $\hat{\epsilon}_t^2$ are uncorrelated. Rejecting the null hypothesis that the $\hat{\epsilon}_t^2$ are uncorrelated is equivalent to rejecting the null hypothesis of no ARCH or GARCH errors. In practice, you should consider values of n up to $T/4$.

The more formal Lagrange multiplier (LM) test for ARCH disturbances has been proposed by Engle (1982). The methodology involves the following two steps:[1]

Step 1: Estimate the most appropriate model for the $\{y_t\}$ sequence using LINREG or BOXJENK and save the residuals.

Step 2: Obtain the squares of the fitted errors $\hat{\epsilon}_t^2$. Regress these squared residuals on a constant and on the n lagged values $\hat{\epsilon}_{t-1}^2, \hat{\epsilon}_{t-2}^2, \hat{\epsilon}_{t-3}^2, \dots , \hat{\epsilon}_{t-n}^2$; i.e., estimate:

$$\hat{\epsilon}_t^2 = \alpha_0 + \alpha_1 \hat{\epsilon}_{t-1}^2 + \alpha_2 \hat{\epsilon}_{t-2}^2 + \dots + \alpha_n \hat{\epsilon}_{t-n}^2$$

If there are no ARCH or GARCH effects, the estimated values of α_1 through α_n should be zero. Hence, this regression will have little explanatory power so that the coefficient of determination (i.e., the usual R^2-statistic) will be quite low. With a sample of T residuals, under the null hypothesis of no ARCH errors, the test statistic TR^2 converges to a χ^2 distribution with n degrees of freedom. If TR^2 is sufficiently large, rejection of the null hypothesis that α_1 through α_n are jointly equal to zero is equivalent to rejecting the null hypothesis of no ARCH errors. On the other hand, if TR^2 is sufficiently low, it is possible to conclude that there are no ARCH effects.

---

[1] Unfortunately, there is no available method to test the null of white-noise errors versus the specific alternative of GARCH(p, q) errors. Bollerslev (1986) proves that the ACF of the squared residuals resulting from (3.5) is an ARMA(m, p) model, where $m = \max(p, q)$.

The ARCH-M Model

Engle, Lilien, and Robins (1987) extend the basic ARCH framework to allow the mean of a sequence to depend on its own conditional variance. This class of model, called ARCH-M, is particularly suited to the study of asset markets. The basic insight is that risk-averse agents will require compensation for holding a risky asset. Given that an asset's *riskiness* can be measured by the variance of returns, the risk premium will be an increasing function of the conditional variance of returns. Engle, Lilien, and Robins express this idea by writing the excess return from holding a risky asset as:

$$y_t = \mu_t + \epsilon_t \tag{3.7}$$

where y_t = excess return from holding a long-term asset relative to a one-period treasury bill; μ_t = risk premium necessary to induce the risk-averse agent to hold the long-term asset rather than the one-period bill; and ϵ_t = unforecastable shock to the excess return on the long-term asset.

To explain (3.7), note that the expected excess return from holding the long-term asset must be just equal to the risk premium:

$$E_{t-1}y_t = \mu_t$$

Engle, Lilien, and Robins assume that the risk premium is an increasing function of the conditional variance of ϵ_t; in other words, the greater the conditional variance of returns, the greater the compensation necessary to induce the agent to hold the long-term asset. Mathematically, if h_t is the conditional variance of ϵ_t, the risk premium can be expressed as:

$$\mu_t = \beta + \delta h_t \qquad \delta > 0 \tag{3.8}$$

where h_t is the ARCH(q) process:

$$h_t = \alpha_0 + \sum_{i=1}^{q} \alpha_i \epsilon_{t-i}^2 \tag{3.9}$$

As a set, equations (3.7), (3.8), and (3.9) constitute the basic ARCH-M model. From (3.7) and (3.8), the conditional mean of y_t depends on the conditional variance h_t. From (3.9), the conditional variance is an ARCH(q) process. It should be pointed out that if the conditional variance is constant (i.e., if $\alpha_1 = \alpha_2 = ... = \alpha_q = 0$), the ARCH-M model degenerates into the more traditional case of a constant risk premium.

The presence of ARCH-M effects can be determined using Lagrange Multiplier tests exactly as in the case of ARCH and GARCH errors. The LM tests are relatively simple to conduct since they do not require estimation of the full model. The statistic TR^2 is asymptotically distributed as χ^2 with degrees of freedom equal to the number of restrictions.

Figure 3.2 illustrates two different ARCH-M processes. The upper-left-hand panel of the figure (labeled "White-Noise Process") shows 60 realizations of a simulated white-noise process denoted by $\{\epsilon_t\}$. Note the temporary increase in volatility during periods 20 to 30. After setting $\epsilon_0 = 0$, the conditional variance is constructed as the first-order ARCH process: $h_t = 1 + 0.65\epsilon_{t-1}^2$.

Figure 3.2: Simulated ARCH-M Processes

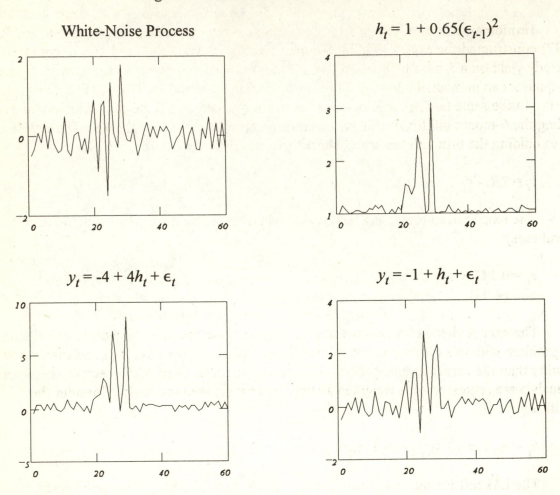

White-Noise Process

$h_t = 1 + 0.65(\epsilon_{t-1})^2$

$y_t = -4 + 4h_t + \epsilon_t$

$y_t = -1 + h_t + \epsilon_t$

As you can see in the upper-right-hand panel, the volatility in $\{\epsilon_t\}$ translates itself into increases in conditional variance. Note that large positive *and* negative realizations of ϵ_{t-1} result in a large value of h_t; it is the square of each $\{\epsilon_t\}$ realization that enters the conditional variance. In the lower-left panel, the values of β and δ are set equal to -4 and +4, respectively. As such, the

y_t sequence is constructed as $y_t = -4 + 4h_t + \epsilon_t$. You can clearly see that y_t is above its long-run value during the period of volatility. In the simulation, conditional volatility translates itself into increases in the values of $\{y_t\}$. In the latter portion of the sample, the volatility of $\{\epsilon_t\}$ diminishes and the values y_{30} through y_{60} fluctuate around their long-run mean.

The lower-right-hand panel reduces the influence of ARCH-M effects by reducing the magnitude of δ and β. Obviously, if $\delta = 0$, there are no ARCH-M effects at all. As you can see by comparing the two lower panels, y_t more closely mimics the $\{\epsilon_t^2\}$ sequence when the magnitude of δ is diminished from $\delta = 4$ to $\delta = 1$.

Implementation: Using quarterly data from 1960:1 to 1984:2, Engle, Lilien, and Robins (1987) constructed the excess yield on 6-month treasury bills as follows. Let r_t denote the quarterly yield on a 3-month T-bill held from t to $(t+1)$. Rolling over all proceeds, at the end of two quarters an individual investing \$1 at the beginning of period t will have $(1+r_t)(1+r_{t+1})$ dollars. In the same fashion, if R_t denotes the quarterly yield on a 6-month T-bill, buying and holding the 6-month bill for the full two quarters will result in $(1 + R_t)$ dollars. The excess yield due to holding the 6-month bill is approximately:

$$y_t = 2R_t - r_{t+1} - r_t$$

The results from regressing the excess yield on a constant are (the t-statistic is in parentheses):

$$y_t = 0.142 + \epsilon_t \tag{3.10}$$
$$(4.04)$$

The excess yield is 0.142% per quarter which is over four standard deviations from zero. The problem with this estimation method is that the post 1979 period showed markedly higher volatility than the earlier sample period. To test for the presence of ARCH errors, the squared residuals were regressed on a weighted average of past squared residuals. Consider the specification:

$$h_t = \alpha_0 + \alpha_1(0.4\epsilon_{t-1}^2 + 0.3\epsilon_{t-2}^2 + 0.2\epsilon_{t-3}^2 + 0.1\epsilon_{t-4}^2)$$

The LM test for the restriction $\alpha_1 = 0$ yields a value of $TR^2 = 10.1$, which has a χ^2 distribution with one degree of freedom. At the 1% significance level, the critical value of χ^2 with one degree of freedom is 6.635; hence, there is strong evidence of heteroskedasticity. Thus, there appear to be ARCH errors so that (3.10) is misspecified if individuals demand a risk premium.

The maximum likelihood estimates of the ARCH-M model and the associated t-statistics are given by:

$$y_t = -0.0241 + 0.687h_t + \epsilon_t$$
$$(-1.29) \quad (5.15)$$

$$h_t = 0.0023 + 1.64\,(0.4\epsilon_{t-1}^2 + 0.3\epsilon_{t-2}^2 + 0.2\epsilon_{t-3}^2 + 0.1\epsilon_{t-4}^2)$$
$$(1.08) \quad (6.30)$$

The estimated coefficients imply a time-varying risk premium. The estimated parameter of the ARCH equation of 1.64 implies that the unconditional variance is infinite. This is somewhat troublesome. However, the conditional variance is finite. Shocks to ϵ_{t-i} act to increase the conditional variance so that there are periods of tranquility and volatility. During volatile periods, the risk premium rises as risk-averse agents seek assets that are conditionally less risky.

Maximum Likelihood Estimation in RATS

To explain maximum likelihood estimation using RATS, it is convenient to begin with the classical regression model. Suppose that $\{\epsilon_t\}$ is generated by:

$$\epsilon_t = y_t - \beta x_t \tag{3.11}$$

In the classical regression model, the mean of ϵ_t is assumed to be zero, the variance is the constant σ^2, and the various realizations of $\{\epsilon_t\}$ are independent. Under the usual normality assumption, the log likelihood of observation t is:

$$-(1/2)\,\ln(2\pi) - (1/2)\,\ln\sigma^2 - \frac{1}{2\sigma^2}(y_t - \beta x_t)^2 \tag{3.12}$$

If we use a sample with T independent observations, the log likelihood equation is:

$$\log \mathcal{L} = -\frac{T}{2}\ln(2\pi) - \frac{T}{2}\ln\sigma^2 - \frac{1}{2\sigma^2}\sum_{t=1}^{T}(y_t - \beta x_t)^2$$

Maximizing the likelihood equation with respect to σ^2 and β yields:

$$\frac{\partial \log \mathcal{L}}{\partial \sigma^2} = -\frac{T}{2\sigma^2} + \frac{1}{2\sigma^4}\sum_{t=1}^{T}(y_t - \beta x_t)^2$$

and

$$\frac{\partial \log \mathcal{L}}{\partial \beta} = \frac{1}{\sigma^2}\sum_{t=1}^{T}(y_t x_t - \beta x_t^2)$$

Setting these partial derivatives equal to zero and solving for the values of β and σ^2 that yield the maximum value of log $\mathcal{L}$ results in the familiar OLS estimates of the variance and β (denoted by $\hat{\sigma}^2$ and $\hat{\beta}$). Hence:

$$\hat{\sigma}^2 = \frac{1}{T} \sum_{t=1}^{T} \epsilon_t^2 \quad \text{and} \quad \hat{\beta} = \frac{\sum x_t y_t}{\sum x_t^2}$$

All of this should be familiar ground since most econometric texts concerned with regression analysis discuss maximum likelihood estimation. The point to emphasize here is that the first-order conditions are easily solved since they are all linear. Calculating the appropriate sums may be tedious, but the methodology is straightforward. Unfortunately, this is not the case in estimating an ARCH-type model since the first-order equations are nonlinear. Instead, the solution requires some sort of search algorithm. The simplest way to illustrate the issue is to introduce an ARCH(1) error process into the regression model above. Continue to assume that ϵ_t is generated by the linear equation $\epsilon_t = y_t - \beta x_t$. Now let ϵ_t be given by (3.2):

$$\epsilon_t = v_t(\alpha_0 + \alpha_1 \epsilon_{t-1}^2)^{0.5}$$

so that the conditional variance of ϵ_t is:

$$h_t = \alpha_0 + \alpha_1(\epsilon_{t-1})^2$$

Although the conditional variance of ϵ_t is not constant, the necessary modification of (3.12) is clear. Since each realization of ϵ_t has the variance h_t, the likelihood of observation t is:

$$-(1/2) \ln(2\pi) - (1/2) \ln h_t - \frac{1}{2h_t}(y_t - \beta x_t)^2$$

If we sum over all usable observations, the appropriate log likelihood function is:

$$\log \mathcal{L} = -\frac{T-1}{2} \ln(2\pi) - 0.5 \sum_{t=2}^{T} \ln h_t - 0.5 \sum_{t=2}^{T} \frac{(y_t - \beta x_t)^2}{h_t}$$

where: $h_t = \alpha_0 + \alpha_1(\epsilon_{t-1})^2$
$\quad\quad\quad = \alpha_0 + \alpha_1(y_{t-1} - \beta x_{t-1})^2$

Note that the initial observation is lost since ϵ_0 is outside the sample. It is possible to make the appropriate substitutions for h_t and then maximize log $\mathcal{L}$ with respect to α_0, α_1, and β. Fortunately, the RATS MAXIMIZE command is able to select the parameter values that maximize this log likelihood function. Before presenting the syntax of the individual RATS instructions, it is worthwhile to consider the following hypothetical segment of a RATS program designed to estimate the model of $y_t = \beta x_t + \epsilon_t$ where the error term has the form of (3.2). To avoid using a new notation, pretend that you can use Greek letters in RATS. Consider the program segment:

> NONLIN β $\alpha 0$ $\alpha 1$
> FRML ϵ = y - β*x
> FRML h = $\alpha 0$ + $\alpha 1$*ϵ**2{1}
> FRML LIKELIHOOD = -0.5*(log(h) + ϵ(t)**2/h)
> COMPUTE β = *initial guess*, $\alpha 0$ = *initial guess*, $\alpha 1$ = *initial guess*
> MAXIMIZE LIKELIHOOD 2 *end*

The first statement prepares the program to estimate a nonlinear model with the parameters β, α_0, and α_1. The second statement sets up the formula (FRML) for ϵ_t; ϵ_t is defined to be $y_t - \beta x_t$. The third statement sets up the formula for h_t as an ARCH(1) process. The fourth statement is the key to understanding the program. The formula LIKELIHOOD defines the log likelihood for observation t; the program "understands" that it will maximize this sum over all $T-1$ observations. Note that the constant term $-(1/2)/\log(2\pi)$ is excluded from the definition of LIKELIHOOD; a constant has no effect on the solution to an optimization problem. The program requires initial guesses for β, α_0, and α_1. In practice, a reasonable initial guess for β could come from an OLS regression of $\{y_t\}$ on $\{x_t\}$. The initial guess for α_0 could be the variance of the residuals estimated from this OLS regression. After all, if there is no ARCH effect, OLS and the maximum likelihood methods are identical. The initial guess for α_1 could be a small positive number. The final statement tells the program to maximize LIKELIHOOD from observation 2 (since the initial observation is lost) to the end of the sample.

The same structure can be used for the estimation of more sophisticated models. The key to writing a successful program is to correctly specify the error process and the variance. For example, in Chapter 2 you estimated an ARMA[1, (1, 4)] of the logarithmic change in the inflation rate (*dlwpi*). Suppose you wanted to estimate the same type of model but wanted the error process to be such that:

$$h_t = \alpha_0 + \alpha_1(0.4\epsilon_{t-1}^2 + 0.3\epsilon_{t-2}^2 + 0.2\epsilon_{t-3}^2 + 0.1\epsilon_{t-4}^2)$$

To keep matters simple, again pretend you can use Greek letters in RATS. To properly define the model, you need to replace lines (2) and (3) of the program segment above with:[1]

---

[1] In actuality the program steps in RATS must be preceded by the type of placeholder described in the next section since ϵ cannot be defined in terms of its own lagged values. Also, the estimated parameters must be listed on the NONLIN instruction. Similar remarks hold for all of the program segments below.

FRML ϵ = dlwpi - a0 - a1*dlwpi{1} - b1*ϵ{1} - b4*ϵ{4}
FRML h = α0 + α1*(0.4*ϵ{1}**2 + 0.3*ϵ{2}**2 + 0.2*ϵ{3}**2 + 0.1*ϵ{4}**2)

Here, the first formula statement defines ϵ_t as the residual from an ARMA[(1, (1, 4)] process. The second statement constrains the lagged coefficients to exhibit a smooth decay. Similarly, if you wanted to estimate the ARMA[1, (1, 4)] with a GARCH(1, 1) error process, replace lines (2) and (3) with:

FRML ϵ = dlwpi - a0 - a1*dlwpi{1} - b1*ϵ{1} - b4*ϵ{4}
FRML h = α0 + α1*ϵ{1}**2 + β1*h{1}

The program steps for the ARCH-M model of Engle, Lilien, and Robbins (1987) have the form:

FRML ϵ = y - a0 - a1*h
FRML h = α0 + α1*(0.4*ϵ{1}**2 + 0.3*ϵ{2}**2 + 0.2*ϵ{3}**2 + 0.1*ϵ{4}**2)

The first statement defines ϵ_t as the value of y_t less value of a_0 and the conditional variance. The second statement defines the conditional variance.

Finally, it is possible to include explanatory variables in the formula for the conditional variance. In the GARCH(1, 1) inflation model, it is possible to write:

FRML h = α0 + α1*ϵ{1}**2 + β1*h{1} + β2*z

where z is an explanatory variable.

RATS Instructions and Procedures

1. **MAXIMIZE**: The RATS MAXIMIZE command is the key to performing any nonlinear optimization including the maximum likelihood estimation of an ARCH, GARCH or ARCH-M process.[1] Suppose your data set contains T observations of the variables y_t and x_t and you have used the FRML instruction to define the function:

$$L = f(y_t, x_t; \beta)$$

where: x_t and β can be vectors (and x_t can represent a lagged value of y_t).

---

[1] The MAXIMIZE instruction was added to RATS beginning with version 4.0. Earlier versions of RATS are not able to estimate ARCH-type models.

MAXIMIZE is able to find the value(s) of β that solve:

$$\max_{\beta} \sum_{t=1}^{T} f(y_t, x_t; \beta)$$

The syntax and principal options of MAXIMIZE are:

maximize(options) *frml start end funcval*
where: *frml*   A previously defined formula
   start end The range of the series to use in the estimation
   funcval   (Optional) The series name for the computed values of $f(y_t, x_t; \beta)$

The key options for our purposes are:

METHOD=   RATS is able to use any one of three different algorithms to find the maximum: BFGS, BHHH, or SIMPLEX. The technical details of each maximization algorithm are provided in the RATS manual. Use either the default BFGS method or the BHHH method for twice-differentiable functions and SIMPLEX in other cases. If you have convergence problems with BFGS, try BHHH. Note that SIMPLEX is extremely slow and often requires many iterations.

ITERATIONS=   The upper limit of the number of iterations used in the maximization.

RECURSIVE   Use this option if the formula must be solved recursively. It is necessary to use RECURSIVE if the value of the value of $f(\ )$ depends on the value of a variable at *t-i*.

Note: You can use TEST and RESTRICT with the BFGS and BHHH options. Coefficients are numbered by their position in the NONLIN statement.

As indicated in the previous section, MAXIMIZE needs to be used in conjunction with several other commands. To illustrate using the simplest possible case, temporarily abstract from the issue of conditional heteroskedasticity. Suppose you wanted the maximum likelihood estimate of β from the model:

$$y_t = \beta x_t + \epsilon_t \text{ such that } E\epsilon_t^2 = \sigma^2$$

Of course, you could estimate β using LINREG as follows:

```
linreg y
# x
```

Instead, to use MAXIMIZE, you must first:

1. List the name(s) of the parameters over which RATS is to perform the maximization. This is done using the NONLIN command.

2. Define the likelihood function *f*( ) using a FRML statement.

3. Set the initial values of the parameters using the COMPUTE command.

Consider the following RATS statements:

```
NONLIN b var
FRML L = -log(var) - (y - b*x)**2/var
COMPUTE b = initial guess, var = initial guess
MAXIMIZE L start end
```

Since RATS cannot process Greek characters, *b* and *var* are used to denote β and σ^2, respectively. The first statement prepares RATS to estimate a nonlinear model; the parameters over which to perform the maximization are *b* and *var*. The second statement is the key to understanding the program; the formula for *L* corresponds to equation (3.12). FRML defines *L* as the log likelihood for observation *t*; the program "understands" that it will maximize this sum over all *T* observations. Note that the constant term $-\log(2\pi)$ can be excluded from the definition of *L* since a constant has no effect on the solution to an optimization problem. Similarly, there is no need to divide each of the expressions by 2. The program requires initial guesses for *b* and *var*; these are provided by the COMPUTE statement. The final statement instructs RATS to maximize *L* over the entire sample period.

2. FRML: This instruction allows you to write and store a function. When used with MAXIMIZE, use the form:

frml *depvar = function(T)*
where: *depvar*   The dependent variable defined by the formula
      function(T)   The formula written using the same syntax as in SET

In constructing your model, it is often helpful to define the log likelihood function using several FRML statements instead of one complicated expression. Consider:

Examples:
1. The example above used the single instruction FRML L = -log(var) - (y - b*x)**2/var. As illustrated in the sample program ARCHREG.PGM, it is possible to define the same likelihood function using the two instructions:

```
frml e = y - b*x
frml L = -log(var) - e**2/var
```

The first FRML instruction defines e_t as the difference between y_t and bx_t. The second uses this definition of e to define the log likelihood function.

2. Consider the three FRML instructions used in the sample program ARCHREG.PGM to estimate a simple regression model with an ARCH(1) error process:

```
frml e = y - b*x
frml v = a0 + a1*e(t-1)**2
frml L = -0.5*(log(v) + e**2/v)
```

Again, the first FRML instruction defines e_t as the difference between y_t and bx_t. The second defines the conditional variance v as an ARCH(1) process. The third uses the definitions of e and v to define the log likelihood function L.

Note that it is possible to use a **subformula** on a FRML instruction in order to reduce computing time. In the example above, the third FRML instruction must refer to the previous calculation of the value of v two separate times per calculation of L. A more efficient program is to combine the three FRML instructions as:

```
frml e = y - b*x
frml L =  (v = a0 + a1*e(t-1)**2), -0.5*(log(v) + e**2/v)
```

The subformula defining v is referred to only once per calculation of L. There is a second important use of subformulas since you cannot use a FRML instruction to define a variable in terms of itself. Suppose you want to estimate the MA(1) model $y_t = e_t - \beta e_{t-1}$. The following is an **illegal** statement because e_t is defined in terms of its own lagged value:

```
frml e = y - b*e{1}
```

The way to circumvent this problem is to create a "placeholder" series using the SET instruction. Then, define the desired series in terms of the placeholder series. Finally, use a subformula to equate the placeholder and the desired series. For example, a simple way to create the formula for the MA(1) process is:

```
set temp = 0.0
nonlin b var
frml e = y - b*temp{1}
frml L = (temp = e), -0.5*(log(var) + e**2/var)
```

The SET instruction generates the placeholder series *temp* containing all zeros. The first FRML instruction creates the desired series e_t equal to y_t - *temp{1}*. The second FRML statement uses the subformula to equate *temp* with e (so that $e_t = y_t - b*e_{t-1}$) and creates the log likelihood L. Detailed examples of the use of subformulas and placeholder series are found in the second sample program (entitled WPI.PRG) below.

3. NLPAR: You will not need to use NLPAR unless you experience convergence problems or want to obtain more precise numerical answers. Numerical optimization algorithms use iteration routines that cannot guarantee precise solutions for β. NLPAR allows you to select the various criteria RATS uses to determine when (and if) the solution converges. There are two principal options; the syntax is:

nlpar(options)

CRITERION=	In the default mode, CRITERION=COEFFICIENTS. Here, convergence is determined using the change in the numerical value of the coefficients between iterations. Setting CRITERION=VALUE means that convergence is determined using the change in the value of the function being maximized.
CVCRIT=	Converge is assumed to occur if the change in the COEFFICIENTS or VALUE is less than the number specified. The default is 0.00001.

Examples:
1. nlpar(cvcrit=0.0001)

Setting CVCRIT=0.0001 means that RATS will continue to search for the values of the coefficients that maximize $f(\ )$ until the change in the coefficients between iterations is not more than 0.0001.

2. nlpar(criterion=value,cvcrit=0.0000001)

Setting CVCRIT=0.0000001 and CRITERION=VALUE means that RATS will continue to search for the values of the coefficients that maximize $f(\ )$ until the change in the value of $f(\ )$ between iterations is less than 0.0000001.

Sample Programs

1. ARCH errors in a regression model: The file labeled ARCHREG.PRN contains 100 simulated values of the sequences $\{x_t\}$ and $\{y_t\}$. The data was constructed to have the theoretical distribution $y_t = 0.9x_t + \epsilon_t$ where ϵ_t is the ARCH(1) process:

$$\epsilon_t = v_t[1 + 0.8(\epsilon_{t-1})]^{0.5}$$

The following program: (i) uses LINREG to regress y_t on x_t, (ii) uses MAXIMIZE to illustrate the maximum likelihood estimation of the same regression equation, (iii) formally tests for ARCH errors, and (iv) uses MAXIMIZE to estimate the ARCH(1) model. Note that the complete program is on the file labeled ARCHREG.PRG and the program and all output can be found on the file labeled ARCHREG.OUT:

allocate 100   ;* Since the data is undated, the calendar statement is unnecessary.
open data a:\archreg.prn   ;* It is assumed that the data is on drive a:\ .
data(format=prn,org=obs) /   ;* All 100 values of y and x are read into memory.

linreg y / resids   ;* Estimate the model $y_t = \beta x_t$ using OLS and save the residuals in
 # x   ;*   the series *resids*. The key portions of the output are given by:

```
Std Error of Dependent Variable 4.8940913917
Standard Error of Estimate       1.7145336381
Sum of Squared Residuals         291.02293401
Durbin-Watson Statistic          1.701689
```

Coefficient	Estimate	Standard Error	t-statistic	Significance Level
X	0.9445457829	0.0354478305	26.64608	0.00000000

* Now compare these OLS estimates to those using maximum likelihood estimation. The next
* four lines of ARCHREG.PRG are:

```
nonlin b var
frml e = y - b*x
frml L = -0.5*(log(var) + e(t)**2/var)
compute b = 0.5, var = 3.0
```

/* The NONLIN instruction indicates that the parameters *b* and *var* are to be estimated. The two FRML statements are used to define the log likelihood function. The fourth statement initializes the values of *b* and *var* to 0.5 and 3.0, respectively. RATS begins iterating using these initial values; good initial guesses are often the key to finding the solution to the maximization problem.
*/

maximize L 1 100

```
Estimation by BFGS
Iterations Taken     15
Usable Observations     100     Degrees of Freedom     98
Function Value              -103.41159446
```

Coefficient		Estimate	Standard Error	t-statistic	Significance Level
1.	B	0.9445453118	0.0353507685	26.71923	0.00000000
2.	VAR	2.9102272613	0.4141063974	7.02773	0.00000000

/*   The first two lines of output indicate that RATS used the BFGS algorithm and took 15 iterations. The fourth line indicates that the maximized summed values of the *L*'s equals

-103.41159446. As compared to the output from LINREG, the point estimate of *b* and its standard error are within the default value of CVCRIT. Also, the estimate of *var* (2.9102272613) closely resembles the output from LINREG. OLS yields a Standard Error of Estimate equal to 1.7145336381. Squaring this OLS estimate yields 2.939625596. Note that alternative initial guesses and/or convergence criteria will yield slightly different answers from those reported here.

The next section of the program checks the residuals from the LINREG instruction for the presence of serial correlation. Note that only 12 ACF coefficients are shown; the complete output is on the file ARCHREG.OUT.

/*

cor(qstats,number=24,span=4,dfc=1) resids

```
Autocorrelations
1:   0.1478052   0.0045328  -0.0183097  -0.0113991   0.0681821  -0.0001274
7:  -0.0981806  -0.1492260   0.0628801   0.1017613   0.0883744  -0.0378697

Ljung-Box Q-Statistics
Q(4)   =    2.3020.  Significance Level 0.51213088
Q(12)  =    9.0054.  Significance Level 0.62139482
Q(24)  =   18.4724.  Significance Level 0.73138501
```

;* There is no evidence of serial correlation in the residuals. Next, check the squared residuals for
;* ARCH errors:

set ressq = resids*resids   ;* Form the squared residuals as the series *ressq*.
cor(partial=pacf,qstats,number=24,span=4,dfc=1) ressq

```
Autocorrelations
1:   0.4734797   0.1293539  -0.0541507  -0.0762162   0.0600453   0.2348990
7:   0.2723641   0.2125219   0.1372632  -0.0030104  -0.0647228  -0.0910312

Ljung-Box Q-Statistics
Q(4)   =   25.7647.  Significance Level 0.00001068
Q(12)  =   48.8363.  Significance Level 0.00000101
Q(24)  =   50.5759.  Significance Level 0.00077377
```

/* The large autocorrelation coefficient at lag 1 (and possibly those at lags 6 and 7) suggests ARCH errors. A Lagrange multiplier test can be conducted by regressing *ressq* on its lagged value. Of course, longer lags can also be used. Here, with one lag, it is possible to accept the alternative hypothesis of ARCH errors at any conventional significance level.
*/
linreg ressq
 # constant ressq{1}

Coefficient	Estimate	Standard Error	t-statistic	Significance Level
Constant	1.5425009425	0.5421819009	2.84499	0.00541831
RESSQ{1}	0.4749026274	0.0893672090	5.31406	0.00000068

compute trsq = %nobs*%rsquared   ;* Compute TR^2 and obtain the cumulative density
cdf chisqr trsq 1   ;* of *trsq* as χ^2 with 1 degree of freedom.
    Chi-Squared(1)= 22.322744 with Significance Level 0.00000230

* Thus, the Lagrange multiplier test indicates the presence of ARCH errors. The following
* six statements can be used to estimate the ARCH(1) model:

nonlin b a0 a1   ;* Here three parameters are to be estimated.
frml e = y - b*x   ;* The explanation of the three FRML instructions is
frml v = a0 + a1*e(t-1)**2   ;*   given above.
frml L = -0.5*(log(v) + e**2/v)
compute b = 0.5, a0 = 2, a1 = 0.5   ;* Initial guesses for the parameters.
maximize L 2 100   ;* Estimation begins with entry *2* since one
    ;*   observation is lost due to the calculation of $e(t-1)$.

```
Estimation by BFGS
Iterations Taken       14
Usable Observations    99      Degrees of Freedom    96
Function Value              -90.55955258
```

Coefficient	Estimate	Standard Error	t-statistic	Significance Level
B	0.8859262129	0.0235152819	37.67449	0.00000000
A0	1.1622384219	0.2861464014	4.06169	0.00004872
A1	0.6701673869	0.2268125860	2.95472	0.00312954

* The coefficient for the ARCH error process equals 0.670673839 and the *t*-statistic is 2.95472
* (significant at the 0.00312954 level).

2. ARCH and GARCH models of the WPI: The file WPI.WK1 contains the quarterly values
of the U.S. Wholesale Price Index from 1960:1 to 1992:2. In the previous chapter, a plausible
ARMA model for the logarithmic change in the index (*dlwpi*) was shown to be:

$$dlwpi_t = 0.010 + 0.7875 dlwpi_{t-1} + \epsilon_t - 0.4373\epsilon_{t-1} + 0.2957\epsilon_{t-4}$$

where $Var(\epsilon_t) = 0.00019193$.

The following program will (i) estimate the ARMA(1, ||1, 4||) model of *dlwpi* and test for
ARCH errors, (ii) illustrate the use of placeholders and subformulas in estimating an ARMA
model with ARCH errors, and (iii) estimate the ARMA(1, ||1, 4||) model and allow the errors to

be GARCH(1, 1). The complete details are on the files labeled ARCH_WPI.OUT and ARCH_WPI.PRG:

```
cal 1960 1 4                    ;* Set the calendar to begin 1960:1.
all 1992:2                      ;* The data runs until 1992:2.
open data a:wpi.wk1             ;* The data set is assumed to be on drive a:\ .
data(format=wks,org=obs)
set dlwpi = log(wpi) - log(wpi{1})    ;* Form the logarithmic change of the WPI.
/*
```

The next two lines estimate the ARMA(1, ||1, 4||) model of the inflation rate, save the residuals as *resids*, and obtain the ACF, PACF, and Q-statistics. The output from the BOXJENK instruction is presented in Chapter 2 and is also contained in the file ARCH_WPI.OUT.
```
*/
```

boxjenk(constant,ar=1,ma=||1,4||) dlwpi / resids
cor(partial=pacf,qstats,number=36,span=12,dfc=4) resids

```
Autocorrelations
1:  0.0089624 -0.0328139  0.0703164 -0.0371207 -0.1003303  0.1643790
7: -0.0416431 -0.0704238 -0.0637490  0.0023137 -0.0800136  0.0130417

Ljung-Box Q-Statistics
Q(12)  =  8.4732.  Significance Level 0.38866218
Q(24)  = 15.0892.  Significance Level 0.77128316
Q(36)  = 28.5406.  Significance Level 0.64238563
```

/* Only the first twelve autocorrelations are shown here; autocorrelations 13 through 36 and the PACF coefficients are contained in the file ARCH_WPI.OUT. As you can see here, the individual ACF coefficients are all small and the Q-statistics do not suggest correlation in the residuals. It is reasonable to conclude that there is no correlation in the residuals. However, as shown in Chapter 2, there is evidence of volatility in the residual series. As such, form the squared residuals and obtain their ACF, PACF, and Q-statistics using:
```
*/
```

set ressq = resids*resids   ;* Form the squared residuals as the *ressq* series.
cor(partial=pacf,qstats,number=24,span=4,dfc=4) ressq

```
Autocorrelations
1:  0.1265324  0.3076689  0.1151171  0.2917305  0.1098073  0.0999289
7:  0.0243902  0.1831903 -0.0778343 -0.0275092 -0.0874216 -0.0033036

Ljung-Box Q-Statistics
Q(4)   = 27.7838.  Significance Level 0.00000403
Q(12)  = 37.5546.  Significance Level 0.00009299
Q(24)  = 40.6895.  Significance Level 0.01284773
```

/* The second and fourth autocorrelations are quite large and the Q-statistics are such that the null hypothesis of no correlation in the squared residuals can be rejected at conventional significance levels. Note that you can plot the ACF and PACF of the squared residuals using the BJIDENT.SRC procedure. The next four instructions perform the Lagrange multiplier test for ARCH(4) errors by estimating an AR(4) model of the squared residuals and computing the significance level of TR^2.
*/

```
linreg ressq
# constant ressq{1 to 4}
```

Coefficient	Estimate	Standard Error	t-statistic	Significance Level
1. Constant	0.0000551562	0.0000281453	1.95969	0.05236938
2. RESSQ{1}	0.0596457653	0.0896003417	0.66569	0.50689960
3. RESSQ{2}	0.2319774754	0.0896657945	2.58713	0.01088114
4. RESSQ{3}	0.0419486403	0.0896457039	0.46794	0.64068474
5. RESSQ{4}	0.2090754203	0.0895832164	2.33387	0.02128004

/* As suggested by the correlations of the squared residuals, the second and fourth lags of *ressq* are significant at conventional levels. Next, compute *trsq* = TR^2 as the number of observations multiplied by R^2 and obtain the cumulative density of *trsq* as χ^2 with four degrees of freedom.
*/

```
compute trsq = %nobs*%rsquared
```

cdf chisqr trsq 4
```
        Chi-Squared(4)= 18.029993 with Significance Level 0.00121755
```

/* You can reject the null hypothesis and conclude that there are ARCH or GARCH errors. In spite of the results of the LINREG output, it would be unwise to conclude that the error process has the form $\epsilon_t = v_t[a_0 + a_2(\epsilon_{t-2})^2 + a_4(\epsilon_{t-4})^2]^{0.5}$. The values of a_2 and a_4 were not jointly estimated with the ARMA(1, ||1, 4||) model and the t-statistics on each of the a_i are unreliable (since the *ressq* is serially correlated). At this point, you could simultaneously estimate the ARMA(1, ||1, 4||) model of the inflation rate and various specifications of the error process.

The following estimations are intended to illustrate the use of the placeholders and subformulas and **not** to suggest the appropriate model of *dlwpi*. Suppose you wanted to estimate an AR(1) model of *dlwpi* with an ARCH(4) error process of the form $E\epsilon_t^2 = a_0 + a_1\epsilon_{t-4}^2$. The next nine lines of ARCH_WPI.PRG estimate such a model. NONLIN prepares RATS to estimate the parameters $b0$, $b1$, $a0$, and $a1$; as before the first FRML instruction defines e_t as $dlwpi_t - b_0 - b_1 dlwpi_{t-1}$. The second FRML instruction defines the conditional variance (*var*) as $a_0 + a_1(\epsilon_{t-4})^2$. The third FRML instruction defines the log likelihood L. The next three statements are used to initialize the values of a_1, a_2, b_0, and b_1. The value of a_1 is initialized using a pure guess. The estimation begins with period 10 so that all models are estimated over the same sample period. Note that an asterisk instructs RATS to calculate the ending date of the sample period.
*/

```
nonlin b0 b1 a0 a1
frml e = dlwpi - b0 - b1*dlwpi{1}
frml var = a0 + a1*e(t-4)**2
frml L = -0.5*(log(var)+e(t)**2/var)
boxjenk(noprint,constant,ar=1) dlwpi
compute b0=%beta(1), b1=%beta(2)
compute a0=%seesq, a1=0.8
```
maximize(iterations=75) L 10 *

```
Estimation by BFGS
Iterations Taken   12
Function Value              489.00061501
```

Coefficient	Estimate	Standard Error	t-statistic	Significance Level
1. B0	0.0024835320	0.0009910230	2.50603	0.01220958
2. B1	0.4897545449	0.0532070036	9.20470	0.00000000
3. A0	0.0000615277	0.0000120098	5.12310	0.00000030
4. A1	0.7633542665	0.2268863825	3.36448	0.00076689

/* Next introduce the MA(1) term into the model for *dlwpi*. Since *e* cannot be defined in terms of its own lag, it is necessary to use a placeholder. The next ten statements in ARCH_WPI.PRG are:
*/

```
set u = 0.0
nonlin b0 b1 b2 a0 a1
frml e = dlwpi - b0 - b1*dlwpi{1} - b2*u{1}
frml var = a0 + a1*e(t-4)**2
frml L = (u = e), -0.5*(log(var)+e(t)**2/var)
boxjenk(noprint,constant,ar=1,ma=1) dlwpi
compute b0=%beta(1), b1=%beta(2), b2 = %beta(3)
compute a0=%seesq, a1=0.8
```
maximize(iterations=75) L 10 *

```
Estimation by BFGS
Iterations Taken     18
Function Value                490.57045626
```

Coefficient	Estimate	Standard Error	t-statistic	Significance Level
1. B0	0.000906855	0.000789394	1.14880	0.25063858
2. B1	0.795327595	0.101833304	7.81009	0.00000000
3. B2	-0.416622671	0.147494972	-2.82466	0.00473313
4. A0	0.000067690	0.000012750	5.30903	0.00000011
5. A1	0.593198426	0.220850624	2.68597	0.00723193

/*   The SET instruction defines the placeholder for e. NONLIN prepares RATS to estimate the parameters $b0$, $b1$, $b2$, $a0$, and $a1$. The first FRML instruction uses the placeholder u to define e_t as: $dlwpi_t - b_0 - b_1 dlwpi_{t-1} - b_2 u_{t-1}$. The second FRML instruction defines the conditional variance (var) as $a_0 + a_1(\epsilon_{t-4})^2$. The third FRML instruction uses a subformula to equate u and e (so that $e_t = dlwpi_t - b_0 - b_1 dlwpi_{t-1} - b_2 e_{t-1}$), and defines the log likelihood L. The next three statements initialize the parameters.

If we use the same logic, it is straightforward to estimate the ARMA(1, ||1, 4||) of $dlwpi$ and toand to define the conditional variance as $a_0 + a_1 var_{t-4}$. Consider:
*/
```
set u = 0.0
nonlin b0 b1 b2 b3 a0 a1
frml e = dlwpi - b0 - b1*dlwpi{1} - b2*u{1} - b3*u{4}
frml var = a0 + a1*e(t-4)**2
frml L = (u = e), -0.5*(log(var)+e(t)**2/var)
boxjenk(noprint,constant,ar=1,ma=||1,4||) dlwpi
compute b0=%beta(1), b1=%beta(2), b2 = %beta(3) , b3 = %beta(4)
compute a0=%seesq, a1=.8
```
maximize(iterations=75) L 10 *

Coefficient		Estimate	Standard Error	t-statistic	Significance Level
1.	B0	0.001002473	0.000915532	1.09496	0.27353300
2.	B1	0.782611824	0.115757312	6.76080	0.00000000
3.	B2	-0.407753735	0.156637869	-2.60316	0.00923683
4.	B3	0.042109194	0.131088239	0.32123	0.74803772
5.	A0	0.000069371	0.000015506	4.47390	0.00000768
6.	A1	0.567436254	0.247490106	2.29276	0.02186163

/* The model appears to perform quite well. As an exercise, you should compare this specification of the conditional variance to other plausible candidates. Finally, a GARCH(1, 1) error process can be estimated by changing the definitions of var and L. The next ten lines of ARCH_WPI.PRG are given below. Note that a second placeholder is needed to define h_t in terms of its own lags. The first FRML instruction defines e in terms of u and the second defines the conditional variance (var) in terms of e_{t-1} and w_{t-1}. The third FRML instruction uses two subformulas to equate u with e and w with var and to define the likelihood function.
*/
```
set w = 0.0
set u = 0.0
nonlin b0 b1 b2 b3 a0 a1 a2
frml e = dlwpi - b0 - b1*dlwpi{1} - b2*u{1} - b3*u{4}
frml var = a0 + a1*e{1}**2 + a2*w{1}
frml L = (u = e), (w = var), -0.5*(log(var)+e(t)**2/var)
boxjenk(noprint,constant,ar=1,ma=||1,4||) dlwpi
```

compute b0=%beta(1), b1=%beta(2), b2 = %beta(3) , b3 = %beta(4)

compute a0=%seesq, a1=0.3 , a2 = 0.5

maximize(iterations=75) L 10 *

```
Estimation by BFGS
Iterations Taken     19
Quarterly Data From 1962:02 To 1992:02
Usable Observations       121      Degrees of Freedom      114
Function Value                      496.96874920


Coefficient    Estimate      Standard        t-statistic     Significance
                             Error                           Level
1. B0          1.3490e-003   9.6391e-004     1.39947         0.16167154
2. B1          0.7968        0.0945          8.43121         0.00000000
3. B2         -0.4014        0.1290         -3.11141         0.00186196
4. B3          0.2357        0.1175          2.00592         0.04486519
5. A0          1.5674e-005   9.2657e-006     1.69158         0.09072557
6. A1          0.2225        0.1104          2.01422         0.04398639
7. A2          0.6633        0.1433          4.62948         0.00000367
```

/* Although the marginal significance of a_0 approximately 0.0907, it would be a mistake to reestimate the model constraining $a_0 = 0$. If $a_0 = 0$, it is possible for the conditional variance to equal zero; a result clearly at odds with reality. You can perform diagnostic tests using TEST and RESTRICT. Further, you can calculate the residuals and use COR to obtain their ACF using:
*/

set resids = 0.0

set resids 62:2 92:2 = dlwpi - %beta(1) - %beta(2)*dlwpi{1} $

  - %beta(3)*resids{1} - %beta(4)*resids{4}

cor(qstats,dfc=4,number=32,span=8) resids 62:2 92:2

```
Autocorrelations
1: -0.0283425 -0.0490607  0.0474186  0.0005863 -0.0854563  0.1753938
7: -0.0450641 -0.0760394 -0.0726409  0.0073674 -0.0982972 -0.0019676


Ljung-Box Q-Statistics
Q(8)   =           6.6292.  Significance Level 0.15683050
Q(24)  =          14.4770.  Significance Level 0.80551317
```

/* As in Chapter 2, you can compare alternative models using the properties of the various residual series. The next four instructions in ARCH_WPI.PRG calculate the conditional variance for each point in the sample period and construct upper and lower bands of two conditional standard deviations around *dlwpi*. Note that %beta(5) is the estimated value of a_0, %beta(6) is the estimated value of a_1, and %beta(7) is the estimated value of a_2.
*/

set convar = 0.0

set convar 62:2 92:2 = %beta(5) + %beta(6)*resids{1}**2 $

  + %beta(7)*convar{1}

```
set upper = dlwpi + 2*convar**0.5
set lower = dlwpi - 2*convar**0.5

graph(header='Two Conditional Standard Deviations Around DLWPI', $
        key=upleft,patterns) 3
# upper  62:2 92:2  1
# lower  62:2 92:2  1
# dlwpi
```

/* The graph contains the *dlwpi* series and the upper and lower bands each equal to two conditional standard deviations (i.e., the square root of the conditional variance) from *dlwpi*. You can see that as *dlwpi* becomes more volatile, the width of the bands increases. For example, in the early part of the 1970's the inflation rate became highly volatile. At the same time, the width of the bands expanded dramatically.

Figure 3.3: Two Conditional Standard Deviations Around DLWPI

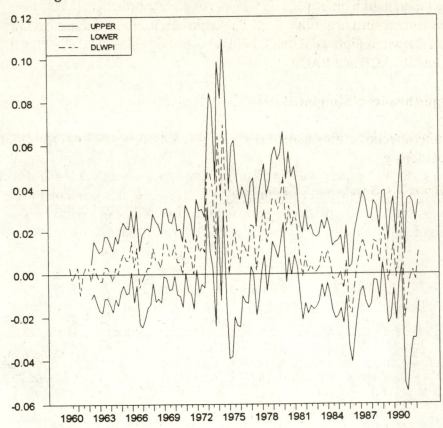

3. Estimation of an ARCH-M process:

In fitting an ARCH or GARCH process, you first estimate the $\{y_t\}$ sequence using the "best fitting" ARMA or regression model. The ACF and PACF of the residuals from this first stage can provide useful information concerning the form of the conditional variance. You then jointly estimate the $\{y_t\}$ sequence and several plausible candidates for the conditional variance jointly. Fitting an ARCH-M model is somewhat more difficult since the variance interacts with the level of the $\{y_t\}$ sequence. As you will see in the sample program below, you cannot hope to gain much useful information concerning the form of the ARCH-M model from the residuals from the best fitting ARMA (or regression) model.

The file labeled ARCH_M.PRN contains 100 simulated values of an ARCH-M process called y. The following program (i) uses the Box-Jenkins methodology to estimate the $\{y_t\}$ sequence as an ARMA process, (ii) checks the residuals ARCH errors, and (iii) illustrates how to estimate several ARCH-M models of the $\{y_t\}$ series. The program statements are on the file labeled ARCH_M.PRG and the program statements and output are on the file labeled ARCH_M.OUT. The first three lines of the program are:

```
all 100                    ;* Since the data is undated, the calendar statement is unnecessary.
open data a:arch_m.prn      ;* It is assumed that the data is in drive a:\ .
data(format=prn,org=obs)   ;* The entire data set is read into memory.
* As shown in Figures 3.3 and 3.4, the next four lines of ARCH_M.PRG plot the {y_t} sequence
*   and its ACF and PACF.
```

graph(header='Simulated ARCH-M Process') 1
 # y
source(noecho) c:\rats\bjident.src   ;* Modify this line if BJIDENT.SRC is not on c:\rats.
@bjident y

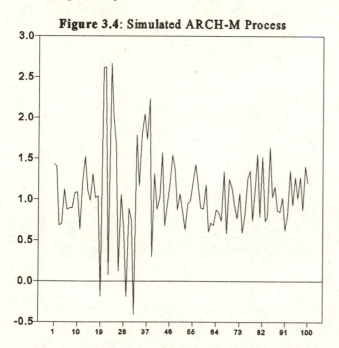

Figure 3.4: Simulated ARCH-M Process

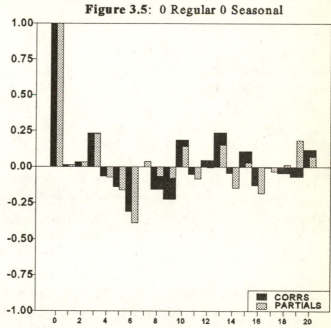

Figure 3.5: 0 Regular 0 Seasonal

/* Note that the $\{y_t\}$ sequence has a mean of approximately unity. The variance seems to be fairly stable except for a period of volatility beginning near entry 18. It is characteristic of an ARCH-M process that the mean value of $\{y_t\}$ seems to respond to this volatility (the conditional variance affects the conditional mean). Note the spikes in the ACF and PACF at lags 3 and 6. It seems reasonable to model the $\{y_t\}$ sequence as an MA($\|$3, 6$\|$) process. Although there might be concern about the correlations at the longer lags, it is wise to begin with the rather parsimonious model:

$$y_t = a_0 + \epsilon_t + \beta_1 \epsilon_{t-3} + \beta_2 \epsilon_{t-6}.$$

The RATS instruction to estimate the model and save the residuals in the series *resids* is:
*/

boxjenk(constant,ma=||3,6||) y / resids

Coefficient	Estimate	Standard Error	t-statistic	Significance Level
1. CONSTANT	1.071771081	0.048009924	22.32395	0.00000000
2. MA{3}	0.254214138	0.098929960	2.56964	0.01170287
3. MA{6}	-0.262006589	0.099273537	-2.63924	0.00968214

/* Check the ACF and PACF of the residuals setting DFC=3 (since three coefficients are estimated in the MA(||3, 6||) model. Here, only the first 18 autocorrelations are shown. As expected, diagnostic checking of the residuals indicates that some of the autocorrelations at the longer lag lengths (especially lags 9 and 13) may be important.
*/

cor(partial=pacf,qstats,number=24,span=8,dfc=3) resids

```
Correlations of Series RESIDS
Autocorrelations
     1: -0.0021437  0.0100467  0.0524147 -0.0505272 -0.1330722 -0.0584164
     7:  0.0512465 -0.1457758 -0.2049787  0.1039352 -0.0511237  0.0490354
    13:  0.2518386 -0.0487310  0.0500207 -0.1158226  0.0074287 -0.0398232

Partial Autocorrelations
     1: -0.0021437  0.0100422  0.0524631 -0.0505223 -0.1349946 -0.0624984
     7:  0.0606562 -0.1348029 -0.2270602  0.0782847 -0.0382361  0.0585397
    13:  0.2117148 -0.1212002  0.0518530 -0.1327334 -0.0348594  0.0105360

Ljung-Box Q-Statistics
Q(8)  =           5.4868.  Significance Level 0.35939565
Q(16) =          21.6455.  Significance Level 0.06110467
Q(24) =          27.7187.  Significance Level 0.14831075
```

/* Instead of focusing on the relative merits of modeling the longer lags, the key issue here involves the autocorrelations of the squared residuals. The next two lines of ARCH_M.PRG form the ACF and PACF of the squared residuals. Only some of the output from the COR instruction is shown here.
*/

set ressq = resids*resids   ;* Form the squared residuals as the *ressq* series.

cor(partial=pacf,qstats,number=24,span=4,dfc=3) ressq

```
Correlations of Series RESSQ
Autocorrelations
    1:   0.4981203   0.2509847   0.2895971   0.1625192   0.0430988   0.1141240
    7:   0.0907499   0.0532747   0.1365066   0.0261814   0.1592152   0.2503240

Partial Autocorrelations
    1:   0.4981203   0.0038049   0.2170029  -0.0878890  -0.0413535   0.1013672
    7:  -0.0172378   0.0348213   0.0984692  -0.1475101   0.2890676   0.0322684

Ljung-Box Q-Statistics
Q(4)   =        43.7460.   Significance Level 0.00000000
Q(12)  =        58.9113.   Significance Level 0.00000000
Q(24)  =        64.5293.   Significance Level 0.00000257
```

/* The first two ACF coefficients (approximately equal to 0.5 and 0.5^2) suggest an AR(1) coefficient; this impression is reenforced by the fact that the second PACF coefficient is approximately zero. At lag 3 there is a spike in the PACF and a cessation in the decay of the ACF. This suggests an MA(3) coefficient. As such, it seems reasonable to estimate the conditional variance as a GARCH(1, ||3||) process. The next four lines in ARCH_M.PRG conduct the Lagrange multiplier test for ARCH or GARCH errors:
*/

```
linreg(noprint) ressq              ;* Perform the Lagrange multiplier test for ARCH errors
# constant ressq{1 to 4}           ;*   using four lags of ressq.
compute trsq = %nobs*%rsquared     ;* Compute TR² and obtain the cumulative density
cdf chisqr trsq 4                  ;*      of trsq as chi-square with four degrees of freedom.
      Chi-Squared(4)= 27.839453 with Significance Level 0.00001344
```

/* Conclude that you can reject the null hypothesis of no ARCH effects. As an exercise, you should try estimating the $\{y_t\}$ sequence as an MA(||3, 6||) model with GARCH(1, 3) errors. However, the plot of the $\{y_t\}$ series suggests the possibility of an ARCH-M model. The next ten lines from ARCH_M.PRG estimate the model:

$$y_t = b_0 + b_1 var_t + \epsilon_t$$
$$var_t = a_0 + a_1 \epsilon_{t-1}^2 \qquad \text{(where var refers to the conditional variance)}$$

The first two lines SET the placeholder u and prepare RATS to estimate the parameters $b0$, $b1$, $a0$, and $a1$. The first FRML statement uses the placeholder to define the conditional variance as an ARCH(1) process. The second FRML statement defines y_t as: $b_0 + b_1 var_t + \epsilon_t$. The third FRML statement uses a subformula to equate u and e (so that $var_t = a_0 + a_1 \epsilon_{t-1}^2$) and defines the log likelihood. The next four lines initialize the parameters; $b0$ and $a0$ are initialized using the estimates from LINREG and $b1$ and $a1$ are initialized by guessing at the parameter values. The MAXIMIZE instruction instructs RATS to estimate the model beginning with observation 2 (an observation is lost because of the lagged variance term).
*/

```
set u = 0.0
nonlin b0 b1 a0 a1
frml var = a0 + a1*u{1}**2
frml e = y - b0 - b1*var(t)
frml L = (u = e), -0.5*(log(var)+e**2/var)
linreg(noprint) y
# constant
compute b0=%beta(1), b1=0.2
compute a0=%seesq, a1=0.3
```
maximize L 2 *

```
Estimation by BFGS
Iterations Taken     13
Usable Observations       99      Degrees of Freedom      95
Function Value                    33.59449767
```

Coefficient	Estimate	Standard Error	t-statistic	Significance Level
1. BO	0.9191270839	0.0611853819	15.02200	0.00000000
2. B1	0.6177376381	0.2695028672	2.29214	0.02189771
3. AO	0.1111855415	0.0253414650	4.38749	0.00001147
4. A1	0.5684221634	0.2332299201	2.43718	0.01480251

/* To illustrate a point, suppose you took the results of the previous Box-Jenkins model seriously and wanted to include an MA(3) coefficient in the model for the $\{y_t\}$ sequence. The second and third lines of ARCH_M.PRG introduce the second placeholder w and prepare RATS to estimate the parameters b0, b1, b2, a0, and a1. The first FRML statement is unchanged but the second redefines e such that (when u and e are equated on the third FRML statement) :

$$y_t = b_0 + b_1 var_t + \epsilon_t + b_2 \epsilon_{t-3}$$

The third FRML statement equates u with e and w with e and defines the log likelihood. The remainder of the program initializes the parameters and specifies the sample period for the estimation. As you can see from the partial listing of the output, the MA(||3||) coefficient can clearly be excluded from the model.
*/

```
set u = 0.0
set w = 0.0
nonlin b0 b1 b2 a0 a1
frml var = a0 + a1*u{1}**2
frml e = y - b0 - b1*var(t) - b2*w{3}
frml L = (u = e), (w = e), -0.5*(log(var)+e**2/var)
boxjenk(noprint,constant,ma=||3||) y
compute b0=%beta(1), b1=0.2 , b2 = %beta(2)
compute a0=%seesq, a1=0.3
```

maximize L 3 *

Coefficient	Estimate	Standard Error	t-statistic	Significance Level
1. B0	0.8853338664	0.0768037159	11.52723	0.00000000
2. B1	0.7621193867	0.3540530310	2.15256	0.03135350
3. B2	0.1088069153	0.0971599311	1.11987	0.26276731
4. A0	0.1113436911	0.0302953926	3.67527	0.00023760
5. A1	0.5288328823	0.2685171350	1.96946	0.04890067

Additional Exercises

1. In sample program 2, *dlwpi* was estimated as an ARMA(1, ||1, 4||) model with GARCH(1, 1) errors. Continue to estimate *dlwpi* as an ARMA(1, ||1, 4||) model, but consider the following specifications for the conditional variance:

(a) $h_t = a_0 + a_1 \epsilon_{t-2}^2$

(b) $h_t = a_0 + a_1 \epsilon_{t-2}^2 + a_2 \epsilon_{t-4}^2$

(c) $h_t = a_0 + a_1 (0.4 \epsilon_{t-1}^2 + 0.3 \epsilon_{t-2}^2 + 0.2 \epsilon_{t-3}^2 + 0.1 \epsilon_{t-4}^2)$

Estimate each of the above specifications and compare the results to those of the GARCH(1, 1) model.

2. In sample program 3, it was suggested that it is reasonable to estimate the conditional variance as a GARCH(1, ||3||) process.

(a) Write the appropriate program to estimate $\{y_t\}$ as an MA(||3, 6||) process with GARCH(1, ||3||) errors.

(b) Estimate the model (*Hint*: You may need to use the NLPAR instruction) and compare the result to the ARCH-M model reported in sample program 3.

(c) The program suggested the most appropriate model is:

$$y_t = b_0 + b_1 var_t + \epsilon_t$$
$$var_t = a_0 + a_1 \epsilon_{t-1}^2$$

Can you improve the model by including an autogressive term at lag 3 in the $\{y_t\}$ equation?

## Chapter 4

Tests For Trends and Unit Roots

There are important differences between stationary and nonstationary time series. Shocks to a stationary time series are necessarily temporary; over time the effects of the shocks will dissipate and the series will revert to its long-run mean level. On the other hand, a nonstationary series necessarily has permanent components. The mean and/or variance of a nonstationary series are time-dependent. To aid in the identification of a nonstationary series, note that:

1. There is no long-run mean to which the series returns.
2. The variance is time dependent and goes to infinity as time goes to infinity.
3. Theoretical autocorrelations do not decay but, in finite samples, the sample correlogram dies out slowly.

Inspection of the autocorrelation function serves only as a rough indicator of whether a trend is present in a series. A slowly decaying ACF is indicative of a large characteristic root, a true unit root process, or a trend stationary process. Formal tests can help determine whether or not a series contains a trend and whether the trend is deterministic or stochastic. However, the existing tests have little power to distinguish between near-unit root and unit root processes. The low power of the tests is due to the fact that a near-unit root process will have the same shaped ACF as a unit root process.

Theoretical Background

Suppose a series is generated by the process:

$$y_t = a_1 y_{t-1} + \epsilon_t \tag{4.1}$$

where: $\{\epsilon_t\}$ is a white noise process.

The methods of the previous chapter are appropriate if $-1 < a_1 < 1$. Suppose you want to test the hypothesis $a_1 = 1$. Now, under the null hypothesis, the $\{y_t\}$ sequence is generated by the nonstationary process:

$$y_t = y_0 + \sum_{i=1}^{t} \epsilon_i \tag{4.2}$$

Under the null hypothesis, it is inappropriate to use classical statistical methods to estimate and perform significance tests on the coefficient a_1. If the $\{y_t\}$ sequence is generated as in (4.2), it is simple to show that the OLS estimate of (4.1) will yield a biased estimate of a_1.

Taking expected values we obtain: $E[y_t] = E[y_{t-s}] = y_0$; thus, the mean is a constant. Although the mean is constant, notice that the variance is time-dependent:

$$\text{Var}(y_t) = \text{Var}(\epsilon_t + \epsilon_{t-1} + \ldots + \epsilon_1) = t\sigma^2$$

Since the variance is not constant, the process is nonstationary. Moreover, as $t \to \infty$, the variance of y_t approaches infinity. It is also instructive to calculate the covariance between y_t and y_{t-s}. Since the mean is constant, we can form the covariance γ_{t-s} as:

$$
\begin{aligned}
E[(y_t - y_0)(y_{t-s} - y_0)] &= E[(\epsilon_t + \epsilon_{t-1} + \ldots + \epsilon_1)(\epsilon_{t-s} + \epsilon_{t-s-1} + \ldots + \epsilon_1)] \\
&= E[(\epsilon_{t-s})^2 + (\epsilon_{t-s-1})^2 + \ldots + (\epsilon_1)^2] \\
&= (t-s)\sigma^2
\end{aligned}
$$

To form the correlation coefficient ρ_s, we can divide γ_{t-s} by the standard deviation of y_t multiplied by the standard deviation of y_{t-s}. Thus, the correlation coefficient ρ_s is:

$$\rho_s = (t-s)/\sqrt{(t-s)t}$$

$$= [(t-s)/t]^{0.5} < 1$$

Since the sample size t will be large relative to the number of autocorrelations formed, for all reasonable values of t and s, the ratio $(t-s)/t$ is approximately equal to unity. For example, for adjacent periods, ($s=1$) so that the correlation coefficient ρ_1 clearly approaches unity as $t \to \infty$. Hence, in using sample data, *the autocorrelation function for a random walk process will show a slight tendency to decay*. Thus, it will not be possible to use the ACF to distinguish between a unit root process ($a_1 = 1$) and a process such that a_1 is close to unity. In the Box-Jenkins identification stage, a slowly decaying ACF or PACF can be an indication of nonstationarity.

Since the estimate of a_1 is directly related to the value of ρ_1, the estimated value of a_1 is biased to be below its true value of unity. The estimated model will mimic that of a stationary AR(1) process with a near-unit root.

Figure 4.1 shows the time plot of a simulated random walk process. One hundred normally distributed random deviates were obtained so as to mimic the $\{\epsilon_t\}$ sequence. Assuming that $y_0 = 0$, the next 100 values in the $\{y_t\}$ sequence are calculated as $y_t = y_{t-1} + \epsilon_t$. The correlogram shown in Figure 4.2 is characteristic of most sample correlograms constructed from nonstationary data. The estimated value of ρ_1 is close to unity and the sample autocorrelations die out slowly. If we did not know the way in which the data was generated, an inspection of the two figures might lead us to falsely conclude that $\{y_t\}$ was generated from a stationary process.

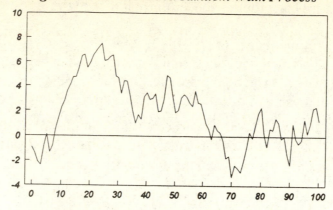

Figure 4.1: *A Simulated Random Walk Process*

Figure 4.2: *Correlogram of the Process*

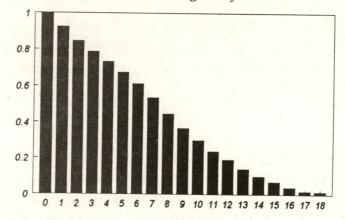

Using the simulated data to estimate an AR(1) model with and without an intercept, we obtain (standard errors are in parentheses):

$$y_t = 0.9546y_{t-1} + \epsilon_t, \qquad R^2 = 0.86 \tag{4.3}$$
$$(0.030)$$

$$y_t = 0.164 + 0.9247y_{t-1} + \epsilon_t, \quad R^2 = 0.864 \tag{4.4}$$
$$(0.037)$$

Examining (4.3), a careful researcher would not be willing to dismiss the possibility of a unit root since the estimated value of a_1 is only 1.5133 standard deviations from unity. We might correctly recognize that under the null hypothesis of a unit root, the estimate of a_1 will be biased below unity. If we knew the true distribution of a_1 under the null of a unit root, we could perform such a significance test. Of course, if we did not know the true data-generating process, we might estimate the model with an intercept. In (4.4), the estimate of a_1 is more than two standard deviations from unity: $(1 - 0.9247)/0.037 = 2.035$. However, it would be wrong to use this information to reject the null of a unit root. After all, the point of this section has been to indicate that such t-tests are inappropriate under the null of a unit root.

Fortunately, Dickey and Fuller (1979, 1981) devised a procedure to formally test for the presence of a unit root. Their methodology is similar to that used in constructing the data reported in Figure 4.1. Suppose that we generated thousands of such random walk sequences and for each we calculated the estimated value of a_1. Although most of the estimates would be close to unity, some would be further from unity than others. In performing this experiment, Dickey and Fuller found that in the presence of an intercept:

90% of the estimated values of a_1 are less than 2.58 standard errors from unity.
95% of the estimated values of a_1 are less than 2.89 standard errors from unity.
99% of the estimated values of a_1 are less than 3.51 standard errors from unity.

The application of these Dickey-Fuller *critical values* to test for unit roots is straightforward. Suppose we did not know the true data generating process and were trying to ascertain whether the data used in Figure 4.1 contained a unit root. Using these Dickey-Fuller statistics, we would not reject the null of a unit root in (4.4). The estimated value of a_1 is only 2.035 standard deviations from unity. In fact, if the true value of a_1 does equal unity, we should find the estimated value to be within 2.58 standard deviations from unity 90% of the time.

Be aware that stationarity necessitates $-1 < a_1 < 1$. Thus, if the estimated value of a_1 is close to -1, you should also be concerned about nonstationarity. Defining $\gamma = a_1 - 1$, it is clear that the equivalent restriction is: $-2 < \gamma < 0$. In conducting a Dickey-Fuller test, *it is possible to check that the estimated value of γ is greater than -2*. Suppose that the estimated value of γ is -1.9 (so that the estimate of a_1 is -0.9) with a standard error of 0.04. Since the estimated value of γ is 2.5 standard errors from -2 [$(2 - 1.9)/0.04 = 2.5$], the Dickey-Fuller statistics indicate that we cannot reject the null hypothesis $a_1 = -2$ at the 95% significance level. Unless stated otherwise, the discussion in the text assumes that a_1 is positive. Also note that if there is no prior information concerning the sign of a_1, a two-tailed test can be conducted.

Dickey and Fuller (1979) actually consider three different regression equations that can be used to test for the presence of a unit root:

$$\Delta y_t = \gamma y_{t-1} + \sum_{i=2}^{p} \beta_i \Delta y_{t-i+1} + \epsilon_t \qquad (4.5)$$

$$\Delta y_t = a_0 + \gamma y_{t-1} + \sum_{i=2}^{p} \beta_i \Delta y_{t-i+1} + \epsilon_t \qquad (4.6)$$

$$\Delta y_t = a_0 + \gamma y_{t-1} + a_2 t + \sum_{i=2}^{p} \beta_i \Delta y_{t-i+1} + \epsilon_t \qquad (4.7)$$

The difference between the three regressions concerns the presence of the deterministic elements a_0 and $a_2 t$. The first is like a pure random walk model, the second adds an intercept or *drift* term, and the third includes both a drift and a linear time trend. In all cases, the parameter of interest in the regression equations is γ; if $\gamma = 0$, the $\{y_t\}$ sequence contains a unit root. The test involves estimating one (or more) of the equations above using OLS in order to obtain the estimated value of γ and the associated standard error. Comparing the resulting t-statistic with the appropriate value reported in the Dickey-Fuller tables allows the researcher to determine whether to accept or reject the null hypothesis $\gamma = 0$.

The methodology is precisely the same regardless of which of the three forms of the equations is estimated. However, be aware that the critical values of the t-statistics do depend on whether an intercept and/or time trend is included in the regression equation. In their Monte Carlo study, Dickey and Fuller (1979) found that the critical values for $\gamma = 0$ depend on the form of the regression and sample size. The Dickey-Fuller critical values are all reported in Table A at the end of this text. The statistics labeled τ, τ_μ, and τ_τ are the appropriate statistics to use for equations (4.5), (4.6), and (4.7), respectively.

Dickey and Fuller (1981) provide three additional F-statistics (called ϕ_1, ϕ_2 and ϕ_3) to test **joint** hypotheses on the coefficients. With (4.6), the null hypothesis $\gamma = a_0 = 0$ is tested using the ϕ_1 statistic. Including a time trend in the regression-so that (4.7) is estimated-the joint hypothesis $a_0 = \gamma = a_2 = 0$ is tested using the ϕ_2 statistic and the joint hypothesis $\gamma = a_2 = 0$ is tested using the ϕ_3 statistic.

The ϕ_1, ϕ_2, and ϕ_3 statistics are constructed in exactly the same way as ordinary F-tests:

$$\phi_i = \frac{[\ rss(restricted) - rss(unrestricted)\ ]/r}{rss(unrestricted)\ /(T-k)}$$

where *rss(restricted)* and *rss(unrestricted)* are the sums of the squared residuals from the restricted and unrestricted models; r = number of restrictions; T = number of usable observations; and k = number of parameters estimated in the unrestricted model. Hence, T-k = degrees of freedom in the unrestricted model.

Comparing the calculated value of ϕ_i to the appropriate value reported in Dickey and Fuller (1981) allows you to determine the significance level at which the restriction is binding. The null hypothesis is that the data is generated by the restricted model and the alternative hypothesis is that the data is generated by the unrestricted model. If the restriction is not binding, *rss(restricted)* should be close to *rss(unrestricted)* and ϕ_i should be small; hence, large values of ϕ_i suggest a binding restriction and a rejection of the null hypothesis. Thus, if the calculated value of ϕ_i is smaller than that reported by Dickey and Fuller, you can accept the restricted model (i.e., you do not reject the null hypothesis that the restriction is not binding). If the calculated value of ϕ_i is larger than reported by Dickey and Fuller, you can reject the null hypothesis and conclude that the restriction is binding. The critical values of the three ϕ_i statistics are reported in Table B at the end of this text.

Additional Issues in Unit Root Tests

Lag lengths: The coefficients of the lagged values of Δy_{t-i} in equations (4.5) through (4.7) are not generally of interest. Nevertheless, it is important to ensure that the $\{\epsilon_t\}$ series approximates white-noise. Including too many lags reduces the power of the test to reject the null of a unit root since the increased number of lags necessitates the estimation of additional parameters and a loss of degrees of freedom. The degrees of freedom decrease since the number of parameters estimated has increased <u>and</u> because the number of usable observations has decreased. (We lose one observation for each additional lag included in the autoregression.) On the other hand, too few lags will not appropriately capture the actual error process so that γ and its standard error will not be well estimated.

How does the researcher select the appropriate lag length in such circumstances? One approach is to start with a relatively long lag length and pare down the model by the usual t-test and/or F-tests. For example, one could estimate equation (4.6) using a lag length of n^*. If the t-statistic on lag n^* is insignificant at some specified critical value, reestimate the regression using a lag length of n^*-1. Repeat the process until the lag is significantly different from zero. In the pure autoregressive case, such a procedure will yield the true lag length with an asymptotic probability of unity provided the initial choice of lag length includes the true length. With seasonal data, the process is a bit different. For example, using quarterly data one could start with three years of lags ($n=12$). If the t-statistic on lag 12 is insignificant at some specified critical value and if an F-test indicates that lags 9 - 12 are also insignificant, move to lags 1 - 8. Repeat the process for lag 8 and lags 5 - 8 until a reasonable lag length has been determined. An alternative procedure is to use the AIC and/or SBC to determine lag length.

Once a tentative lag length has been determined, diagnostic checking should be conducted. As always, plotting the residuals is a most important diagnostic tool. There should not appear to be any strong evidence of structural change or serial correlation. Moreover, the correlogram of the residuals should appear to be white-noise. The Ljung-Box Q-statistic should not reveal any significant autocorrelations among the residuals. It is inadvisable to use the alternative procedure of beginning with the most parsimonious model and keep adding lags until a significant lag is found. In Monte Carlo studies, this procedure is biased towards selecting a value of n that is less than the true value.

Moving-average components: The Dickey-Fuller tests are also applicable to processes in which there are moving-average terms. Clearly, an invertible MA model can be transformed into an autoregressive model, and the procedure can be generalized to allow for moving-average components. Let the $\{y_t\}$ sequence be generated from the mixed autoregressive/moving-average process:

$$A(L)y_t = C(L)\epsilon_t$$

where $A(L)$ and $C(L)$ are polynomials of orders p and q, respectively.

If the process is invertible, it is possible to write y_t as:

$$\Delta y_t = \gamma y_{t-1} + \sum_{i=2}^{\infty} \beta_i \Delta y_{t-i+1} + \epsilon_t$$

As it stands, this infinite-order autoregression cannot be estimated using a finite data set. Fortunately, Said and Dickey (1984) have shown that an unknown ARIMA(p, 1, q) process can be well approximated by an ARIMA(n, 1, 0) autoregression of an order no more than $T^{1/3}$. Thus, we can use a finite-order autoregression to approximate the infinite-order process. The test for $\gamma = 0$ can be conducted using the aforementioned Dickey-Fuller τ, τ_μ, or τ_τ test statistics.

Unit roots in a regression model: The unit root issue arises quite naturally in the context of the standard regression model. Consider the regression equation:

$$y_t = a_0 + a_1 z_t + e_t \tag{4.8}$$

where the notation e_t is used to highlight the fact that the residuals from such a regression will not generally be white-noise.

The assumptions of the classical regression model necessitate that both the $\{y_t\}$ and $\{z_t\}$ sequences be stationary and that the errors have a zero mean and a finite variance. In the presence of nonstationary variables, there might be what Granger and Newbold (1974) call a **spurious regression**. A spurious regression has a high R^2, t-statistics that appear to be significant, but the results are without any economic meaning. The regression output "looks good" because the least-squares estimates are not consistent and the customary tests of statistical inference do not hold.

Worksheet 4.1 illustrates the problem of spurious regressions. The top two panels show 100 realizations of the $\{y_t\}$ and $\{z_t\}$ sequences generated as:

$$y_t = y_{t-1} + \epsilon_{yt} \quad \text{and} \quad z_t = z_{t-1} + \epsilon_{zt}$$

Although $\{\epsilon_{yt}\}$ and $\{\epsilon_{zt}\}$ are drawn from white-noise distributions, the realizations of the two sequences are such that y_{100} is positive and z_{100} is negative. A regression of y_t on z_t will capture the *within-sample* tendency of the sequences to move in opposite directions. The straight line shown in the scatter plot is the OLS regression line: $y_t = -0.31 - 0.46z_t$. The correlation

Worksheet 4.1: Spurious Regressions

Consider the two random walk processes:

$$y_t = y_{t-1} + \varepsilon_{yt} \qquad\qquad z_t = z_{t-1} + \varepsilon_{zt}$$

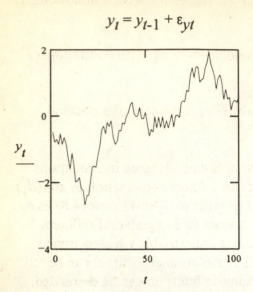

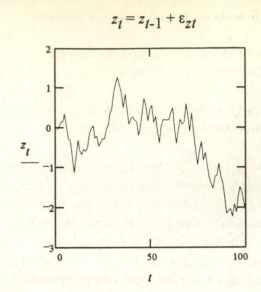

Since the $\{\varepsilon_{yt}\}$ and $\{\varepsilon_{zt}\}$ sequences are independent, the regression of y_t on z_t is spurious. Given the realizations of the random disturbances, it appears as if the two sequences are related. In the scatter plot of y_t against z_t, you can see that y_t tends to rise as z_t decreases. A regression equation of y_t on z_t will capture this tendency. The correlation coefficient between y_t and z_t is -0.372 and a linear regression yields

$$y_t = -0.46z_t - 0.31.$$

However, the residuals from the regression equation are nonstationary; the regression is spurious.

Scatter Plot of y_t and z_t

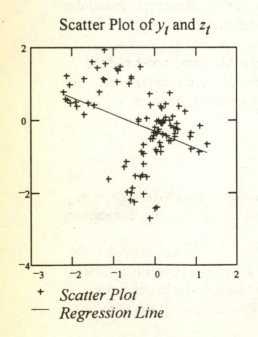

+   *Scatter Plot*
—   *Regression Line*

Regression Residuals

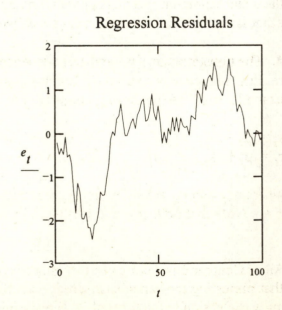

92 Tests for Trends and Unit Roots

coefficient between $\{y_t\}$ and $\{z_t\}$ is -0.372. The residuals from this regression have a unit root; as such, the coefficients -0.31 and -0.46 are spurious.

The point is that the econometrician has to be very careful in working with nonstationary variables. In terms of (4.8), there are four cases to consider:

1. Both $\{y_t\}$ and $\{z_t\}$ are stationary. When both variables are stationary, the classical regression model is appropriate.

2. The $\{y_t\}$ and $\{z_t\}$ sequences are integrated of different orders. Regression equations using such variables are meaningless. It can be shown that a linear combination of an $I(d_1)$ and an $I(d_2)$ variable where $d_1 > d_2$ must be integrated of order d_1. Now, view (4.8) as $e_t = y_t - a_0 - a_1 z_t$. Since e_t is assumed to be $I(0)$, y_t and z_t cannot be integrated of different orders. For the same reason, it is also inappropriate to use one variable which is trend stationary and another which is difference stationary. In such instances, "time" can be included as a so-called *explanatory* variable or the variable in question can be detrended.

3. The nonstationary $\{y_t\}$ and $\{z_t\}$ sequences are integrated of the same order and the residual sequence contains a stochastic trend. This is the case in which the regression is spurious. The results from such spurious regressions are meaningless in that all errors are permanent. In this case, it is often recommended that the regression equation be estimated in first differences. Consider the first difference of (4.8):

$$\Delta y_t = a_1 \Delta z_t + \Delta e_t$$

Since y_t, z_t, and e_t each contain unit roots, the first difference of each is stationary. Hence, the usual asymptotic results apply. Of course, if one of the trends is deterministic and the other is stochastic, first-differencing each would not be appropriate.

4. The nonstationary $\{y_t\}$ and $\{z_t\}$ sequences are integrated of the same order and the residual sequence is stationary. In this circumstance, $\{y_t\}$ and $\{z_t\}$ are **cointegrated**. For example, suppose that both z_t and y_t are the random walk plus noise processes:

$$y_t = \mu_t + \epsilon_{yt}$$
$$z_t = \mu_t + \epsilon_{zt}$$

where ϵ_{yt} and ϵ_{zt} are white-noise processes and μ_t is the random walk process: $\mu_t = \mu_{t-1} + \epsilon_t$. Note that both $\{z_t\}$ and $\{y_t\}$ are $I(1)$ processes but that $y_t - z_t = \epsilon_{yt} - \epsilon_{zt}$ is stationary.

All of Chapter 6 is devoted to the issue of cointegrated variables. For now it is sufficient to note that pretesting the variables in a regression for nonstationarity is extremely important. Estimating a regression in the form of (4.8) is meaningless if cases 2 or 3 apply. If the variables are cointegrated, the results of Chapter 6 apply. The remainder of this chapter considers the formal test procedures for the presence unit roots and/or deterministic time trends.

Multiple roots: Dickey and Pantula (1987) suggest a simple extension of the basic procedure if more than one unit root is suspected. In essence, the methodology entails nothing more than performing Dickey-Fuller tests on successive differences of $\{y_t\}$. When exactly one root is suspected, the Dickey-Fuller procedure is to estimate an equation such as: $\Delta y_t = a_0 + \gamma y_{t-1} + \epsilon_t$. Instead, if two roots are suspected, estimate the equation:

$$\Delta^2 y_t = a_0 + \beta_1 \Delta y_{t-1} + \epsilon_t \tag{4.9}$$

Use the appropriate statistic (i.e., τ, τ_μ, or τ_τ depending on the deterministic elements actually included in the regression) to determine whether β_1 is significantly different from zero. If you cannot reject the null hypothesis that $\beta_1 = 0$, conclude that the $\{y_t\}$ sequence is $I(2)$. If β_1 does differ from zero, go on to determine whether there is a single unit root by estimating:

$$\Delta^2 y_t = a_0 + \beta_1 \Delta y_{t-1} + \beta_2 y_{t-2} + \epsilon_t. \tag{4.10}$$

Since there are not two unit roots, you should find that β_1 and/or β_2 differ from zero. Under the null hypothesis of a single unit root, $\beta_1 < 0$ and $\beta_2 = 0$; under the alternative hypothesis, $\{y_t\}$ is stationary so that β_1 and β_2 are both negative. Thus, estimate (4.10) and use the Dickey-Fuller critical values to test the null hypothesis $\beta_2 = 0$. If you reject this null hypothesis, conclude that $\{y_t\}$ is stationary.

Seasonality: The most direct method to treat seasonality in a nonstationary sequence occurs when the seasonal pattern is purely deterministic. For example, let D_1, D_2, and D_3 represent quarterly seasonal dummy variables such that the value of D_i is unity in season i and zero otherwise. Estimate the regression equation:

$$y_t = \alpha_0 + \alpha_1 D_1 + \alpha_2 D_2 + \alpha_3 D_3 + \hat{y}_t \tag{4.11}$$

where $\hat{y}_t$ is the regression residual so that $\hat{y}_t$ can be viewed as the deseasonalized value of y_t.

Next, use these regression residuals to estimate the regression:

$$\Delta \hat{y}_t = \gamma \hat{y}_{t-1} + \sum_{i=2}^{p} \beta_i \Delta \hat{y}_{t-i+1} + \epsilon_t$$

The null hypothesis of a unit root (i.e., $\gamma = 0$) can be tested using the Dickey-Fuller τ_μ statistic. Rejecting the null hypothesis is equivalent to accepting the alternative that the $\{y_t\}$ sequence is stationary. The test is possible as Dickey, Bell, and Miller (1986) show that the limiting distribution for γ is not affected by the removal of the deterministic seasonal components. If you want to include a time trend in (4.11), use the τ_τ statistic.

If you suspect a seasonal unit root, it is necessary to use an alternative procedure. To keep the notation simple, suppose you have quarterly observations on the $\{y_t\}$ sequence and want to test for the presence of a seasonal unit root. To explain the methodology, note that the polynomial $(1 - \gamma L^4)$ can be factored so that there are four distinct characteristic roots:

$$(1 - \gamma L^4) = (1 - \gamma^{-1/4}L)(1 + \gamma^{1/4}L)(1 - i\gamma^{-1/4}L)(1 + i\gamma^{1/4}L) \tag{4.12}$$

If y_t has a seasonal unit root, $\gamma = 1$. Equation (4.12) is a bit restrictive in that it only allows for a unit root at an annual frequency. Hylleberg, Engle, Granger, and Yoo (1990) develop a clever technique that allows you to test for unit roots at various frequencies; you can test for a unit root (i.e., a root at a zero frequency), a unit root at a semiannual frequency, or a seasonal unit root. To understand the procedure, suppose y_t is generated by:

$$A(L)y_t = \epsilon_t$$

where $A(L)$ is a fourth-order polynomial such that:

$$(1 - a_1L)(1 + a_2L)(1 - a_3iL)(1 + a_4iL)y_t = \epsilon_t \tag{4.13}$$

Now, if $a_1 = a_2 = a_3 = a_4 = 1$, (4.13) is equivalent to setting $\gamma = 1$ in (4.12). Hence, if $a_1 = a_2 = a_3 = a_4 = 1$, there is a seasonal unit root. Consider some of the other possible cases:

Case 1: If $a_1 = 1$, one homogeneous solution to (4.13) is $y_t = y_{t-1}$. As such, the $\{y_t\}$ sequence tends to repeat itself each and every period. This is the case of a nonseasonal unit root.

Case 2: If $a_2 = 1$, one homogeneous solution to (4.13) is $y_t + y_{t-1} = 0$. In this instance, the sequence tends to replicate itself at 6-month intervals so that there is a semiannual unit root. For example, if $y_t = 1$, it follows that $y_{t+1} = -1$, $y_{t+2} = +1$, $y_{t+3} = -1$, $y_{t+4} = 1$, and so forth.

Case 3: If either a_3 or a_4 is equal to unity, the $\{y_t\}$ sequence has an annual cycle. For example, if $a_3 = 1$, a homogeneous solution to (4.13) is $y_t = iy_{t-1}$. Thus, if $y_t = 1$, $y_{t+1} = i$, $y_{t+2} = i^2 = -1$, $y_{t+3} = -i$, and $y_{t+4} = -i^2 = 1$ so that the sequence replicates itself every fourth period.

To develop the test, view (4.13) as a function of a_1, a_2, a_3, and a_4 and take a Taylor series approximation of $A(L)$ around the point $a_1 = a_2 = a_3 = a_4 = 1$. It can be shown that:

$$(1 - L^4)y_t = \gamma_1(1 + L + L^2 + L^3)y_{t-1} - \gamma_2(1 - L + L^2 - L^3)y_{t-1} + (1 - L^2)(\gamma_5 - \gamma_6 L)y_{t-1} + \epsilon_t$$

Thus, as illustrated in sample program 2, to implement the procedure, perform the following three steps:

Step 1: Form the following variables:

$$y_{1t-1} = (1 + L + L^2 + L^3)y_{t-1} = y_{t-1} + y_{t-2} + y_{t-3} + y_{t-4}$$
$$y_{2t-1} = (1 - L + L^2 - L^3)y_{t-1} = y_{t-1} - y_{t-2} + y_{t-3} - y_{t-4}$$
$$y_{3t-1} = (1 - L^2)y_{t-1} = y_{t-1} - y_{t-3} \text{ so that } y_{3t-2} = y_{t-2} - y_{3t-4}$$

Step 2: Estimate the regression:

$$(1-L^4)y_t = \gamma_1 y_{1t-1} - \gamma_2 y_{2t-1} + \gamma_5 y_{3t-1} - \gamma_6 y_{3t-2} + \epsilon_t$$

You might want to modify the form of the equation by including an intercept, deterministic seasonal dummies, and a linear time trend. As in the augmented form of the Dickey-Fuller test, lagged values of $(1-L^4)y_{t-i}$ may also be included. Perform the appropriate diagnostic checks to ensure that the residuals from the regression equation approximate a white-noise process.

Step 3: Form the t-statistic for the null hypothesis $\gamma_1 = 0$; the appropriate critical values are reported in Hylleberg, Engle, Granger, and Yoo (1990). If you do not reject the hypothesis $\gamma_1 = 0$, conclude that $a_1 - 1$ so there is a nonseasonal unit root. Next form the t-test for the hypothesis $\gamma_2 = 0$. If you do not reject the null hypothesis, conclude that $a_2 = 1$ and there is a unit root with a semiannual frequency. Finally, perform the F-test for the hypothesis $\gamma_5 = \gamma_6 = 0$. If the calculated value is less than the critical value reported in Hylleberg $et\ al.$ (1990), conclude that γ_5 and/or γ_6 is zero so there is a unit root with an annual frequency. Be aware that the three null hypotheses are not alternatives; a series may have nonseasonal, semiannual, and annual unit roots.

At the 5% significance level, Hylleberg $et\ al.$ (1990) report that the critical values using 100 observations are:

	$\gamma_1 = 0$	$\gamma_2 = 0$	$\gamma_5 = \gamma_6 = 0$
Intercept	-2.88	-1.95	3.08
Intercept plus seasonal dummies	-2.95	-2.94	6.57
Intercept plus seasonal dummies plus time trend	-3.53	-2.94	6.60

Structural breaks: Perron (1989) shows that unit root tests are biased toward accepting the null hypothesis of a unit root in the presence of a structural break. Sample program 3 illustrates Perron's methodology to test for a unit root against the alternative hypothesis of a stationary series with a one-time change in the mean.

RATS Instructions and Procedures

1. LINREG: The most direct way to conduct the Dickey-Fuller tests is to use the LINREG instruction. Create the lagged changes of y_t and, if necessary, a time trend.

Example:
Consider the program segment from the first sample program (REAL.PRG). The goal is to check for a unit root in the *rcan* series:

```
diff rcan / drcan
set trend = t
linreg drcan
# constant trend rcan{1} drcan{1 to 2}
```

The first instruction creates the first difference of *rcan* and stores the result in *drcan*. The second instruction creates the series *trend* as the integers 1, 2, 3, ... The LINREG instruction uses the dependent variable $drcan_t$ and the supplementary card specifies estimating the model:

$$drcan_t = a_0 + \gamma rcan_{t-1} + a_2 t + \beta_2 drcan_{t-1} + \beta_3 drcan_{t-2} + \epsilon_t$$

The *t*-statistic for γ should be compared to the Dickey-Fuller τ_τ statistic in Table A.

2. ADF.SRC: Some versions of RATS come with the procedure ADF.SRC. This procedure computes the augmented Dickey-Fuller *t*-tests of the regression equation:

$$y_t = a_0 + \gamma y_{t-1} + \sum_{i=2}^{p} \beta_i \Delta y_{t-i} + \epsilon_t$$

The advantage of ADF.SRC is that it automatically determines the appropriate number of lagged differences using one of the following four methods: the AIC, BIC (the default), adding lags until the Ljung-Box test fails to reject no serial correlation at a user-defined level, or by adding lags until a Lagrange multiplier test fails to reject no serial correlation at a user-defined level.[1] After compiling, the procedure is used as:

```
@adf(options) series start end residuals
```
where: *series*   The series to be analyzed
      start end   The range of the series to use. The default is the entire range.
      residuals   The name of the series used to store the regression residuals. If *residuals* is not specified, the regression residuals are not saved.

---

[1] As calculated in ADF.SRC, the SBC and BIC will always select the identical model.

The principal options are:

DET=   Specifies the deterministic terms to include in the model. The default is to include only a constant. DET=NONE specifies neither a constant nor trend and DET=TREND a constant and a trend.

CRITERION=   Specifies whether the AIC, BIC, Ljung-Box Q-statistic, or a Lagrange multiplier test is used to select lag length. The syntax is CRITERION= AIC, BIC, LBTEST, or LMTEST.

MAXLAG=   The maximum lag considered by the AIC or BIC option. The default is 12.

ARSIGNIF=   The significance level for the Ljung-Box and LM tests. The default is 0.05.

SCLAGS=   The number of lags to use in the Ljung-Box and LM tests. The default is 8.

Examples:
1. @adf(criterion=aic) y /

Estimate a model in the form of (4.6) using the AIC to select a lag length no greater than 12. The estimation takes place over the entire sample.

2. @adf(det=trend,criterion=lbtest,sclags=4) y 20 100 resids

Estimate a model in the form of (4.7) using the Ljung-Box Q-statistic to select a lag length no greater than 4. The test uses the 0.05 significance level. The estimation takes place over sample periods 20 through 100. The residuals are saved in *resids*.

3. DFUNIT.SRC: The advantage of this procedure is that it can compute either the usual Dickey-Fuller *t*-test or the alternative $T(\text{rho} - 1)$ test. [*Note*: In our notation, this alternative is a test on the value of $T\gamma$. The critical values for $T(\text{rho} - 1)$ are available in Fuller (1976).] DFUNIT.SRC necessarily includes a constant in the regression equation. After compiling, the procedure is used as:

@dfunit(options) *series start end*
where: *series*   The series to be analyzed
       start end   The range of the series to use. The default is the entire range.

The principal options are:

TTEST   Computes the regression *t*-test, as opposed to the $T(\text{rho}-1)$ test. The default is the $T(\text{rho}-1)$ test

TREND   If TREND is specified, the model includes a time trend and a constant. The default is to include only a constant. [It is not possible to specify a model in the form of (4.5).]

LAGS=   The number of lagged changes to include. The default is zero.

Examples:
1. @dfunit(lags=12,ttest) y /

Estimate a model in the form of (4.6) using 12 lagged changes. The estimation takes place over the entire sample.

2. @dfunit(trend,lags=4) y 20 100

Estimate a model in the form of (4.7) using 4 lagged changes. The estimation takes place over sample periods 20 through 100.

4. PPUNIT.SRC: Computes the Phillips-Perron (1988) modifications of the Dickey-Fuller *t*-test or the alternative $T(rho - 1)$ test (*Note*: In our notation, this alternative is a test on the value of $T\gamma$.) PPUNIT.SRC necessarily includes a constant in the regression equation. After compiling, the procedure is used as:

@ppunit(options) *series start end*

The syntax and usage are precisely the same as in the DFUNIT.SRC procedure.

5. Others: Several additional procedures can be downloaded from the RATS Bulletin Board. The phone number is 708-864-8816. A very useful procedure is:

URAUTO.SRC: URAUTO.SRC runs a set of unit root tests in sequence attempting to classify the series based upon trend and unit root properties. After compiling, the procedure is used as:

@urauto(options) *series start end*
where: *series*　　　　The series to be analyzed
　　　 start end　　　The range of the series to use. The default is the entire range.

The key options are:

LAG=　　　　The number of lags to use. The default is 4.
NOPARAM　　The default is the Dickey-Fuller test. NOPARAM specifies the Phillips-Perron
　　　　　　　　test.

Other unit root procedures include: BAYESTST.SRC (generalizes Sims' Bayesian method to allow for intercept and trend), UNITROOT.SRC (runs Dickey-Fuller regressions with constant+trend, constant only or neither constant nor trend), URSB.SRC (performs Sargan-Bhargava unit root tests), and URTT.SRC (provides descriptive statistics including the correlogram, and all combinations of trend and constant).

Sample Programs

1. Dickey-Fuller and Phillips-Perron tests: The purpose of this exercise is to illustrate some of the various RATS commands and procedures that can be used to test for unit roots. The columns in the file labeled REAL.PRN contain the logarithm of the real exchange rates for Canada, Germany, Japan, and the UK. The four series are called *rcan, rger, rjap,* and *ruk,* respectively. Each series is constructed as $r_t = e_t + p^*_t - p_t$ where r = log of the real exchange rate, e = log of the dollar price of foreign exchange, p^* = log of the foreign wholesale price index, p = log of the U.S. wholesale price index. All series run from February 1973 through December 1989 and each is expressed as an index number such that February 1973 = 1.00.

The file labeled REAL.PRG contains all of the statements used below and all of the statements and output are on the file labeled REAL.OUT. The first four lines of the program read the data into RATS memory. The SET statement creates the variable *trend* as the series of integers and the DIFFERENCE instruction creates the first difference of *rcan.* The remainder of the program analyzes only the *rcan* series. As an exercise, you should repeat the subsequent steps for each of the other real exchange rates:

```
calendar 73 2 12          ;*  Set the calendar for monthly data beginning
allocate 89:12            ;*    with 1973:2.
open data a:\real.prn     ;*  Modify this line if the data is not on drive a:\ .
data(format=prn,org=obs) /
set trend = t
diff rcan / drcan
```

/* The high-resolution graph of the *rcan* series shown in Figure 4.3 was created using:
*/
```
graph(header='The Canadian Real $
        Exchange  Rate') 1
# rcan
```

/* You can see there is little tendency for mean reversion in the *rcan* series. The mean is approximately unity during the mid-1970's, falls to approximately 0.885 throughout the mid-1980's, and then rises in the late 1980's.

Figure 4.3: The Canadian Real Exchange Rate

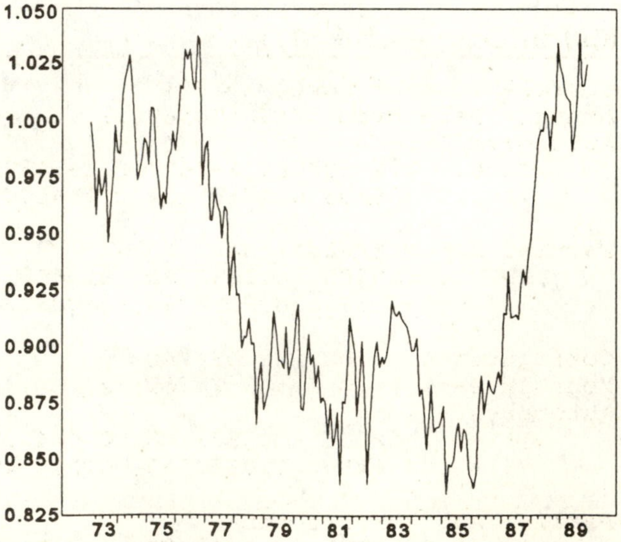

The next set of instructions compile the BJIDENT.SRC procedure and plot the ACF and PACF of the *rcan* series and its first difference.

```
/*
source(noecho) c:\rats\bjident.src     ;* Change this instruction if BJIDENT.SRC is not in the
@bjident(diff=1) rcan                   ;*    c:\rats directory.
```

/* The option DIFF=1 instructs RATS to create the ACF and PACF of the level of *rcan* and its first difference. (Here, only the autocorrelations of the level of the series are shown.) The autocorrelations confirm that there is little tendency for mean reversion in the *rcan* series.

One way to obtain a display of the ACF and PACF of *rcan* and its first difference is to use the COR instructions:

```
cor(partial=pacf) rcan
cor(partial=pacf) drcan
```

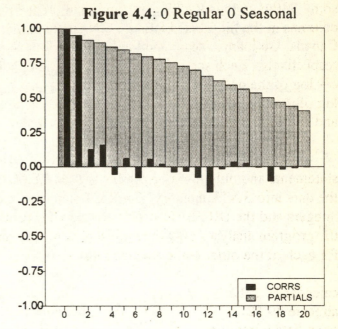

Figure 4.4: 0 Regular 0 Seasonal

A useful trick to is to use the BJIDENT.SRC procedure and to specify the no graph option. The ACF and PACF of *rcan* and *drcan* are displayed. If you use this shortcut, note that BJIDENT.SRC inappropriately labels the series and its first difference as *DIFFED*. Consider:
```
*/
```
@bjident(nograph,diffs=1) rcan

```
Correlations of Series DIFFED
Monthly Data From 73:02 To 89:12
Autocorrelations
     1: 0.95109959 0.91691527 0.89743824 0.86897993 0.84708012 0.81911904
     7: 0.79706303 0.77888188 0.75410092 0.72946966 0.70020306 0.65782904

Partial Autocorrelations
     1:   0.9510996  0.1291783  0.1615114 -0.0546352  0.0613725 -0.0779928
     7:   0.0571170  0.0198234 -0.0359361 -0.0323219 -0.0771024 -0.1815772

Correlations of Series DIFFED
Monthly Data From 73:03 To 89:12
Autocorrelations
     1: -0.1562001 -0.1531103  0.0443029 -0.0152957  0.1053500 -0.0740475
     7: -0.0475489  0.0597755 -0.0255490  0.0142241  0.1810469 -0.1151413

Partial Autocorrelations
     1: -0.1562001 -0.1819480 -0.0131290 -0.0395388  0.1079517 -0.0469954
     7: -0.0339943  0.0210078 -0.0201967  0.0099899  0.2019143 -0.0428092
```

/* To conserve space, only the first 12 autocorrelations are shown. All 20 of the autocorrelations are shown in the file labeled REAL.OUT. The Dickey-Fuller test in the form of (4.6) can be conducted using the LINREG instruction:
*/

linreg drcan   ;* Estimate $\Delta y_t = a_0 + \gamma y_{t-1} + \epsilon_t$ using LINREG. All
 # constant rcan{1}   ;*   output is in the file labeled REAL.OUT.

Coefficient	Estimate	Standard Error	t-statistic	Significance Level
Constant	0.033045933	0.018189262	1.81678	0.07074734
RCAN{1}	-0.035397124	0.019523543	-1.81305	0.07132361

* The estimate of γ is -0.0353 with a t-statistic of -1.81305. From the Dickey-Fuller tables, you
* can see that it is not possible to reject the null of a unit root at conventional significance levels.
* Now use the augmented Dickey-Fuller test with two lags:

linreg drcan
 # constant rcan{1} drcan{1 to 2}

Coefficient	Estimate	Standard Error	t-statistic	Significance Level
Constant	0.018082360	0.018192635	0.99394	0.32147828
RCAN{1}	-0.019051510	0.019544685	-0.97477	0.33087743
DRCAN{1}	-0.181729177	0.070444941	-2.57973	0.01061947
DRCAN{2}	-0.174737282	0.069878053	-2.50060	0.01321796

* To perform the test including a time trend, use:

linreg drcan
 # constant trend rcan{1} drcan{1 to 2}

Coefficient	Estimate	Standard Error	t-statistic	Significance Level
Constant	0.008103034	0.019882814	0.40754	0.68405876
TREND	0.000024515	0.000019842	1.23550	0.21813259
RCAN{1}	-0.011040106	0.020567412	-0.53678	0.59203379
DRCAN{1}	-0.195259591	0.071197820	-2.74249	0.00666534
DRCAN{2}	-0.187597988	0.070556478	-2.65883	0.00849258

* The identical tests can be performed using the DFUNIT.SRC procedure. Do **not** change the
* *start* date to allow for lagged values. Consider:

source(noecho) c:\rats\dfunit.src   ;* Modify this line if DFUNIT.SRC is not in c:\rats.
@dfunit(ttest) rcan 73:2 89:12   ;* The output is the same as that of LINREG with no lags.
        Dickey-Fuller Test with 0 Lags = -1.81305

@dfunit(ttest,lags=2) rcan 73:2 89:12   ;* The augmented test with two lags yields the same
                                             ;* result as the second LINREG instruction above.

```
        Dickey-Fuller Test with 2 Lags = -0.97477
```

@dfunit(ttest,lags=2,trend) rcan 73:2 89:12   ;* Now include a trend.

```
        Dickey-Fuller Test with 2 Lags = -0.53678
```

* The Phillips-Perron PPUNIT.SRC procedure uses the same syntax as DFUNIT.SRC. Consider:

source c:\rats\ppunit.src   ;* Modify this if PPUNIT.SRC is not in c:\rats.
@ppunit(ttest,lags=0) rcan 73:2 89:12   ;* Lags = 0 is needed since the default is 4.

```
        Phillips-Perron Test with 0 Lags = -1.82209
```

@ppunit(ttest,lags=2) rcan 73:2 89:12   ;* Now use two lags.

```
        Phillips-Perron Test with 2 Lags = -1.51739
```

@ppunit(ttest,lags=2,trend) rcan 73:2 89:12   ;* Now include a trend.

```
        Phillips-Perron Test with 2 Lags = -1.09831
```

/* Regardless of lag length, the presence of a trend, and whether DFUNIT.SRC or PPUNIT.SRC is used, the null hypothesis of a unit root cannot be rejected. The next two lines of REAL.PRG use the ADF.SRC procedure to display similar results. As opposed to DFUNIT.SRC or PPUNIT.SRC, note that ADF.SRC selects the lag length and reports the t-statistic and the critical value of the intercept and γ.
*/

source(noecho) c:\rats\adf.src   ;* Modify this line if ADF.SRC in not on c:\rats.
@adf rcan 73:02 89:12   ;* The defaults options use the BIC criterion to determine
                                   ;* lag length and include only a constant in the model.

```
Using data from  73:02 to 89:12

INFORMATION CRITERIA
Minimum AIC at lag:        2
Minimum BIC at lag:        2

AUGMENTED DICKEY-FULLER TEST FOR RCAN WITH 2 LAGS:-0.9748
AT LEVEL 0.05 THE TABULATED CRITICAL VALUE:       -2.8760

Coefficient and T-Statistic on the Constant:
     0.01808          0.9939
```

/* The URAUTO.SRC procedure performs the F-tests on the intercept and trend in order to select the appropriate deterministic regressors to include in the model. The critical values of Φ_3 and Φ_1 are reported (denoted by psi3 and psi1). As opposed to ADF.SRC, the procedure does not select lag length. Note that URAUTO.SRC uses the $T(\text{rho-}1)$ test as opposed to the t-test to determine the significance of γ.
*/

```
source(noecho) c:\rats\urauto.sr        ;* Modify this line if URAUTO.SRC is not on c:\rats.
@urauto(lag=2) rcan 73:02 89:12
```

```
REGRESSIONS WITH CONSTANT,TREND
  t(rho-1)/tao =        -0.53678 with critical value      -3.41000
  Cannot reject a unit root with t(rho-1)/tao
  Next is joint test of trend=0 and root=1
  psi3 =            1.23959 with critical value            6.25000
    PSI3 cannot reject unit root and no linear trend

REGRESSIONS WITH CONSTANT,NO TREND
  t(rho-1)/mu =        -0.97477 with critical value       -2.86000
  Cannot reject a unit root with t(rho-1)/mu
   Next is joint test of constant=0 and root=1
  psi1 =            0.53703 with critical value            4.59000
    PSI1 cannot reject constant=0 and root=1

REGRESSIONS WITH NO CONSTANT, NO TREND
  t(rho-1) =         0.29353 with critical value          -1.95000
  Cannot reject a unit root with t(rho-1)

     CONCLUSION: Series contains a unit root with zero drift
```

/* The file REAL.OUT also contains output from the URTT.SRC procedure. This procedure can only be obtained from the RATS Bulletin Board.
*/

2. Tests for seasonal unit roots: This exercise is designed to illustrate the Hylleberg, Engle, Granger, and Yoo methodology to test for seasonal unit roots. The file labeled US.PRN contains real U.S. GDP measured in 1985 dollars; the variable name is *gdp85*. The following program and all output are contained in the file labled SEASONS.OUT:

```
cal 60 1 4                          ;* Set the calendar for quarterly data beginning with 1960:1.
all 91:4                            ;* The data set runs through 91:4.
open data a:us.prn                  ;* Modify this line if the data is not on drive a:\ .
data(format=prn,org=obs) / gdp85
statistics gdp85                    ;* Obtain the sample statistics of gdp85.
set lgdp = log(gdp85)              ;* Perform the test on the log of gdp85.  The log
                                    ;*  transformation helps correct for heteroskedasticity.
```

* The next four statements create the variables *y1, y2, y3* and the fourth difference of *lgdp*.
* Note that the lagged values of each can be used in the LINREG instruction:

```
set y1 = lgdp + lgdp{1} + lgdp{2} + lgdp{3}
set y2 = lgdp - lgdp{1} + lgdp{2} - lgdp{3}
set y3 = lgdp - lgdp{2}
set y4 = lgdp - lgdp{4}
```

* Regress *y4* on the lagged values of *y1, y2, y3*, and a constant and save the residuals as *resids*.

linreg y4 / resids   ;* Here a constant is included in the regression equation.
 # constant y1{1} y2{1} y3{1} y3{2}

```
Coefficient    Estimate      Standard      t-statistic    Significance
                             Error                        Level
Constant       0.114021571   0.047717865    2.38949       0.01844225
Y1{1}         -0.001820743   0.000793942   -2.29329       0.02358638
Y2{1}          0.514108743   0.086916822    5.91495       0.00000003
Y3{1}          0.717694355   0.082057862    8.74620       0.00000000
Y3{2}          0.417578117   0.081453080    5.12661       0.00000116
```

/* The null hypothesis $\gamma_1 = 0$ cannot be rejected but the null $\gamma_2 = 0$ can be rejected. Conclude that there is a a unit root but not a semiannual unit root. To perform the *F*-test $\gamma_5 = \gamma_6 = 0$, use the EXCLUDE instruction:
*/

exclude
 # y3{1} y3{2}
```
        Null Hypothesis : The Following Coefficients Are Zero
        Y3                    Lag(s) 1 to 2
        F(2,119)=      78.84897 with Significance Level 0.00000000
```

* Conclude there is not a seasonal unit root. It is left as an exercise for you to perform the
*   appropriate diagnostic tests concerning the residuals.

3. Structural breaks and unit root tests: This exercise is designed to illustrate the difficulty of discerning between unit root processes and a series with a structural break. The second column of the file labeled BREAK.PRN contains the simulated values of the $\{y1_t\}$ sequence. In order to simulate a series with a structural break, 100 random numbers were drawn to represent the $\{\epsilon_t\}$ sequence. By setting $y1_0 = 0$, the next 100 values in the $\{y1_t\}$ sequence were constructed as:

$$y1_t = 0.5y1_{t-1} + \epsilon_t + D_L$$

where $D_L = 0$ for $t = 1, \ldots, 50$ and $D_L = 1$ for $t = 51, \ldots, 100$.

If you did not know that the series contained a structural break at $t = 51$, you might inadvertently conclude that the series contains a unit root. The following program first tests for a unit root and then uses the Perron methodology to test for a structural break. The files BREAK.PRG and BREAK.OUT contain the program and the program plus output, respectively.

```
cal 1900 1 1            ;* Although the data is undated, it is convenient to set the
all 1999:1              ;*    calendar for 100 observations of annual data beginning
open data a:\break.prn  ;*    with 1900. It is assumed that the data disk is on drive a:\.
data(format=prn,org=obs) /
```

* A plot of the data is always a useful tool. Here, the plot reveals strong evidence of the
* structural break. Create the graph using:

graph(header='A Structural Break') 1
 # y1

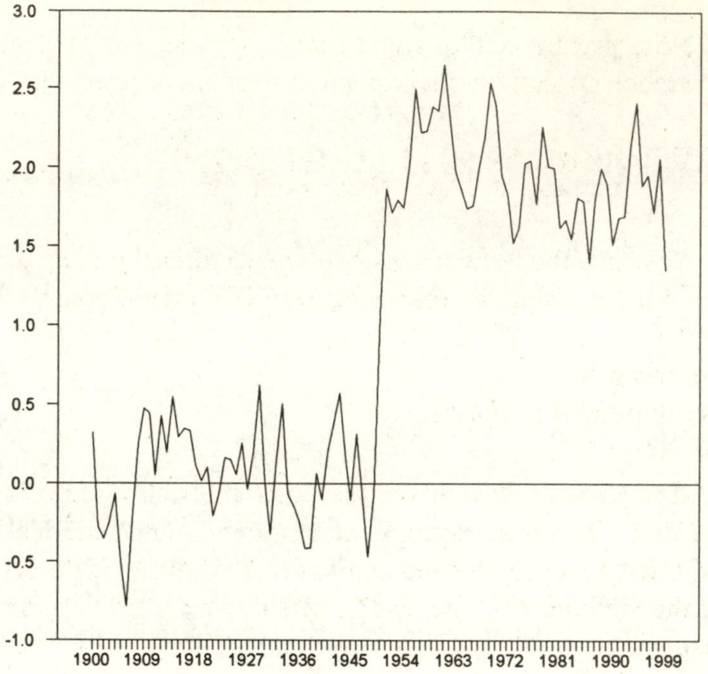

/* Although the structural break is
evident, one purpose of this exercise
is to illustrate the point that unit root
tests are biased towards accepting
the null of a unit root in the presence
of a structural break. Intuitively, in
the regression $y1_t = a_0 + a_1 y1_{t-1} + e_t$, the coefficient a_1 is biased
towards unity in the presence of a
structural break. To illustrate this
point, first use the methodology of
sample program 1 to test for unit
roots.
*/

Figure 4.5: A Structural Break

source c:\rats\bjident.src   ;* Obtain the ACF and PACF of *y1* with BJIDENT.SRC
@bjident(nograph,diffs=1) y1   ;* using the NOGRAPH option. Note that the *y1* series and
                                       ;* its first difference are both labeled *DIFFED*.

```
Correlations of Series DIFFED
Annual Data From 1900:01 To 1999:01
Autocorrelations
     1: 0.94212749 0.87753118 0.83551124 0.80535774 0.76777678 0.72387744
     7: 0.68530152 0.65934155 0.64746814 0.61984913 0.57096329 0.52765052

Partial Autocorrelations
     1:  0.9421275 -0.0896210  0.1713612  0.0590698 -0.0598575 -0.0372158
     7:  0.0180367  0.0663115  0.1142814 -0.1272497 -0.1448405  0.0108252

Correlations of Series DIFFED
Annual Data From 1896:01 To 1994:01
Autocorrelations
     1: -0.0016951 -0.2010085 -0.1116985  0.0792064  0.0102899 -0.0604869
     7: -0.0670984 -0.0999167  0.1622744  0.1772953 -0.0803472 -0.1654044

Partial Autocorrelations
     1: -0.0016951 -0.2010119 -0.1171837  0.0377173 -0.0348776 -0.0540135
     7: -0.0642963 -0.1390859  0.1292766  0.1417676 -0.0460950 -0.0804313
```

* The ACF and PACF are clearly indicative of a unit root process. Next, perform the Dickey-
* Fuller tests on the *y1* series.

```
source(noecho) c:\rats\dfunit.src            ;* Modify this line if DFUNIT.SRC is not on c:\rats.
@dfunit(ttest) y1 1900:01 1999:01            ;* Perform a Dickey-Fuller test with only a constant.
       Dickey-Fuller Test with  0 Lags = -1.70630
```

* Note that the null of a unit root is not rejected. The next instruction includes a trend in the
* model. Again, the null of a unit root is not rejected:

```
@dfunit(ttest,trend) y1 1900:01 1999:01
       Dickey-Fuller Test with  0 Lags = -2.73397
```

* Now use the Perron methodology to filter the {*y1*} series. First create a trend and a level
*   dummy using the following two SET instructions:

```
set trend = t
set dummy = t>1949:1
```

/* The variable *dummy* is equal to zero for all values of $t \le 1949{:}1$ and equal to 1 beginning in
1950:1. This is an example of creating dummy variables using logical operators. For each value
of *t*, RATS evaluates the expression *t*>1949:1. If the statement is false, RATS sets dummy = 0.
If the statement is true, RATS sets dummy = 1. A pulse dummy, called *pulse*, can be created
using:
*/
```
set pulse = t.EQ.1950:1
```

/*   Here, for each value of *t*, RATS evaluates the expression t.EQ.1950:1. The expression is
true for only 1950:1. Thus, *pulse* is set equal to zero for all periods except 1950:1.

        Now, estimate a regression with an intercept, time trend, and the level dummy. Save the
residuals as *resids*. The *resids* series is the filtered *y1* series.
*/
```
linreg(noprint) y1 / resids
# constant dummy trend
```

* To perform unit root tests with LINREG, it is necessary to create the first difference of *resids*:

```
set dresids = resids - resids{1}         ;* Store the first difference of resids in dresids.
linreg resids                            ;* Perform a Dickey-Fuller tests of resids.
# resids{1}
```

Coefficient	Estimate	Standard Error	t-statistic	Significance Level
RESIDS{1}	0.4842616924	0.0897395180	5.39630	0.00000047

The critical value of the *t*-statistic is 3.96. Conclude that the filtered series does not contain a unit root. [*Note*: The critical values for the *t*-statistics used for such structural break tests are reported in Perron (1989). The *t*-values are generally larger than the corresponding Dickey-Fuller values.] The diagnostic checks to determine whether it is appropriate to omit the lagged values of *dresids* is left as an exercise.

Additional Exercises

1. The sample program REAL.PRG tested for a unit root in the log of the real Canadian/U.S. exchange rate (*rcan*). Use the LINREG instruction to estimate a model of the form:

$$drcan_t = a_0 + \gamma rcan_{t-1} + \sum_{i=1}^{n} \beta_i drcan_{t-i} + \epsilon_t$$

(a) Use the AIC and the SBC to determine the appropriate lag length n.

(b) Use the EXCLUDE instruction to determine the appropriate lag length.

(c) Check the residuals from the models you selected in parts (a) and (b) for the presence of serial correlation.

(d) Determine the appropriate deterministic regressors to include in your model.

2. In addition to *rcan*, the data set REAL.PRN contains the real exchange rates for Germany (*rger*), Japan (*rjap*), and the UK (*ruk*).

(a) Select one or two of these other series and perform unit root tests using the LINREG instruction as in sample program 1. Be sure to determine the appropriate lag length.

(b) Show that you can obtain the identical results using the DFUNIT.SRC procedure.

(c) Determine the appropriate deterministic regressors to include in your model.

3. The file labeled US.PRN used in sample program 2 also contains quarterly U.S. money supply data as measured by M1 (*m1*). Define *lm1* as the natural log of *m1*.

(a) Check for multiple unit roots in the *lm1* series.

(b) Check for seasonal unit roots in the *lm1* series.

(c) Estimate the regression $lgdp85_t = a_0 + a_1 lm1_t + \epsilon_t$. Present evidence to show that this is a spurious regression.

## Chapter 5

Vector Autoregression Analysis

As you have seen in previous chapters, many interesting dynamic relationships can be captured using single equation time-series methods. In the recent past, many time-series texts would end with nothing more than a brief discussion of multiequation models. Yet, one of the most fertile areas of contemporary time-series research concerns multiequation models. The specific aim of this chapter is to generalize univariate methods to consider multivariate systems of equations. Towards this end you will be introduced to the concept of a Vector Autoregression (VAR). The most basic form of a VAR treats all variables symmetrically without making reference to the issue of dependence versus independence.

The tools employed by VAR analysis-Granger causality, impulse response analysis, and variance decompositions-can be helpful in understanding the interrelationships among economic variables and in the formulation of a more structured economic model. RATS is especially powerful in allowing you to perform sophisticated VAR analysis.

Theoretical Background

A natural starting place for multivariate models is to treat each variable symmetrically. In the two-variable case, we can let the time path of the $\{y_t\}$ be affected by current and past realizations of the $\{z_t\}$ sequence **and** let the time path of the $\{z_t\}$ sequence be affected by current and past realizations of the $\{y_t\}$ sequence. Consider the simple bivariate system:

$$y_t = b_{10} - b_{12}z_t + \gamma_{11}y_{t-1} + \gamma_{12}z_{t-1} + \epsilon_{yt} \tag{5.1}$$
$$z_t = b_{20} - b_{21}y_t + \gamma_{21}y_{t-1} + \gamma_{22}z_{t-1} + \epsilon_{zt} \tag{5.2}$$

where it is assumed (i) that both y_t and z_t are stationary; (ii) ϵ_{yt} and ϵ_{zt} are white-noise disturbances with standard deviations of σ_y and σ_z, respectively; and (iii) $\{\epsilon_{yt}\}$ and $\{\epsilon_{zt}\}$ are uncorrelated.

Equations (5.1) and (5.2) constitute a *first-order* VAR since the longest lag length is unity. The structure of the system incorporates feedback since y_t and z_t are allowed to affect each other. For example, $-b_{12}$ is the contemporaneous effect of a unit change of z_t on y_t and γ_{12} is the effect of a unit change in z_{t-1} on y_t. Note that the terms ϵ_{yt} and ϵ_{zt} are pure innovations (or shocks) in y_t and z_t, respectively. Of course, if b_{21} is not equal to zero, ϵ_{yt} has an indirect contemporaneous effect on z_t, and if b_{12} is not equal to zero, ϵ_{zt} has an indirect contemporaneous effect on y_t.

Equations (5.1) and (5.2) are not reduced form equations since y_t has a contemporaneous effect on z_t and z_t has a contemporaneous effect on y_t. Fortunately, it is possible to transform the system of equations into a more usable form. Using matrix algebra, we can write the system in the compact form:

$$Bx_t = \Gamma_0 + \Gamma_1 x_{t-1} + \epsilon_t \tag{5.3}$$

where:

$$B = \begin{bmatrix} 1 & b_{12} \\ b_{21} & 1 \end{bmatrix}; \quad x_t = \begin{bmatrix} y_t \\ z_t \end{bmatrix}; \quad \Gamma_0 = \begin{bmatrix} b_{10} \\ b_{20} \end{bmatrix};$$

$$\Gamma_1 = \begin{bmatrix} \gamma_{11} & \gamma_{12} \\ \gamma_{21} & \gamma_{22} \end{bmatrix}; \quad \text{and} \quad \epsilon_t = \begin{bmatrix} \epsilon_{yt} \\ \epsilon_{zt} \end{bmatrix}$$

Equation (5.3) represents a VAR in **primitive** form. Premultiplication by B^{-1} allows us to obtain the Vector Autoregressive (VAR) model in **standard** form:

$$x_t = A_0 + A_1 x_{t-1} + e_t$$

where:

$$A_0 = B^{-1}\Gamma_0; \quad A_1 = B^{-1}\Gamma_1; \quad \text{and} \quad e_t = B^{-1}\epsilon_t$$

For notational purposes, we can define a_{i0} as element i of the vector A_0; a_{ij} as the element in row i and column j of the matrix A_1; and e_{it} as the element i of the vector e_t. Using this new notation, we can rewrite (5.3) in the equivalent form:

$$y_t = a_{10} + a_{11}y_{t-1} + a_{12}z_{t-1} + e_{1t} \tag{5.4a}$$
$$z_t = a_{20} + a_{21}y_{t-1} + a_{22}z_{t-1} + e_{2t} \tag{5.4b}$$

It is important to note that the error terms (i.e., e_{1t} and e_{2t}) are composites of the two shocks ϵ_{yt} and ϵ_{zt}. Since $e_t = B^{-1}\epsilon_t$, we can compute e_{1t} and e_{2t} as:

$$e_{1t} = (\epsilon_{yt} - b_{12}\epsilon_{zt})/(1-b_{12}b_{21}) \tag{5.5}$$
$$e_{2t} = (\epsilon_{zt} - b_{21}\epsilon_{yt})/(1-b_{12}b_{21}) \tag{5.6}$$

Since ϵ_{yt} and ϵ_{zt} are white-noise processes, it follows that both e_{1t} and e_{2t} have zero means, constant variances, and are individually serially uncorrelated. The covariance of the two terms is:

$$Ee_{1t}e_{2t} = E[(\epsilon_{yt} - b_{12}\epsilon_{zt})(\epsilon_{zt} - b_{21}\epsilon_{yt})]/(1-b_{12}b_{21})^2 \qquad (5.7)$$
$$= -(b_{21}\sigma_y^2 + b_{12}\sigma_z^2)/(1-b_{12}b_{21})^2$$

In general, (5.7) will not be zero so that the two shocks will be correlated. Since all variance and covariance terms are time-invariant, we can write the variance/covariance matrix as:

$$\Sigma = \begin{bmatrix} \sigma_1^2 & \sigma_{12} \\ \sigma_{21} & \sigma_2^2 \end{bmatrix} \qquad (5.8)$$

where $Var(e_{it}) = \sigma_i^2$ and $\sigma_{12} = \sigma_{21} = Cov(e_{1t}, e_{2t})$.

Estimation: Note that the right-hand sides of (5.4a) and (5.4b) contain only pre-determined variables and that the error terms are serially uncorrelated with constant variance. Hence, *each equation in the system can be estimated using OLS*. Moreover, OLS estimates are consistent and asymptotically efficient. Even though the errors are correlated across equations, estimation using seemingly unrelated regressions (SUR) does not add to the efficiency of the estimation procedure since both regressions have identical right-hand-side variables.

If one or more of the equations is constrained so as to have different right-hand-side variables than the others (including the possibility of differing lag lengths), the system is called a **near-VAR**. A near-VAR can be estimated using RATS SUR instruction. In this case, SUR improves the efficiency of the estimates.

There is an issue of whether the variables in a VAR need to be stationary. Sims (1980) and others (including the *RATS User's Manual* itself) recommend against differencing *even if the variables contain a unit root*. They argue that the goal of a VAR analysis is to determine the interrelationships among the variables, **not** to determine the parameter estimates. The main argument against differencing is that it "throws away" information concerning the comovements in the data (such as the possibility of cointegrating relationships). Similarly, it is argued that the data need not be detrended. In a VAR, a trending variable will be well approximated by a unit root plus drift. However, the majority view is that the form of the variables in the VAR should mimic the true data generating process. This is particularly true if the aim is to estimate a structural model. We return to these issues in the next chapter; for now it is assumed that all variables are stationary. In an exercise, you are asked to compare a VAR in levels to a VAR in first differences.

Identification: To illustrate the identification procedure, return to the two-variable/first-order VAR of the previous section. Due to the feedback inherent in a VAR process, the primitive equations (5.1) and (5.2) cannot be estimated directly. However, OLS can be used to estimate the VAR in standard form [i.e., equations (5.4a) and (5.4b)]. OLS can provide estimates of the two elements of A_0 and of the four elements of A_1. Moreover, by obtaining the residuals from the two regressions, it is possible to calculate estimates of the variance of e_{1t}, e_{2t}, and of the covariance between e_{1t} with e_{2t}. The issue is whether it is possible to recover all of the information present in the primitive system represented by (5.1) and (5.2) from the estimates of (5.4a) and (5.4b).

The answer to this question is, "No, unless we are willing to appropriately restrict the primitive system." The reason is clear if we compare the number of parameters of the primitive system with the number of parameters recovered from the estimated VAR model. Estimating (5.4a) and (5.4b) yields six coefficient estimates (a_{10}, a_{20}, a_{11}, a_{12}, a_{21}, and a_{22}) and the calculated values of $\text{Var}(e_{1t})$, $\text{Var}(e_{2t})$, and $\text{Cov}(e_{1t}, e_{2t})$. However, the primitive system (5.1) and (5.2) contains ten parameters. In addition to the two intercept coefficients b_{10} and b_{20}, the four autoregressive coefficients γ_{11}, γ_{12}, γ_{21}, and γ_{22}, the two feedback coefficients b_{12} and b_{21}, there are the two standard deviations σ_y and σ_z. In all, the primitive system contains ten parameters whereas the VAR estimation yields only nine parameters. In this two-variable case, if exactly one parameter of the primitive system is restricted, the system is exactly identified, and if more than one parameter is restricted, the system is overidentified.

One way to identify the model is to use the type of **recursive** system proposed by Sims (1980). Suppose that you are willing to impose a restriction on the primitive system such that the coefficient b_{21} is equal to zero. Writing (5.1) and (5.2) with the constraint imposed yields:

$$y_t = b_{10} - b_{12}z_t + \gamma_{11}y_{t-1} + \gamma_{12}z_{t-1} + \epsilon_{yt} \tag{5.9}$$
$$z_t = b_{20} \qquad\quad + \gamma_{21}y_{t-1} + \gamma_{22}z_{t-1} + \epsilon_{zt} \tag{5.10}$$

Imposing the restriction $b_{21} = 0$ means that B^{-1} is given by:

$$B^{-1} = \begin{bmatrix} 1 & -b_{12} \\ 0 & 1 \end{bmatrix}$$

Now, premultiplication of the primitive system by B^{-1} yields:

$$\begin{bmatrix} y_t \\ z_t \end{bmatrix} = \begin{bmatrix} b_{10} - b_{12}b_{20} \\ b_{20} \end{bmatrix} + \begin{bmatrix} \gamma_{11} - b_{12}\gamma_{21} & \gamma_{12} - b_{12}\gamma_{22} \\ \gamma_{21} & \gamma_{22} \end{bmatrix} \begin{bmatrix} y_{t-1} \\ z_{t-1} \end{bmatrix} + \begin{bmatrix} \epsilon_{yt} - b_{12}\epsilon_{zt} \\ \epsilon_{zt} \end{bmatrix} \tag{5.11}$$

Estimating the system using OLS yields the theoretical parameter estimates:

$$y_t = a_{10} + a_{11}y_{t-1} + a_{12}z_{t-1} + e_{1t}$$
$$z_t = a_{20} + a_{21}y_{t-1} + a_{22}z_{t-1} + e_{2t}$$

where:
$$a_{10} = b_{10} - b_{12}b_{20}$$
$$a_{11} = \gamma_{11} - b_{12}\gamma_{21}$$
$$a_{12} = \gamma_{12} - b_{12}\gamma_{22}$$
$$a_{20} = b_{20}$$
$$a_{21} = \gamma_{21}$$
$$a_{22} = \gamma_{22}$$

$$\text{Var}(e_1) = \sigma_y^2 + b_{12}^2\sigma_z^2$$
$$\text{Var}(e_2) = \sigma_z^2$$
$$\text{Cov}(e_1, e_2) = -b_{12}\sigma_z^2$$

Thus, we have nine parameter estimates a_{10}, a_{11}, a_{12}, a_{20}, a_{21}, a_{22}, $\text{Var}(e_1)$, $\text{Var}(e_2)$, and $\text{Cov}(e_1, e_2)$ that can be substituted into the nine equations above in order to simultaneously solve for b_{10}, b_{12}, γ_{11}, γ_{12}, b_{20}, γ_{21}, γ_{22}, σ_y^2, and σ_z^2.

Note too that the estimates of the $\{\epsilon_{yt}\}$ and $\{\epsilon_{zt}\}$ sequences can be recovered. The residuals from the second equation (i.e., the $\{e_{2t}\}$ sequence) are estimates of the $\{\epsilon_{zt}\}$ sequence. Combining these estimates along with the solution for b_{12} allows us to calculate the estimates of the $\{\epsilon_{yt}\}$ sequence using the relationship $e_{1t} = \epsilon_{yt} - b_{12}\epsilon_{zt}$.

In (5.10), the assumption $b_{21} = 0$ means that y_t does not have a contemporaneous effect on z_t. In (5.11), both ϵ_{yt} and ϵ_{zt} shocks affect the contemporaneous value of y_t, but only ϵ_{zt} shocks affect the contemporaneous value of z_t. The observed values of e_{2t} are completely attributed to pure shocks to the $\{z_t\}$ sequence. Decomposing the residuals in this fashion is called a **Choleski** decomposition. Here the alternative form (or "ordering") of the Cholseki decomposition is to allow $b_{12} = 0$.

Innovation Accounting

An essential tool to analyze the dynamic interrelationships among the variables in a VAR is the **vector moving-average** (VMA) representation. Just as an autoregression has a moving-average representation, a VAR can be written as a VMA. The VMA representation of (5.3) expresses the variables y_t and z_t in terms of the current and past values of the two shocks ϵ_{yt} and ϵ_{zt}. For illustrative purposes, write (5.4a) and (5.4b) in matrix form:

$$\begin{bmatrix} y_t \\ z_t \end{bmatrix} = \begin{bmatrix} a_{10} \\ a_{20} \end{bmatrix} + \begin{bmatrix} a_{11} & a_{12} \\ a_{21} & a_{22} \end{bmatrix} \begin{bmatrix} y_{t-1} \\ z_{t-1} \end{bmatrix} + \begin{bmatrix} e_{1t} \\ e_{2t} \end{bmatrix}$$

Let μ_y and μ_z be the mean values of $\{y_t\}$ and $\{z_t\}$, respectively. If we iterate backwards, it is possible to form:

$$\begin{bmatrix} y_t \\ z_t \end{bmatrix} = \begin{bmatrix} \mu_y \\ \mu_z \end{bmatrix} + \frac{1}{1-b_{12}b_{21}} \sum_{i=0}^{\infty} \begin{bmatrix} a_{11} & a_{12} \\ a_{21} & a_{22} \end{bmatrix}^i \begin{bmatrix} 1 & -b_{12} \\ -b_{21} & 1 \end{bmatrix} \begin{bmatrix} \epsilon_{yt} \\ \epsilon_{zt} \end{bmatrix} \tag{5.12}$$

Now, define the 2 x 2 matrix ϕ_i with elements $\phi_{jk}(i)$ such that:

$$\phi_i = \frac{A_1^i}{1-b_{12}b_{21}} \begin{bmatrix} 1 & -b_{12} \\ -b_{21} & 1 \end{bmatrix}$$

If we let $\mu = [\mu_y \; \mu_z]'$ the moving-average representation of (5.12) can be written as:

$$x_t = \mu + \sum_{i=0}^{\infty} \phi_i \epsilon_{t-i}$$

The moving-average representation is an especially useful tool to examine the interaction between the $\{y_t\}$ and $\{z_t\}$ sequences. The coefficients of ϕ_i can be used to generate the effects of ϵ_{yt} and ϵ_{zt} shocks on the entire time paths of the $\{y_t\}$ and $\{z_t\}$ sequences. If you understand the notation, it should be clear that the four elements $\phi_{jk}(0)$ are **impact multipliers**. For example, the coefficient $\phi_{12}(0)$ is the instantaneous impact of a one-unit change in ϵ_{zt} on y_t. In the same way, the elements $\phi_{11}(1)$ and $\phi_{12}(1)$ are the one-period responses of unit changes in ϵ_{yt-1} and ϵ_{zt-1} on y_t, respectively. Updating by one period indicates that $\phi_{11}(1)$ and $\phi_{12}(1)$ also represent effects of unit changes in ϵ_{yt} and ϵ_{zt} on y_{t+1}.

The four sets of coefficients $\phi_{11}(i)$, $\phi_{12}(i)$, $\phi_{21}(i)$, and $\phi_{22}(i)$ are called the **impulse response functions**. Plotting the impulse response functions [i.e., plotting the coefficients of $\phi_{jk}(i)$ against i] is a practical way to visually represent the behavior of the $\{y_t\}$ and $\{z_t\}$ series in response to the various shocks. In principle, it might be possible to know all of the parameters of the primitive system (5.1) and (5.2). With such knowledge, it would be possible to trace out the time paths of the effects of pure ϵ_{yt} or ϵ_{zt} shocks. However, this methodology is not available to the researcher since an estimated VAR is underidentified. You must impose an additional restriction on the two-variable VAR system in order to identify the impulse responses. Again, one possible identification restriction is to use the Choleski decomposition such that:

$$e_{1t} = \epsilon_{yt} - b_{12}\epsilon_{zt} \tag{5.13}$$
$$e_{2t} = \epsilon_{zt} \tag{5.14}$$

Thus, if we use (5.14), all of the observed errors from the $\{e_{2t}\}$ sequence are attributed to ϵ_{zt} shocks. Given the calculated $\{\epsilon_{zt}\}$ sequence, knowledge of the values of the $\{e_{1t}\}$ sequence and the correlation coefficient between e_{1t} and e_{2t} allows for the calculation of the $\{\epsilon_{yt}\}$ sequence using (5.13). Although this Choleski decomposition constrains the system such that an ϵ_{yt} shock has no direct effect z_t, there is an indirect effect in that lagged values of y_t affect the contemporaneous value of z_t. The key point is that the decomposition forces a potentially important asymmetry on the system since an ϵ_{zt} shock has contemporaneous effects on both y_t and z_t. Alternatively, you could set $b_{12} = 0$ and decompose the errors using:

$$e_{1t} = \epsilon_{yt}$$
$$e_{2t} = -b_{21}\epsilon_{yt} + \epsilon_{zt}$$

It is crucial to note that *the importance of the ordering depends on the magnitude of the correlation coefficient between e_{1t} and e_{2t}*. For example, if the correlation coefficient is equal to zero, the ordering is immaterial. Formally, we would replace (5.13) and (5.14) with $e_{1t} = \epsilon_{yt}$ and $e_{2t} = \epsilon_{zt}$. On the other hand, if the correlation coefficient is unity (so that the two shocks are equivalent), it is inappropriate to attribute the shock to a single source. If $|\rho_{12}| > 0.2$, the usual procedure is to obtain the impulse response function using a particular ordering. Compare the results to the impulse response function obtained by reversing the ordering. If the implications are quite different, additional investigation into the relationships between the variables is necessary.

Variance decomposition: Suppose you knew the coefficients of A_0 and A_1 and wanted to forecast the various values of x_{t+i} conditional on the observed value of x_t. If we update (5.3) one period (i.e., $x_{t+1} = A_0 + A_1 x_t + e_{t+1}$) the conditional expectation of x_{t+1} is:

$$E_t x_{t+1} = A_0 + A_1 x_t$$

Note that the one-step ahead forecast error is $x_{t+1} - E_t x_{t+1} = e_{t+1}$. Similarly, the two-step ahead forecast of x_{t+2} is:

$$E_t x_{t+2} = [I + A_1]A_0 + A_1^2 x_t$$

The two-step ahead forecast error (i.e., the difference between the realization of x_{t+2} and the forecast) is $e_{t+2} + A_1 e_{t+1}$. More generally, it is easily verified that the n-step ahead forecast is:

$$E_t x_{t+n} = [I + A_1 + A_1^2 + ... + A_1^{n-1}]A_0 + A_1^n x_t$$

and that the associated forecast error is:

$$e_{t+n} + A_1 e_{t+n-1} + A_1^2 e_{t+n-2} + ... + A_1^{n-1} e_{t+1}.$$

Of course it is possible to write these forecast errors in terms of the ϵ_{yt} and ϵ_{zt} shocks. The **forecast error variance decomposition** tells us the proportion of the movements in a sequence due to its "own" shocks versus shocks to the other variable. *If ϵ_{zt} shocks explain none of the forecast error variance of $\{y_t\}$ at all forecast horizons, we can say that the $\{y_t\}$ sequence is exogenous.* In such a circumstance, the $\{y_t\}$ sequence would evolve independently of the ϵ_{zt} shocks and of the $\{z_t\}$ sequence. At the other extreme, ϵ_{zt} shocks could explain all of the forecast error variance in the $\{y_t\}$ sequence at all forecast horizons so that $\{y_t\}$ would be entirely endogenous. In applied research, it is typical for a variable to explain almost all of its forecast error variance at short horizons and smaller proportions at longer horizons.

Note that the variance decomposition contains the same problem inherent in impulse response function analysis. In order to identify the $\{\epsilon_{yt}\}$ and $\{\epsilon_{zt}\}$ sequences, it is necessary to restrict the B matrix. The Choleski decompostion used in (5.13) and (5.14) necessitates that all of the one-period forecast error variance of z_t is due to ϵ_{zt}. If we use the alternative ordering, all of the one-period forecast error variance of y_t would be due to ϵ_{yt}. The dramatic effects of these alternative assumptions are reduced at longer forecasting horizons. In practice, it is useful to examine the variance decomposition at various forecast horizons. As n increases, the variance decompositions should converge. Moreover, if the correlation coefficient ρ_{12} is significantly different from zero, it is customary to obtain the variance decompositions under various orderings. The analysis of impulse response functions and variance decompositions is called **innovation accounting**. In RATS, innovation accounting can be performed using a Choleski decomposition with the IMPULSE and ERRORS instructions. Alternatively, you can choose your own restrictions using the BERNANKE.SRC procedure.

Hypothesis Testing

In a VAR, long lag lengths quickly consume degrees of freedom. If lag length is p, each of the n equations contains np coefficients plus the intercept term. Appropriate lag length selection can be critical. If p is too small, the model is misspecified; if p is too large, degrees of freedom are wasted. To check lag length, begin with the longest plausible length or the longest feasible length given degrees-of-freedom considerations. Estimate the VAR and form the variance/covariance matrix of the residuals. Using quarterly data, you might start with a lag length of 12 quarters based on the a priori notion that three years is sufficiently long to capture the system's dynamics. Call the variance/covariance matrix of the residuals from the 12-lag model Σ_{12}. Now suppose you want to determine whether 8 lags are appropriate. After all, restricting the model from 12 to 8 lags would reduce the number of estimated parameters by $4n$ in each equation.

Since the goal is to determine whether lag 8 is appropriate for all equations, an equation-by-equation F-test on lags 9 through 12 is not appropriate. Instead, the proper test for this **cross-equation** restriction is a likelihood ratio test. Reestimate the VAR *over the same sample period* using 8 lags and obtain the variance/covariance matrix of the residuals Σ_8. Note that Σ_8 pertains to a system of n equations with $4n$ restrictions in each equation for a total of $4n^2$ restrictions. Sims (1980) recommends using:

$$(T-c)(\log|\Sigma_8| - \log|\Sigma_{12}|)$$

where T = number of usable observations; c = number of parameters estimated in each equation of the unrestricted system; and $\log|\sum_n|$ is the natural logarithm of the determinant of $\sum_n$. In the example at hand, $c = 12\,n{+}1$ since each equation of the unrestricted model has 12 lags for each variable term plus an intercept.

This statistic has the asymptotic χ^2 distribution with degrees of freedom equal to the number of restrictions *in the system*. Clearly, if the restriction of a reduced number of lags is not binding, we would expect $\log|\sum_8|$ to be equal to $\log|\sum_{12}|$. Large values of this sample statistic would mean the restriction of only 8 lags is binding; hence, we can reject the null hypothesis that lag length = 8. If the calculated value of the statistic is less than χ^2 at a prespecified significance level, we would not be able to reject the null of only 8 lags.

This type of likelihood ratio test is applicable to any type of cross-equation restriction. As explained below, use the RATS RATIO instruction to perform such tests. Let $\sum_u$ and $\sum_r$ be the variance/covariance matrices of the unrestriced and restricted systems, respectively. (*Note*: If the equations of the unrestricted model contain different regressors, let c denote the maximum number of regressors contained in the longest equation.) The test statistic:

$$(T{-}c)(\log|\textstyle\sum_r| - \log|\textstyle\sum_u|) \tag{5.15}$$

can be compared to a χ^2 distribution with degrees of freedom equal to the number of restrictions.

The likelihood ratio test is based on asymptotic theory which may not be very useful in the small samples available to time-series econometricians. Moreover, the likelihood ratio test is only applicable when one model is a restricted version of the other. Alternative test criteria are the multivariate generalizations of the AIC and SBC:

$$\text{AIC} = T\log|\textstyle\sum| + 2\,N$$
$$\text{SBC} = T\log|\textstyle\sum| + N\log(\text{T})$$

where $|\sum|$ = determinant of the variance/covariance matrix of the residuals and N = total number of parameters estimated *in all equations*. Thus, if each equation in an n-variable VAR has p lags and an intercept, $N = n^2 p{+}n$; each of the n equations has np lagged regressors and an intercept.

Granger causality: If $\{y_t\}$ does not improve the forecasting performance of $\{z_t\}$, then $\{y_t\}$ does not Granger-cause $\{z_t\}$. The practical way to determine Granger causality is to consider whether the lags of one variable enter into the equation for another variable. In terms of (5.4a) and (5.4b), $\{y_t\}$ does not Granger-cause $\{z_t\}$ if $a_{21} = 0$. More generally, let z_t be given by:

$$z_t = a_{20} + a_{21}(1)y_{t-1} + a_{21}(2)y_{t-2} + a_{21}(3)y_{t-3} + \dots + a_{22}(1)z_{t-1} + a_{22}(2)z_{t-2} + \dots + \epsilon_{zt}$$

To determine if $\{y_t\}$ Granger-causes $\{z_t\}$, use a standard F-test to test the restriction:

$$a_{21}(1) = a_{21}(2) = a_{21}(3) = \dots = 0$$

Note that Granger causality is something quite different from a test for exogeneity. A necessary condition for the exogeneity of z_t is that *current and past* values of y_t do not affect z_t. Thus, $\{z_t\}$ may not be exogenous to $\{y_t\}$ even though $\{y_t\}$ does not Granger-cause $\{z_t\}$. If $\phi_{21}(0)$ is not zero, pure shocks to y_t (i.e., ϵ_{yt}) affect the value of z_t even though the $\{y_t\}$ sequence does not Granger-cause the $\{z_t\}$ sequence.

A **block exogeneity** test is useful for detecting whether to incorporate a variable into a VAR. Given the aforementioned distinction between causality and exogeneity, this multivariate generalization of the Granger causality test should actually be called a "block causality" test. In any event, the issue is to determine whether lags of one variable-say w_t-Granger-cause any other of the variables in the system. In the three-variable case with w_t, y_t, and z_t, the test is whether lags of w_t Granger-cause either y_t or z_t. In essence, the block exogeneity restricts all lags of w_t in the y_t and z_t equations to be equal to zero. This cross-equation restriction is properly tested using the likelihood ratio test given by (5.15). Estimate the y_t and z_t equations using lagged values of $\{y_t\}$, $\{z_t\}$, and $\{w_t\}$ and calculate Σ_u. Reestimate excluding the lagged values of $\{w_t\}$ and calculate Σ_r. Next, form the likelihood ratio statistic:

$$(T-c)(\log|\Sigma_r| - \log|\Sigma_u|)$$

This statistic has a chi-square distribution with degrees of freedom equal to $2p$ (since p lagged values of $\{w_t\}$ are excluded from each equation). Here $c = 3p + 1$ since the unrestricted y_t and z_t equations contain p lags of $\{y_t\}$, $\{z_t\}$, and $\{w_t\}$ plus a constant. Another way to determine whether or not to include a variable in the system is to use the multivariate generalizations of the AIC and/or SBC.

RATS Instructions and Procedures

1. Instructions to estimate a VAR: Preparing RATS to perform a VAR analysis consists of the following three steps:

Step 1: To perform likelihood ratio tests and to obtain the impulse response functions and variance decompositions, you need to save the residuals from each equation of the estimated model. You must first reserve "room" for each of the residual series using the ALLOCATE statement. If there are n equations in your VAR system, be sure to reserve room for at least $2n$ series on the ALLOCATE statement. For example, sample program 1 below uses quarterly data through 91:4. The appropriate ALLOCATE statement to reserve 10 series is:

all 10 91:4

Step 2: After making the necessary data transformations, you must define the equations to use in the VAR. Typically, you will use the following five instructions to set up a VAR:

    SYSTEM 1 to *number of equations in the system*
    VARIABLES *list of dependent variables*
    LAGS 1 to *lag length*
    DETERMINISTIC *list of deterministic (constant, seasonals) and exogenous variables*
    END(SYSTEM)

For example, to set up the two-variable first-order VAR represented by equations (5.4a) and (5.4b) use:

    SYSTEM 1 to 2   ;*There are two variables in the VAR.
    VARIABLES y z   ;*The endogenous variables are y and z.
    LAGS 1   ;*Use only one lag of each variable.
    DETERMINISTIC constant   ;*Include an intercept.
    END(SYSTEM)   ;*End the block of statements.

Modification of the SYSTEM-END(SYSTEM) block is straightforward. If you want to:

i. Include four lags, simply replace the LAGS instruction with:

LAGS 1 to 4

ii. Set up a three-variable VAR with w as a dependent variable, replace lines 1 and 2 with

SYSTEM 1 to 3
VARIABLES w y z

iii. Include an exogenous variable w such that (5.4a) and (5.4b) become:

$$y_t = a_{10} + a_{11}y_{t-1} + a_{12}z_{t-1} + a_{13}w_t + a_{14}w_{t-1} + e_{1t}$$
$$z_t = a_{20} + a_{21}y_{t-1} + a_{22}z_{t-1} + a_{23}w_t + a_{24}w_{t-1} + e_{2t}$$

replace line 4 with:

DETERMINISTIC constant w{0 to 1}

Step 3: Finally, you instruct RATS to estimate the system using ESTIMATE. Consider the ESTIMATE statement appearing in the three-variable VAR of sample program 2:

estimate(noprint,outsigma=V) 61:2 91:4 1

The statement instructs RATS to estimate the three equations using OLS over the sample period 61:2 to 91:4. Although the OLS results are not printed, the results of the Granger causality tests are displayed. The residuals from equations 1, 2, and 3 are stored in series 1 through 3, respectively. The 3 x 3 covariance matrix of these residual series is saved and given the name V. The syntax and principal options are:

estimate(OUTSIGMA=V,other options) *start end residuals*
where: *start end*   The range of entries to use.

     residuals   The series number in which to begin saving the residuals. The residuals from the first equation are stored in the series given by *residuals*, the residuals from the second equation are stored in series number *residuals+1*, and so forth. The appropriate number of series should be declared on the ALLOCATE instruction.

    OUTSIGMA=   The name of the variance/covariance matrix. This option computes and saves the covariance matrix of the residuals. You *must* use this option if you want to perform innovation accounting or hypothesis tests

The other principal options are:

NOPRINT   By default, RATS prints out the results of the OLS estimation of each equation. Use NOPRINT to suppress the output.

NOFTESTS   By default, RATS prints the results of all Granger causality tests. To prevent a great deal of output, use the NOPRINT option..

SIGMA   This option computes and displays (but does not save) the covariance matrix of the residuals. Use both OUTSIGMA= and SIGMA if you want to compute, save, and print the variance/covariance matrix.

Examples:
1. Sample program 1 (VAR1.PRG) estimates a two-equation VAR. The following instruction is used to suppress the printing of the OLS output and the F-tests, to estimate the model over the period 1963:2 to 1991:4, and to save the residuals from equation 1 in series number 1 and from equation 2 in series number 2:

estimate(noprint,noftests) 63:2 91:4 1

2. Sample program 2 (VAR2.PRG) estimates a three-variable VAR. The following instruction is used to suppress the printing of the OLS output and the F-tests, to estimate the model over the period 1963:2 to 1991:4. The residuals are saved in the series

numbered 3 and 4 and the variance/covariance matrix (v) is calculated and saved (but not displayed).

estimate(noprint,noftests,outsigma=v) 63:2 91:4 3

2. The impulse response functions and variance decompositions: The variance decomposition and impulse response functions are best obtained using the ERRORS instruction. The syntax and principal options are:

errors(IMPULSES) *equations steps name*
where: *equations*   Number of equations in the VAR.
     steps   The forecast horizon and the number of impulse responses.
     name   The name of the covariance matrix used on the ESTIMATE instruction.

The principal option is IMPULSES. If you exclude IMPULSES, RATS calculates and prints only the variance decompositions. The option DECOMP= is explained on page 146 below.

    Example: Although there is a fair amount of flexibility in the use of the supplementary cards, the easiest method is illustrated in sample program 2. Consider the statements:

errors(impulses) 3 24 V
1
2
3

The forecast error variances (from 1-step ahead through 24-step ahead horizons) will be displayed for each of the three variables in the system. Using the three supplementary cards in this fashion results in a Choleski decomposition using the ordering of the variables implied by the VARIABLES instruction. The first VARIABLES instruction in sample program 2 is:

vars gm1 inf dtbill

    Hence, the *errors(impulses) 3 24 V* statement and the three supplementary cards are for the ordering *gm1 → inf → dtbill*.

3. Likelihood ratio tests: RATS will perform likelihood ratio tests using the RATIO instruction. RATIO calculates the statistic:

$$(T-c)(\log|\textstyle\sum_r| - \log|\textstyle\sum_u|)$$

    To use the instruction, estimate the unrestricted model being sure to save the residuals using the ESTIMATE statement. For convenience, suppose you save the residuals in series *1* through *n*. Next, estimate the restricted model and save the residuals in series *n+1* through *2n*.

(*Note*: this is why you need to reserve *2n* series on the ALLOCATE statement.) The likelihood ratio test is conducted using:

ratio(*degrees*=df ,*mcorr*=c,other options) *start end*
1 2 ... n
n+1 n+2 ... 2n

where: *start end* The range over which the test is to be performed.
  degrees= The number of degrees of freedom (equal to the number of restrictions in the system).
  mcorr= Sims' small sample correction for likelihood ratio tests (i.e., the value of *c*). Set *mcorr* equal to the largest number of parameters estimated in any one of the equations (usually equal to the number of parameters estimated in each of the unrestricted equations).

  The other principal option, NOPRINT, supresses the printing of the covariance matrices and the marginal significance level of the test. As described in sample program 4, if you use NOPRINT, it is possible to obtain the marginal significance level with the instruction:

  display %signif

  Example: Sample program 1 performs various hypothesis tests. First, a two-variable VAR using 12 lags of each variable is estimated and the residuals are saved in series 1 and 2. The estimation is over the sample period 63:2 to 91:4. Next, the same sample period is used to estimate a model with a lag length of 8 and the residuals are saved in series 3 and 4. The lag length test is conducted using:

  ratio(degrees=16,mcorr=28) 63:2 91:4
  # 1 2
  # 3 4

  There are 16 degrees of freedom (four lags of each variable in each equation) and mcorr= 28 since the longest equation in the model contains 28 parameters (12 coefficients for each variable, a constant, and three seasonal dummy variables). The supplementary cards instruct RATS to use series 1 and 2 to construct the first covariance matrix and series 3 and 4 to construct the second.

4. Multivariate AIC and SBC: Although RATS does not directly calculate the multivariate versions of the AIC and SBC, as illustrated in sample program 4, they are easily constructed. When you use the OUTSIGMA= option on the ESTIMATE statement, RATS computes the covariance matrix of the residuals. You can fetch the logarithmic determinant of this covariance matrix using %LOGDET. The following three statements will compute and display the multivariate versions of the AIC and SBC, respectively:

```
compute aic =  %nobs*%logdet + 2*N
compute sbc =  %nobs*%logdet + N*log(%nobs)
display 'aic = ' aic ' sbc = ' sbc
```

where you must set N equal to the number of parameters estimated in the entire system.

5. Seemingly Unrelated Regressions (SUR): In a near-VAR, the right-hand sides of the equations in the system are not identical. Examples include:

   i. Different lag lengths:
$$y_t = a_{11}(1)y_{t-1} + a_{11}(2)y_{t-2} + a_{12}z_{t-1} + e_{1t}$$
$$z_t = a_{21}y_{t-1} + a_{22}z_{t-1} + e_{2t}$$

   ii. The $\{z_t\}$ series does not Granger-cause $\{y_t\}$:
$$y_t = a_{11}y_{t-1} + e_{1t}$$
$$z_t = a_{21}y_{t-1} + a_{22}z_{t-1} + e_{2t}$$

   iii. A third variable $\{w_t\}$ affects only $\{z_t\}$:
$$y_t = a_{11}y_{t-1} + a_{12}z_{t-1} + e_{1t}$$
$$z_t = a_{21}y_{t-1} + a_{22}z_{t-1} + a_{23}w_t + e_{2t}$$

The efficiency of the estimates can be improved using the SUR instruction. Sample program 3 illustrates how to estimate a near-VAR. The three steps in estimating a near-VAR are similar to those discussed for VAR estimation (see subsection 1 above).

Step 1: As in Step 1 of a VAR estimation, use the ALLOCATE instruction to reserve room for each of the residual series.

Step 2: You must define the equations to use in the near-VAR. The simplest way to set up your equations is using the DEFINE= option of the LINREG instruction.

Examples:
1. To set up the first near-VAR system above, use:
```
      linreg(define=1) y
      # y{1 to 2} z{1}
      linreg(define=2) z
      # y{1} z{1}
```

2. To set up the third near-VAR system above, use:
```
      linreg(define=1) y
      # y{1} z{1}
      linreg(define=2) z
      # y{1} z{1} w
```

Step 3: Finally, you instruct RATS to estimate the system using the SUR instruction. There is one supplementary card for each equation in the system. The typical syntax of SUR is:

sur(options) *equations start end*
 # equation resids

where: *equations*   The number of equations in the system you want to estimate.
      start end   The range of entries to use.
      equation   The number of the equation.
      resids   The number of the series in which to store the residuals.

6. The Sims-Bernanke Decomposition: In order to exactly identify the primitive system from an *n*-equation VAR in standard form, it is necessary to impose $(n^2 - n)/2$ restrictions on the structural model [see page 323 of Enders (1995)]. You can easily verify that a Choleski decomposition always results in an exactly identified system. Of course, the ordering implied by such a decomposition may be inconsistent with economic theory. Sims (1986) and Bernanke (1986) developed a procedure that allows you to impose $(n^2 - n)/2$ **or more** restrictions on the structural model. If more than $(n^2 - n)/2$ restrictions are imposed, the system is overidentified and the overidentifying restrictions can be tested. The BERNANKE.SRC procedure allows you to perform the Sims-Bernanke decomposition. Sample program 4 provides an illustration of the procedure. The steps in using the procedure are:

    Step 1: Estimate a VAR (or near-VAR) being sure to save the residual series. You must also use the OUTSIGMA= option on the ESTIMATE instruction.

    Step 2: You must indicate the pattern of the B^{-1} matrix. If we use the notation from equation (5.3), the relationship between the regression residuals and the pure innovations is given by:

$$e_t = B^{-1} \epsilon_t$$

    For example, let y_t, z_t, and w_t be the left-hand-side variables in a three-equation system. Let the regression residuals be e_{1t}, e_{2t}, and e_{3t} and let the pure innovations be ϵ_{yt}, ϵ_{zt}, and ϵ_{wt}. Suppose you want the relationship between the regression residuals and the pure innovations to be such that:

$$\begin{bmatrix} e_{1t} \\ e_{2t} \\ e_{3t} \end{bmatrix} = \begin{bmatrix} 1 & 0 & 0 \\ 0 & 1 & 0 \\ \beta_{31} & \beta_{32} & 1 \end{bmatrix} \begin{bmatrix} \epsilon_{yt} \\ \epsilon_{zt} \\ \epsilon_{wt} \end{bmatrix}$$

where the β_{ij} are the coefficients of B^{-1}.

Note that the ordering of the variables is such that w_t responds contemporaneously to shocks in ϵ_{yt}, ϵ_{zt}, and ϵ_{wt}. However, y_t responds contemporaneously to ϵ_{yt} shocks only and z_t responds contemporaneously to ϵ_{zt} shocks only. The system contains one overidentifying restriction. To enter this pattern of B^{-1}, declare a 3 x 3 matrix and input the pattern of the coefficients using:

```
declare rect betainv(3, 3)
input betainv
1 0 0
0 1 0
1 1 1
```

The first instruction defines the 3 x 3 matrix called *betainv*. The second instruction prepares RATS to read the pattern of the coefficients. The next three lines represent the pattern of the coefficients in B^{-1}. (*Note*: the diagonal elements cannot be set equal to zero.)

Step 3: After compiling BERNANKE.SRC, invoke the procedure using:

@bernanke(options) *sigma pattern factor*
where: *sigma*   The covariance matrix of residuals named on the ESTIMATE instruction.
      pattern   The B^{-1} matrix named on the DECLARE instruction.
      factor   The name you want to give to the output matrix.

The key options are:

TEST   Perform the likelihood ratio test of the overidentification restrictions (if any).
PRINT   Print the coefficients and their standard errors.

BERNANKE.SRC has difficulty estimating a large number of coefficients. If you experience any problems, try estimating a more restrictive system. If you have convergence problems, you can use the options:

INITIAL=   If you experience convergence problems, you can also input initial guesses for the B^{-1} coefficients using the INITIAL= option. Technical details are contained in the *RATS User's Manual*.
ITERS=   The maximum number of iterations. The default is 50.
CVCRIT=   The convergence criterion for coefficients (the default is 0.0001).

To continue with the example above, suppose you used OUTSIGMA=V on the ESTIMATE instruction of Step 1 and inputted B^{-1} in Step 2. You perform the decomposition by invoking the BERNANKE.SRC procedure and then using an ERRORS instruction with the IMPULSES option. Since there are three equations in the system, to obtain 24 impulses, use:

```
@bernanke v betainv factor
errors(decomp=factor,impulses) 3 24
        # 1
        # 2
        # 3
```

Note: The option `decomp=factor` decomposes the errors using the estimated values of the output matrix *factor*.

Sample Programs

1. Hypothesis testing: This exercise uses data from the file labeled US.PRN. The program performs some simple hypothesis tests concerning the relationship between the U.S. money supply (as measured by $M1$), interest rate (as measured by the 3-month T-bill rate), and the U.S. GDP Deflator (1985=100) for the period 1960:Q1 through 1991:Q4. These three variables are labeled *m1*, *tbill*, and *gdpdef*, respectively. All program statements are on the file labeled VAR1.PRG and the statements and all output are on the file labeled VAR1.OUT:

```
cal 60 1 4                   ;* Set CALENDAR for quarterly data beginning with
all 10 91:4                  ;*     60:1 and ending 91:4.  Allocate space for 10 series.
open data a:\us.prn          ;* Modify this line if the data set is not on drive a:\.
data(format=prn,org=obs) / m1 gdpdef tbill
```

* The next three lines transform *m1* and *gdpdef* to growth rates and *tbill* to its first difference:

```
set gm1 = log(m1) - log(m1{1})
set inf = log(gdpdef) - log(gdpdef{1})
diff tbill / dtbill
seasonal seasons             ;* Creates a dummy variable called seasons.
```

/* Note that *seasons* is equal to 1 in the first quarter of each year and 0 in all other quarters. The next five lines of VAR1.PRG set up a bivariate VAR using 12 lags of *gm1* and *inf* with a constant and three seasonal dummy variables. Note that a lead of a dummy variable is equivalent to a variable with 1 in the second quarter of each year and 0 in all other quarters. Thus, the expression *seasons{-2 to 0}* creates three seasonal dummies.
*/

```
system 1 to 2               ;* Define a system of two equations.
vars gm1 inf                ;* Use gm1 and inf as the dependent variables.
lags 1 to 12                ;* Use 12 lags of each variable.
det constant seasons{-2 to 0} ;* Include an intercept and three seasonal dummy variables.
end(system)
```

* The next line instructs RATS to estimate each equation over the period 1963:2 to 1991:4 and to
* save the residuals as series 1 and 2, respectively. At this stage, the regression output is not
* important; the options *noftests* and *noprint* cause the printing of all output to be suppressed:

estimate(noftests,noprint) 63:2 91:4 1

/* Next, define a similar system using only eight lags of each variable. Even though there are
fewer lags, estimate the model over the 1963:2 to 1991:4 sample period. In order to perform
hypothesis tests, both models need to be estimated over the same sample period:
*/
system 1 to 2
vars gm1 inf
lags 1 to 8   ;* Estimate the system using only eight lags.
det constant seasons{-2 to 0}
end(system)
estimate(noftests,noprint) 63:2 91:4 3   ;* Estimate over the same sample period used above
                                          ;*   and save the residuals as series 3 and 4.

/* The likelihood ratio test that lags 9 through 12 are insignificant involves 16 restrictions (there
are four lags of each variable excluded from each of the two equations) and mcorr = 28 since each
equation in the unrestricted model has 28 coefficients (12 lags of each variable plus a constant and
three seasonal dummies).
*/
ratio(degrees=16,mcorr=28) 63:2 91:4
 # 1 2
 # 3 4

```
Covariance\Correlation Matrices
              R_GM1              R_INF
R_GM1   0.00010772851    -0.0803217107
R_INF  -0.00000276324     0.00001098599


              R_GM1              R_INF
R_GM1   0.00011290732    -0.0697025669
R_INF  -0.00000256979     0.00001203861


Log Determinants are -2.056126e+001 -2.042120e+001
Chi-Squared(16)=      12.184668 with Significance Level 0.73117267
```

/*   RATS automatically calls the residuals from the *gm1* and *inf* equations R_GM1 and
R_INF, respectively. When we use the 12-lag model, the variance of R_GM1 is 0.00010772851
and the variance of R_INF is 0.00001098559. The covariance of R_GM1 and R_INF is
-0.00000276324 and the correlation coefficient is -0.0803217107. The covariance/correlation
matrix for the eight lag model is printed immediately below. This positioning is determined by the

supplementary cards. In the remaining discussion, the covariance/correlation matrices will not be displayed. However, all are shown in the file VAR1.OUT.

Next, RATS performs the χ^2 test for the presence of lags 9 through 12. The two log determinants are displayed along with the calculated value of χ^2 and the significance level. Here, the difference between the log determinants is small enough that you can safely conclude the restriction is not binding (i.e., conclude there are no more than eight lags of each variable). As an exercise, you should demonstrate that lags 5 through 8 are not significant. Assuming a maximum of no more than four lags, the test for the significance of lags 2, 3, and 4 can be performed using:
*/

```
system 1 to 2
vars gm1 inf
lags 1 to 4                              ;* Use lags 1 through 4.
det constant seasons{-2 to 0}
end(system)
estimate(noftests,noprint) 61:2 91:4 1      ;* Save the residuals in series 1 and 2.
```

/* If we use only four lags, the sample period can begin in 61:2. The ESTIMATE instruction above saves the residuals in series 1 and 2. Hence, it writes over the values created in the tests using 12 lags. Now, estimate a model using only one lag.
*/

```
system 1 to 2
vars gm1 inf
lags 1                                  ;* Use only one lag.
det constant seasons{-2 to 0}
end(system)
estimate(noftests,noprint) 61:2 91:4 3 ;* Save the residuals in series 3 and 4.
```

* The likelihood ratio test has 12 degrees of freedom (three lags of each variable in each equation)
* and mcorr = 12 since each equation in the unrestricted model has 12 coefficients:

ratio(degrees=12,mcorr=12) 61:2 91:4
 # 1 2
 # 3 4

```
Log Determinants are -2.032279e+001 -1.989689e+001
Chi-Squared(12)=     47.274603 with Significance Level 0.00000418
```

/* Conclude that the restriction is binding; use the model with four lags. To test for the presence of the seasonal dummy variables, simply estimate the VAR with and without the seasonal dummy variables. Save the residuals from each estimation and perform the likelihood ratio test. Note

that series 1 and 2 contain the residuals from the model with four lags and the seasonals. Hence, this estimation does not need to be performed again. Next, estimate the model without the seasonals and save the residuals in series 3 and 4.
*/


```
system 1 to 2
vars gm1 inf
lags 1 to 4
det constant                                    ;* Now, omit the seasonal dummy variables.
end(system)
estimate(noprint,noftests) 61:2 91:4 3          ;* Estimate the restricted model and save residuals
                                                ;*    in series 3 and 4.
```


* Now there are six degrees of freedom (three seasonals in each equation) and each equation in
* the unrestricted model contains 12 coefficients:

ratio(degrees=6,mcorr=12) 61:2 91:4
 # 1 2
 # 3 4

```
Log Determinants are -2.032279e+001 -1.997102e+001
Chi-Squared(6)=      39.045961 with Significance Level 0.00000070
```

/* Conclude that the seasonal dummy variables belong in the model. Now, suppose you believe that the *tbill* rate has an influence on the relationship between money growth and inflation. To test whether the tbill rate (in the form of *dtbill*) belongs in the system, you can use a block exogeneity test. Note that series 1 and 2 still contain the residuals of the two-variable model using four lags, a constant, and three seasonal dummy variables. To perform the block exogeneity test, include the contemporaneous value of *dtbill* and its first four lags on the DETERMINISTIC instruction:
*/


```
system 1 to 2
vars gm1 inf
lags 1 to 4
det constant seasons{-2 to 0} dtbill{0 to 4}    ;*Include dtbill and its first four lags:
end(system)
estimate(noprint,noftests) 61:2 91:4 3          ;* Save the residuals in series 3 and 4.
```

/* There are 10 degrees of freedom (five values of *dtbill* in each equation) and each equation in the unrestricted system has 17 parameters (4 lags of *gm1* + 4 lags of *inf* + constant + 3 seasonals + 5 coefficients for *dtbill* and its 4 lags):
*/

```
ratio(degrees=10,mcorr=17) 61:2 91:4
#1 2
#3 4
```

```
Log Determinants are -2.032279e+001 -2.065940e+001
Chi-Squared(10)=      35.681066 with Significance Level 0.00009549
```

/* There is strong evidence that *dtbill* belongs in the system; either the contemporaneous value of *dtbill* and/or its lags influence the relationship between money growth and inflation. Note that a block causality test can be conducted using:
*/

```
system 1 to 2
vars gm1 inf
lags 1 to 4
det constant seasons{-2 to 0} dtbill{1 to 4} :* Include only lagged values of dtbill.
end(system)
estimate(noprint, noftests) 61:2 91:4 3
```

* Degrees of freedom are reduced by 2 (for the contemporaneous value of *dtbill* in each equation)
*   and *mcorr* is reduced by 1:

```
ratio(degrees=8,mcorr=16) 61:2 91:4
#1 2
#3 4
```

```
Log Determinants are -2.032279e+001 -2.064146e+001
Chi-Squared(8)=      34.098071 with Significance Level 0.00003900
```

* Conclude that the contemporaneous value of *dtbill* affects the contemporaneous value of *gm1* and/or *inf*. At this point, it seems sensible to estimate a three-variable fourth-order VAR that includes *dtbill* and *seasons{-2 to 0}* as in sample program 2.

   2. Innovation accounting and forecasting: This exercise continues with the three-variable VAR developed in sample program 1 above. Granger causality tests are performed, and Choleski decompositions are used to perform innovation accounting. The model is also used for forecasting. The first seven lines repeat those from sample program 1. As explained below, line 8 has been modified for use with the FORECAST instruction. All program statements are on the file labeled VAR2.PRG and the statements and all output are on the file labeled VAR2.OUT:

```
cal 60 1 4
all 10 91:4
open data a:\us.prn
data(format=prn,org=obs) / m1 gdpdef tbill
set gm1 = log(m1) - log(m1{1})
```

```
set inf = log(gdpdef) - log(gdpdef{1})
diff tbill / dtbill
seasonal seasons 60:1 94:1     ;* Seasons extends beyond the end of the sample period so that
                               :*      forecasts after 1991:4 can be obtained.
system 1 to 3                  ;* Define a system of three equations.
vars gm1 inf dtbill            ;* The dependent variables are gm1, inf, and dtbill.
lags 1 to 4                    ;* Use the lag length found in sample program 1.
det constant seasons{-2 to 0}  ;* Include the intercept and seasonal dummies.
end(system)
```

* Next, estimate the model over the sample period 61:2 to 91:4 and save the residuals in series
*   1 through 3. Note that the residuals from the *gm1* equation are in series 1, from the *inf*
*   equation in series 2, and from the *dtbill* equation in series 3. The variance/covariance matrix
*   is called *V*:

estimate(noprint,outsigma=V) 61:2 91:4 1

```
F-Tests, Dependent Variable GM1
Variable              F-Statistic        Signif
GM1                       4.8458         0.0012465
INF                       0.7027         0.5917829
DTBILL                    4.9135         0.0011233

F-Tests, Dependent Variable INF
Variable              F-Statistic        Signif
GM1                       1.2715         0.2857596
INF                      46.6028         0.0000000
DTBILL                    4.0802         0.0040649

F-Tests, Dependent Variable DTBILL
Variable              F-Statistic        Signif
GM1                       2.8679         0.0265898
INF                       3.3814         0.0120133
DTBILL                    6.3197         0.0001326
```

/*   The *F*-tests indicate that, at conventional significance levels, *gm1* Granger-causes itself
and *dtbill*, *inf* Granger-causes itself and *dtbill*, and *dtbill* Granger-causes all variables in the
system. Next, obtain the forecast errors and impulse responses. The parameters on the ERRORS
statement instruct RATS that (i) there are three series, (ii) to obtain 1-step ahead through 24-step
ahead forecast errors, and (iii) to use the decomposition implied by the elements of *V*. The
ordering is a Choleski decomposition such that series 1 innovations (i.e., money growth
innovations) contemporaneously affect all others, *inf* innovations contemporaneously affect *dtbill*,
but *dtbill* innovations have no contemporaneous effects on the other variables.
*/

errors(impulses) 3 24 V
 # 1
 # 2
 # 3

```
Responses to Shock in GM1
    Entry        GM1              INF              DTBILL
      1      0.009914796234  0.0003310652521  -0.069369992663
      2      0.000430038149  0.0004649512266   0.137458832936
      3     -0.000168900209  0.0008911872397   0.177065673289

Responses to Shock in INF
    Entry        GM1              INF              DTBILL
      1      0.000000000000  0.0033226113122   0.064957952911
      2     -0.001238643329  0.0009643014543   0.160012173853
      3     -0.001380099946  0.0011537099029   0.178577880128

Responses to Shock in DTBILL
    Entry        GM1              INF              DTBILL
      1      0.000000000000  0.0000000000000   0.706350529941
      2     -0.004011972849  0.0010042894492   0.228645483058
      3     -0.001230802931  0.0005708467076  -0.199249717052
```

/*   Note that only the first three impulses are shown even though RATS produces impulses for periods 1 through 24 for each of the three shocks. Full details are on the file labeled VAR2.PGM.

A one-standard-deviation-shock in *gm1* (equal to 0.009914796234 units), induces a contemporaneous increase in *inf* of 0.0003310652521 units and a contemporaneous decrease in *dtbill* of 0.069369992663 units. After one period, *gm1* is still 0.000430038149 units above its mean, while *inf* is 0.0004649512266 units higher. When we look at the next set of numbers, a one-standard-deviation increase in *inf* (equal to 0.0033226113122) has no contemporaneous effect on *gm1*, but increases *dtbill* by 0.064957952911 units contemporaneously. In the output below, the variance decompositions are abbreviated; only the 1-step, 8-step, 12-step, and 24-step ahead forecast error variances are reported.
*/

```
Decomposition of Variance for Series GM1
Step  Std Error       GM1        INF       DTBILL
1     0.009914796  100.00000    0.00000    0.00000
8     0.011596003   78.71923    4.46800   16.81276
12    0.011653647   78.58614    4.72555   16.68832
24    0.011718945   78.14103    5.27461   16.58436

Decomposition of Variance for Series INF
Step  Std Error       GM1        INF       DTBILL
1     0.003339064    0.98305   99.01695    0.00000
8     0.005177402   11.41291   74.40874   14.17834
12    0.005507750   13.45608   72.09331   14.45061
24    0.005767766   15.30695   70.51264   14.18041

Decomposition of Variance for Series DTBILL
Step  Std Error       GM1        INF       DTBILL
1     0.712715092    0.94735    0.83068   98.22197
8     0.888913168   10.54384   11.72735   77.72880
12    0.892540927   10.71747   11.71525   77.56728
24    0.892964203   10.72789   11.74220   77.52991
```

/*   Thus, the *gm1* explains all of its own 1-step ahead forecast error variance and 78.14103% of its 24-step ahead forecast error variance. Similarly, at an 8-step ahead horizon, *gm1* and *dtbill* explain 11.41291% and 14.17834% of the forecast error variance in *inf*, respectively.

One difficulty with the impulse responses reported above is that they are not standardized to account for differences in the units of measure. The following program segment, adapted from Example 8.3 of the *RATS User's Manual*, divides each response by the standard deviation of the appropriate residual variance. As such, all responses are measured in terms of standard deviations. The program segment produces high-resolution graphs of the standardized impulse responses. Comments show how you can easily modify the program to suit your individual needs. For example, if you want to print the coefficients, simply delete the NOPRINT option on the IMPULSE instruction below. The syntax of some instructions are beyond the scope of this workbook. Consult the *RATS User's Manual* if you want to learn about the details of the program segment. Note the use of the IMPULSE instruction. This instruction has the same syntax as ERRORS, but produces only the impulse responses.
*/

```
COMPUTE NEQN  = 3        ;* Note that neqn is the number of equations in the system.  You
                         ;*   can modify this line in your own work.
DECLARE RECT[SERIES] IMPBLK(NEQN,NEQN)
DECLARE VECT[SERIES] SCALED(NEQN)
DECLARE VECT[LABELS] IMPLABEL(NEQN)
COMPUTE IMPLABEL=|| $
 'GM1','INF', 'DTBILL'||             ;* In your own work, enter the names of your variables.
LIST IEQN = 1 TO NEQN
DO I=1,NEQN
/* You can easily modify the next IMPULSE instruction.  IMPULSE has the same syntax as
ERRORS described on page 121.
        Delete NOPRINT for a printout of the responses.
        Change the number 24 to the number of impulse responses desired.
*/
IMPULSE(NOPRINT) NEQN 24 I V
 CARDS IEQN IMPBLK(IEQN,I) 1 IEQN
 DISPLAY(STORE=HEADER) 'Plot of Responses to' IMPLABEL(I)
 DO J=1,NEQN
   SET SCALED(J) = (IMPBLK(J,I))/SQRT(V(J,J))
   LABELS SCALED(J)
   # IMPLABEL(J)
 END DO J
* You can modify the options on the following GRAPH instruction.
 GRAPH(HEADER=HEADER,KEY=UPRIGHT,NUMBER=0) NEQN
 CARDS SCALED(IEQN)
END DO I
```

Figure 5.1 Impulse Response Functions

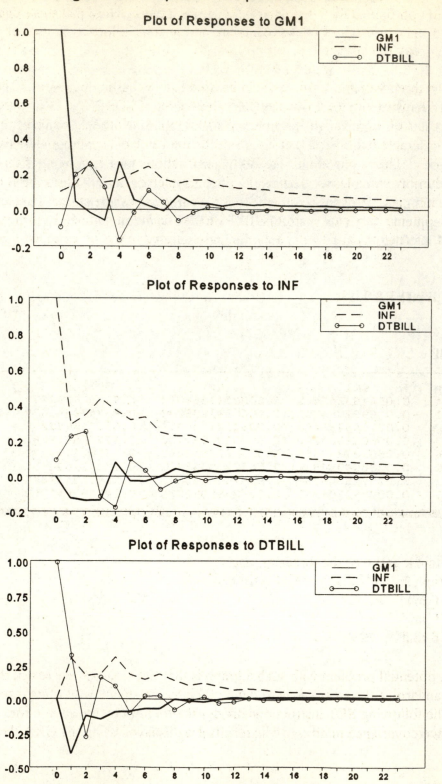

/*   The impulse responses are plotted in Figure 5.1. The last panel shows that a one-standard-deviation *dtbill* shock induces an increase of approximately 0.30 standard deviations in *inf* and a decrease of approximately 0.4 standard deviations in *gm1*. Note that these changes occur after one period since *dtbill* does not have a contemporaneous influence on *gm1* or *inf*. Thereafter, the responses decay towards zero.

The three-variable VAR can also be used for forecasting purposes. The following FORECAST instruction (see Chapter 2 for the syntax of FORECAST) prepares RATS to create eight forecasts of three variables beginning with 1991:4. Note that seven of the forecasts extend beyond the sample period and that RATS needs the value of *seasons* and its two leads for each of these periods. This is why the SEASONAL instruction at the beginning of this program created seasonal dummy variables through 94:1. Each supplementary card lists the equation to be used for forecasting and provides a name so that the forecasts can be stored for later use. For example, the first supplementary card instructs RATS to use equation number 1 (as created by the SYSTEM instruction) and to store the forecasts of *gm1* in the series called *f_m1*.
*/

```
forecast(print) 3 8 91:4
# 1 f_m1
# 2 f_inf
# 3 f_tbill
```

Entry	GM1	INF	DTBILL
91:04	0.054453245465	0.0062311256057	-0.773609093379
92:01	-0.016962064705	0.0062892986988	-0.673478691578
92:02	0.027845468488	0.0064121746372	0.018765830218
92:03	0.006018139260	0.0070697067703	0.577028819081
92:04	0.050187353668	0.0071822700463	-0.125811164931
93:01	-0.023604354574	0.0077700245831	-0.156421614985
93:02	0.025725348769	0.0082344006375	0.035723111896
93:03	0.007782507877	0.0088495392371	0.342392641050

*/ To obtain a graph of the forecasts, use:

```
     graph 3
     # f_m1
     # f_inf
     # f_tbill
```

A potential problem with such a graph is that the variables are scaled differently.   One way to standardize the forecasts is to divide each by the square root of its forecast-error variance. Each of the following SET instructions divides the forecast by the square root of element $v(i, i)$ of the variance/covariance matrix v. The results are displayed using the GRAPH instruction:
*/

```
set s_m1 91:4 93:3 = f_m1/sqrt(v(1,1))
set s_inf 91:4 93:3 = f_inf/sqrt(v(2,2))
set s_tbill 91:4 93:3 = f_tbill/sqrt(v(3,3))
```

graph(style=symbols,key=upright, $
        header='Standardized VAR Forecasts') 3
 # s_m1
 # s_inf
 # s_tbill

Figure 5.2: Standardized VAR Forecasts

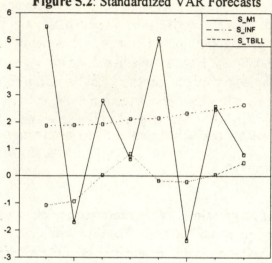

/*   A simple way to reverse the order of the Choleski decomposition is to copy the system block above and to reverse the order of the variables on the VARIABLES instruction. Consider:
*/

```
system 1 to 3
vars dtbill inf gm1     ;* Reverse the order of the variables.
lags 1 to 4
det constant seasons{-2 to 0}
end(system)
estimate(noftests,noprint,outsigma=V) 61:2 91:4 1
```

/* Next, innovation accounting is performed. To save space, only the 1-step, 8-step, 12-step, and 24-step ahead forecast error variances are reported here. All the impulse responses and forecast error variances are displayed in the file VAR2.OUT. If you compare the results to those from the original ordering, there are important differences at short, but not long, forecasting horizons.
*/

errors(impulses) 3 24 V
 # 1
 # 2
 # 3

```
Decomposition of Variance for Series DTBILL
Step  Std Error       DTBILL        INF          GM1
1     0.712715092  100.00000     0.00000      0.00000
8     0.888913168   78.12894    13.28652      8.58455
12    0.892540927   77.91875    13.25898      8.82226
24    0.892964203   77.87929    13.28741      8.83330

Decomposition of Variance for Series INF
Step  Std Error       DTBILL        INF          GM1
1     0.003339064    0.65678    99.34322      0.00000
8     0.005177402   15.80727    74.59880      9.59394
12    0.005507750   15.99842    72.58207     11.41952
24    0.005767766   15.63298    71.34480     13.02222

Decomposition of Variance for Series GM1
Step  Std Error       DTBILL        INF          GM1
1     0.009914796    0.94735     1.15327     97.89938
8     0.011596003   18.92351     4.82827     76.24821
12    0.011653647   18.78193     5.18708     76.03100
24    0.011718945   18.65690     5.79648     75.54662
```

3. Seemingly Unrelated Regressions: This exercise continues with the three-variable VAR developed in Sample Programs 1 and 2 above. The program illustrates the use of the SUR instruction in setting up a near-VAR. All program statements are on the file labeled SUR.PRG and the statements and all output are on the file labeled SUR.OUT.

* The first 8 lines repeat those from sample program VAR1.PRG:

```
cal 60 1 4
all 10 91:4
open data a:\us.prn
data(format=prn,org=obs) / m1 gdpdef tbill
set gm1 = log(m1) - log(m1{1})
set inf = log(gdpdef) - log(gdpdef{1})
diff tbill / dtbill
seasonal seasons
```

/* In sample program 2, the *F*-tests suggested that *gm1* Granger-causes itself and *dtbill*, *inf* Granger-causes itself and *dtbill*, and *dtbill* Granger-causes all variables in the system. Suppose that you wanted to impose these restrictions on the previously estimated three-equation system (so as to estimate a more parsimonious model). The resulting near-VAR can be estimated using the SUR instruction. The following three LINREG instructions and accompanying supplementary cards define the three equations to be estimated.
*/

```
linreg(define=1,noprint) gm1
# constant seasons{-2 to 0} gm1{1 to 4} dtbill{1 to 4}
linreg(define=2,noprint) inf
# constant seasons{-2 to 0} inf{1 to 4} dtbill{1 to 4}
linreg(define=3,noprint) dtbill
# constant seasons{-2 to 0} gm1{1 to 4} inf{1 to 4} dtbill{1 to 4}
```

/* The following SUR instruction prepares RATS to estimate a three-equation system over the maximum possible sample period. The OUTSIGMA= option is necessary in order to perform innovation accounting. The supplementary cards instruct RATS to store the residuals from equation 1 in series 1, equation 2 in series 2, and equation 3 in series 3. Only the output concerning equation 2 and the covariance/correlation matrix is shown below. The file labeled SUR.OUT contains the complete listing.
*/

```
sur(outsigma=v) 3 /
# 1 1
# 2 2
# 3 3
```

```
Dependent Variable INF - Estimation by Seemingly Unrelated Regressions
Quarterly Data From 61:02 To 91:04
Usable Observations       123      Degrees of Freedom     111
Centered R**2       0.710944       R Bar **2      0.682299
Uncentered R**2     0.938948       T x R**2       115.491
Mean of Dependent Variable          0.0122854097
Std Error of Dependent Variable     0.0063832279
Standard Error of Estimate          0.0035979060
Sum of Squared Residuals            0.0014368869
Durbin-Watson Statistic                1.981315
```

Coefficient	Estimate	Standard Error	t-statistic	Significance Level
13. Constant	0.002625138	0.000914266	2.87130	0.00408781
14. SEASONS{-2}	-0.001068471	0.000892672	-1.19694	0.23133184
15. SEASONS{-1}	-0.000459182	0.000879918	-0.52185	0.60177687
16. SEASONS	-0.000572820	0.000894423	-0.64043	0.52189002
17. INF{1}	0.306027835	0.089599785	3.41550	0.00063666
18. INF{2}	0.214675655	0.090131025	2.38182	0.01722743
19. INF{3}	0.196397036	0.086863858	2.26098	0.02376079
20. INF{4}	0.114484691	0.088503778	1.29356	0.19581845
21. DTBILL{1}	0.001401241	0.000404522	3.46394	0.00053232
22. DTBILL{2}	-0.000212455	0.000407730	-0.52107	0.60231954
23. DTBILL{3}	0.000834864	0.000410675	2.03290	0.04206222
24. DTBILL{4}	0.000312792	0.000400178	0.78163	0.43443173

```
Covariance\Correlation Matrix of Residuals
                GM1              INF            DTBILL
GM1      0.00010092496    0.1016011268    -0.0982145703
INF      0.00000348864    0.00001168201    0.0825871708
DTBILL  -0.00070340783    0.00020123490    0.50823426913
```

/*   Notice that each coefficient is numbered. As in LINREG and BOXJENK, SUR creates a vector called *%BETA* and each coefficient *i* can be referenced by *%BETA(i)*. SUR also creates *%NREG* (the number of regressors in the system), *%NOBS* (the number of observations), and *%LOGDET* (the log determinant of the variance/covariance matrix).

Given that the system is estimated and the residuals appropriately stored, innovation accounting proceeds just as before. For example, you can obtain the impulse responses and variance decompositions using the following ERRORS instruction taken from sample program 2:

```
errors(impulses) 3 24 V
# 1
# 2
# 3
```

The standardized impulse responses to a one-standard-deviation *gm1* shock are shown in Figure 5.2. As compared to the unconstrained system, the response of *inf* to a *gm1* shock is diminished in the near-VAR. The figure was constructed using the modified program segment from the Example 8.3 of the *RATS User's Manual*. Note that the program itself produces responses to all three shocks. Only the response of *gm1* is shown here.
*/

```
COMPUTE  NEQN  = 3                        ;* Modify this line such that NEQN equals the
                                          ;*   number of equations in your system
DECLARE RECT[SERIES] IMPBLK(NEQN,NEQN)
DECLARE VECT[SERIES] SCALED(NEQN)
DECLARE VECT[LABELS] IMPLABEL(NEQN)
COMPUTE IMPLABEL=|| 'GM1','INF', 'DTBILL'||    ;* Use the names of the variables in
                                          ;*   your system.

LIST IEQN = 1 TO NEQN
DO I=1,NEQN
```

/*   On the following IMPULSE instruction, the number *24* produces 24 impulse responses. You can modify this line to produce any desired number of impulses. Use the NOPRINT option if you want a high-resolution graph of the responses. Delete NOPRINT if you want a printout of the standardized responses.
*/

```
 impulse(NOPRINT) NEQN 24 I V
 CARDS IEQN IMPBLK(IEQN,I) 1 IEQN
 DISPLAY(STORE=HEADER) 'Plot of Responses to' IMPLABEL(I)
 DO J=1,NEQN
   SET SCALED(J) = (IMPBLK(J,I))/SQRT(V(J,J))
   LABELS SCALED(J)
   # IMPLABEL(J)
 END DO J
```

* You can modify the options on the GRAPH instruction.

```
   GRAPH(HEADER=HEADER,KEY=UPRIGHT,NUMBER=0) NEQN
   CARDS SCALED(IEQN)
END DO I
```

/* Note that the program produces the responses of all variables. Here, only the responses of the *gm1* series are shown.
*/

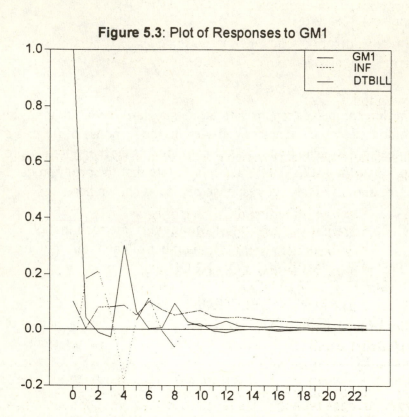

Figure 5.3: Plot of Responses to GM1

4. **The Sims-Bernanke decomposition**:   This exercise is designed to illustrate the use of the BERNANKE.SRC procedure. The data file US.PRN contains some of the relevant variables that might be used to analyze the relationship between the short-term interest rate (the 30-day treasury bill rate denoted by *tbill*) the 10-year government bond yield (denoted by *r10*), goverment purchases (denoted by *govt*), the money supply (as measured by M1 and denoted by *m1*), and the GDP deflator (denoted by *gdpdef* where 1985=100) for the period 1960:Q1 through 1991:Q4. The following program (i) transforms the variables, (ii) tests for the appropriate lag length using the RATS RATIO instruction and by constructing the multivariate AIC and SBC, (iii) estimates an unrestricted VAR and uses a Choleski decomposition to analyze the residuals, and (iv) uses the BERNANKE.SRC procedure to model the innovations and obtain the resulting impulse responses and variance decompositions.

Respectively, the first four instructions of BERNANKE.PRG (1) set the calendar for quarterly data beginning in 1960:4, (2) allocate space to store 10 series and to instruct RATS that the data ends in the fourth quarter of 1991, (3) instruct RATS that the data is in the file labeled US.PRN residing in drive a:\, and (4) read *govt, gdpdef, tbill, r10,* and *m1* into memory.

```
cal 60 1 4
all 10 91:4
open data a:\us.prn
data(format=prn,org=obs) / govt gdpdef tbill r10 m1
```

* Next, create the real value of government purchases and money supply by dividing each by
*   the GDP deflator. Taking logs helps to reduce heteroskedasticity:

```
set rgovt = log(govt/gdpdef)
set rm1 = log(m1/gdpdef)
```

* Next, take the first difference of each variable to be used in the VAR and create the seasonal
*   dummy variable called *seasons*:

```
diff rgovt / drgovt      ;* drgovt is the first difference of rgovt.
diff tbill / dtbill      ;* dtbill is the first difference of tbill.
diff r10 / dr10          ;* dr10 is the first difference of r10.
diff rm1 / drm1          ;* drm1 is the first difference of rm1.
seasonal seasons
```

* Summary statistics of the variables can be produced using:
table / drgovt dr10 drm1 dtbill

Series	Obs	Mean	Std Error	Minimum	Maximum
DRGOVT	127	0.0070901238	0.0113550267	-0.0236582942	0.0470866931
DR10	127	0.0225196850	0.5356319047	-2.4500000000	1.5400000000
DRM1	127	0.0030031118	0.0302736282	-0.0612194631	0.0740133003
DTBILL	127	0.0050393701	0.8885692745	-3.4100000000	4.4700000000

/* The next section of the program performs lag length tests. First, construct a four-variable VAR using 12 lags of each variable, a constant, and three seasonal dummy variables. Store the residuals in series 1 through 4.
*/

```
system 1 to 4                    ;* Define a system of 4 variables.
vars drgovt dr10 drm1 dtbill     ;* Use drgovt, dr10, drm1 and dtbill as the variables.
lags 1 to 12                     ;* Use 12 lags of each.
det constant seasons{-2 to 0}    ;* Include a constant and three seasonal dummies.
end(system)
```

```
estimate(noprint,noftests) / 1          ;* Estimate the model over the entire sample period and
                                         ;*   store the residuals in series 1 through 4.
```

* The next six statements set up the identical VAR using only eight lags of each variable:
```
system 1 to 4
vars drgovt dr10 drm1 dtbill
lags 1 to 8
det constant seasons{-2 to 0}
end(system)
```

* Next, estimate the eight-lag model over the same sample period used in the 12-lag model. You
*   must specify the starting and ending dates. Store the residuals in series 5 through 8;

```
estimate(noprint,noftests) 63:2 91:4 5
```

* Perform the likelihood ratio test. There are 64 degrees of freedom (four lags of four variables
* are excluded from four equations). The small sample correction *mcorr* equals 52; equations in
* the 12-lag system contain 52 parameters (12 lags of four variables, a constant, and three
* seasonal dummies). NOPRINT suppresses the display of the 4 x 4 covariance/correlation
* matrix:

```
ratio(degrees=64,mcorr=52,noprint) 63:2 91:4
# 1 2 3 4
# 5 6 7 8
```

* Although NOPRINT supresses the display of the covariance/correlation matrix, it is possible to
* obtain the marginal significance level of the test if you use:

display %signif
```
    0.23359
```

/* The significance level of the test is 23.359%. You can accept the null hypothesis that the
restriction is not binding (i.e., conclude there are not more than eight lags).

    The next portion of the program illustrates the process of selecting lag length using the
RATIO instruction and using the multivariate AIC and SBC. The next six statements set up
another eight-lag VAR. (*Note*: In this case, these six statements are redundant since equations 1
through 4 already define the four-variable VAR with eight lags. Although it is possible to jump to
the ESTIMATE statement, careful programming suggests repeating the statements.) The
ESTIMATE instruction uses the longest possible sample period and stores the residuals in series 1
through 4. Now, the covariance matrix *v* is calculated using OUTSIGMA= option. The use of
this option is necessary if you want to compute the AIC and SBC.
*/

```
system 1 to 4
vars drgovt dr10 drm1 dtbill
lags 1 to 8
det constant seasons{-2 to 0}
end(system)
estimate(noprint,noftests,outsigma=v) / 1
```

* Next, compute and display the multivariate AIC and the SBC. Note that $N = 144$ since there
* are eight lags of four variables plus a constant and three dummies in the four equations
* [(8*4 + 4)*4 = 144]:

```
compute aic = %nobs * %logdet + 2*144
compute sbc = %nobs * %logdet + 144*log(%nobs)
```
display 'aic = ' aic 'sbc = ' sbc
```
        aic = -2371.29199 sbc = -1971.09821
```

* The next six instructions set up the four-lag VAR:
```
system 1 to 4
vars drgovt dr10 drm1 dtbill
lags 1 to 4
det constant seasons{-2 to 0}
end(system)
```

/* Next, estimate the four-lag model over the same sample period used in the eight-lag model.
You must specify the starting and ending dates. Store the residuals in series 5 through 8. Use the
OUTSIGMA= option to calculate and store the covariance/correlation matrix of the residuals.
This is necessary to calculate the AIC and SBC. Use SIGMA if you want to display the matrix.
*/

estimate(noprint,noftests,outsigma=v,sigma) 62:2 91:4 5

```
Covariance\Correlation Matrix of Residuals
             DRGOVT           DR10            DRM1            DTBILL
DRGOVT  0.00010962709   -0.0386433144    0.0317095769    0.0116769378
DR10   -0.00019693493    0.23690753712  -0.1714385416    0.7648307602
DRM1    0.00000327541   -0.00082321580   0.00009732661  -0.2067635045
DTBILL  0.00009378277    0.28555509323  -0.00156467739   0.58839673101
```

/*   You can see that the correlation of the residuals from the *dr10* equation and the *dtbill*
equation is quite high (0.7648307602). The correlation of the residuals from the *drm1* equation
and the *bill* equation is significant at about the 5% level (the correlation is -0.2067635045).
These correlations suggest that the ordering of the variables in a Choleski decomposition can be
important. Next, perform the likelihood ratio test for four versus eight lags using:
*/

```
ratio(degrees=64,mcorr=36,noprint) 62:2 91:4
# 1 2 3 4
# 5 6 7 8
display %signif
     0.01628
```

* At this point, an econometrician might reasonably reject the null hypothesis and conclude that
* eight lags should be used. This conclusion is reinforced by the AIC but not the SBC. Consider:
compute aic = %nobs * %logdet + 2*80   ;* In the four-lag model, N = 80. Each of the
compute sbc = %nobs * %logdet + 80*log(%nobs) ;* the four equations contains 20 parameters.
display 'aic = ' aic 'sbc = ' sbc
```
        aic = -2369.53046 sbc = -2147.20058
```

/*   If you compare the AIC and SBC to those of the eight-lag model, it is clear that the AIC
selects the eight-lag model and the SBC strongly selects the four-lag model. This same type of
ambiguity occurs in univariate models as well. Here, we adopt the parsimony principal and
proceed with the four-lag model. In your own work, you should carefully check the residuals for
lack of autocorrelation before proceeding with the more parsimonious model. Next,
BERNANKE.PRG proceeds with innovation accounting using a Choleski decomposition:
*/

errors(impulses) 4 12 v   ;* Only 12 steps are used here. The ordering of the variables
 # 1   ;* is implied by the VARS statement; *drgovt* precedes *dr10* which
 # 2   ;* precedes *drm1* which precedes *dtbill*. The output is lengthy
 # 3   ;* and only a partial listing is reported here. All the output
 # 4   ;* is contained on the file BERNANKE.OUT.

```
Decomposition of Variance for Series DRGOVT
Step  Std Error      DRGOVT       DR10       DRM1       DTBILL
  1   0.010470296  100.00000    0.00000    0.00000    0.00000
  8   0.011143336   96.25204    1.69492    0.74848    1.30457
 12   0.011158067   96.13497    1.74415    0.79734    1.32354

Decomposition of Variance for Series DR10
Step  Std Error      DRGOVT       DR10       DRM1       DTBILL
  1   0.486731484    0.14933   99.85067    0.00000    0.00000
  8   0.541193504    3.96439   91.10924    2.05136    2.87501
 12   0.541907757    3.96834   90.92394    2.17668    2.93104

Decomposition of Variance for Series DRM1
Step  Std Error      DRGOVT       DR10       DRM1       DTBILL
  1   0.009865425    0.10055    2.90159   96.99786    0.00000
  8   0.013439260    3.07397   37.27562   55.56634    4.08408
 12   0.013487078    3.34799   37.10563   55.41920    4.12718

Decomposition of Variance for Series DTBILL
Step  Std Error      DRGOVT       DR10       DRM1       DTBILL
  1   0.767070226    0.01364   58.65324    0.60615   40.72698
  8   0.905895524    2.02272   56.26195    6.53355   35.18178
 12   0.908524455    2.05098   56.06864    6.89249   34.98789
```

/*   You can see that *drgovt* and *dr10* each explain the preponderence of their forecast error variances at the three horizons shown (RATS actually displays all 12 forecasting horizons). At longer horizons, *dr10* explains about 37% of the forecast error variance of *drm1* and the variable *dr10* explains about 56% of the forecast error variance of *dtbill*. Of course, these proportions are conditional on the ordering used in the decomposition. Now consider an alternative decomposition. Suppose that a particular economic model implies the following relationship among the innovations of the primitive model:

The contemporaneous value of	Is affected by the contemporaneous value of
drgovt	no other variable
dr10	no other variable
drm1	*drgovt*
dtbill	*dr10*

As implied by the VARS instruction, let equations 1 through 4 represent the *drgovt, dr10, drm1,* and *dtbill* equations, respectively. The relationship between the innovations and the regression residuals is:

$$
\begin{bmatrix} e_{1t} \\ e_{2t} \\ e_{3t} \\ e_{4t} \end{bmatrix} = \begin{bmatrix} 1 & 0 & 0 & 0 \\ 0 & 1 & 0 & 0 \\ 1 & 0 & 1 & 0 \\ 0 & 1 & 0 & 1 \end{bmatrix} \begin{bmatrix} \epsilon_{1t} \\ \epsilon_{2t} \\ \epsilon_{3t} \\ \epsilon_{4t} \end{bmatrix}
$$

Using the notation of equation (5.3), we get:

$$ e_t = B^{-1} \epsilon_t $$

The remainder of BERNANKE.PRG uses this particular structure among the pure innovations to perform innovation accounting.
*/
source(noecho) c:\rats\bernanke.src   ;* Compile the BERNANKE.SRC procedure. Modify this
                                      ;*   line if the procedure is not in c:\rats.

* Next, define and input the B^{-1} matrix (called *betainv*) as a rectangular 4 x 4 matrix. The pattern
* following the INPUT instruction is precisely that of B^{-1} above:

```
declare rect betainv(4,4)
input betainv
1 0 0 0
0 1 0 0
1 0 1 0
0 1 0 1
```

/* Next, invoke the BERNANKE procedure. RATS is instructed to use the covariance matrix *v* to orthogonalize the innovations using the pattern given by *betainv* and to store the result in the matrix *factor*. The TEST option instructs RATS to perform the likelihood ratio test of the restrictions. Note that only six zero restrictions are required; since 10 are imposed, there are four overidentifying restrictions. PRINT instructs RATS to display the off-diagonal coefficient estimates and their standard error. Note that the estimate of β_{31} is -0.02988 with a standard error of 0.08633 and the estimate of β_{42} is -1.20534 with a standard error of 0.09397. The restricted model can be accepted (i.e., the hyopthesis that *betainv* is appropriate is not rejected) at conventional significance levels.
*/

@bernanke(test,print) v betainv factor

```
Coefficient Estimates for Structural Decomposition
 Row Col  Value     Std.Error
  3   1  -0.02988   0.08633
  4   2  -1.20534   0.09307

LR Test of Overidentification
Chi-Square( 4 ) =         5.93263 Signif. Level = 0.2042360
```

/*   Now, obtain the impulse responses and variance decompositions using the ERRORS instruction along with the IMPULSES option. Note that we are no longer interested in a Cholseki decomposition using the covariance matrix *v*. The option *decomp=factor* instructs RATS to perform the decomposition using the matrix *factor* that was obtained by invoking the BERNANKE.SRC procedure. The output is quite lengthy and only a partial listing is reported here. The complete output is contained on the file labeled BERNANKE.OUT.
*/
errors(decomp=factor, impulses) 4 12   ;* Only 12 steps are used here.
 # 1
 # 2
 # 3
 # 4

```
Decomposition of Variance for Series DRGOVT
 Step  Std Error       INNOV_1    INNOV_2    INNOV_3    INNOV_4
    1  0.010470296  100.00000    0.00000    0.00000    0.00000
    8  0.011116699   96.41252    1.51936    0.73230    1.33582
   12  0.011132035   96.28042    1.57495    0.78954    1.35508

Decomposition of Variance for Series DR10
 Step  Std Error       INNOV_1    INNOV_2    INNOV_3    INNOV_4
    1  0.486731484    0.00000  100.00000    0.00000    0.00000
    8  0.542179045    3.79817   91.24314    2.03951    2.91918
   12  0.542920284    3.80328   91.05325    2.16768    2.97579

Decomposition of Variance for Series DRM1
 Step  Std Error       INNOV_1    INNOV_2    INNOV_3    INNOV_4
    1  0.009865425    0.10055    0.00000   99.89945    0.00000
    8  0.013487058    2.88708   36.28524   56.69518    4.13249
   12  0.013532987    3.16846   36.11943   56.53473    4.17738

Dcomposition of Variance for Series DTBILL
 Step  Std Error       INNOV_1    INNOV_2    INNOV_3    INNOV_4
    1  0.767070217    0.00000   58.49661    0.00000   41.50339
    8  0.908281625    2.13584   55.66970    6.53011   35.66436
   12  0.911236636    2.16347   55.49673    6.89684   35.44296
```

/* A high-resolution graph of the impulse responses obtained from the Sims-Bernanke decomposition can be obtained with a slight modification of Example 8.3 from the *RATS User's Manual*. The four graphs in Figure 5.4 were obtained using the program segment below. Be sure to note that the IMPULSE instruction uses the DECOMP= option so as to produce the impulses obtained from the Sims-Bernanke (as opposed to a Choleski) decomposition.
*/

```
COMPUTE NEQN  = 4
DECLARE RECT[SERIES] IMPBLK(NEQN,NEQN)
DECLARE VECT[SERIES] SCALED(NEQN)
DECLARE VECT[LABELS] IMPLABEL(NEQN)
COMPUTE IMPLABEL=|| 'RGOVT','R10', 'DRM1', 'TBILL'||
LIST IEQN = 1 TO NEQN
DO I=1,NEQN
  impulse(NOPRINT,decomp=factor) NEQN 12 I
  CARDS IEQN IMPBLK(IEQN,I) 1 IEQN
  DISPLAY(STORE=HEADER) 'Plot of Responses to' IMPLABEL(I)
  DO J=1,NEQN
    SET SCALED(J) = (IMPBLK(J,I))/SQRT(V(J,J))
    LABELS SCALED(J)
    # IMPLABEL(J)
  END DO J
  GRAPH(HEADER=HEADER,KEY=UPRIGHT,NUMBER=0) NEQN
  CARDS SCALED(IEQN)
END DO I
```

Figure 5.4: Impulse Responses Using the Bernanke Decomposition

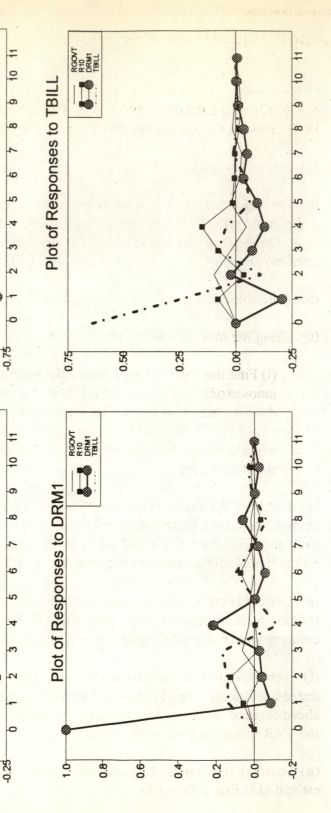

Plot of Responses to RGOVT

Plot of Responses to R10

Plot of Responses to DRM1

Plot of Responses to TBILL

Additional Exercises

1. In this exercise, you are asked to estimate a VAR using three nonstationary variables in order to compare the effects of estimating the model in levels as opposed to first differences. To keep the issue simple, use the three variables *rgovt*, *r10*, and *tbill* from sample program 1.

(a) Pretest the variables for the presence of unit roots using Dickey-Fuller tests.

(b) Estimate the trivariate VAR in levels including three seasonal dummy variables. Construct a likelihood ratio test to determine whether it is possible to restrict the number of lags from 12 to 8. Do the residuals of the regression equations used to construct Σ_{12} and Σ_8 appear to be stationary?

Compare these results to those using the multivatiate AIC and SBC.

(c) Using the model with 12 lags:

(i) Find the correlations between the innovations. Since the correlation between the innovations in *tbill* and *r10* is 0.808, explain why the ordering in a Choleski decomposition is likely to be important.

(ii) Show that each variable Granger-causes each of the other variables conventional significance levels.

(d) Consider the variance decompositions using a Choleski decomposition such that *rgovt* innovations contemporaneously affect all variables, *tbill* innovations contemporaneously affect itself and *r10*, and *r10* innovations contemporaneously affect only *r10*. Using this ordering, obtain the 24-step ahead forecast error variance decompositions of *rgovt*, *tbill*, and *r10*.

(e) Use the reverse ordering such that *r10* innovations affect all variables contemporaneously, *tbill* innovations contemporaneously affect *tbill* and *rgovt*, and *rgovt* innovations contemporaneously affect only *rgovt*. Compare your results to those in part (d).

(f) Now estimate the same trivariate VAR (including seasonals) but use first differences instead of levels. Use the same ordering as in part (d) and obtain the proportions of 24-step ahead forecast error variances of $\Delta rgovt_t$, $\Delta tbill_t$ and $\Delta r10_t$. Compare these results to those of the VAR using the level of the variables.

(g) Compare the impulse responses from the model estimated in levels to those of the model estimated in first differences.

Chapter 6 | Cointegration and Error Correction

This chapter explores an exciting new development in econometrics: the estimation of a structural equation or a VAR containing nonstationary variables. In univariate models, we have seen that a stochastic trend can be removed by differencing. The resulting stationary series can be estimated using univariate Box-Jenkins techniques. At one time, the conventional wisdom was to generalize this idea and difference all nonstationary variables used in a regression analysis. However, the appropriate way to treat nonstationary variables is not so straightforward in a multivariate context. It is quite possible for there to be a linear combination of integrated variables that is stationary; such variables are said to be **cointegrated**.

The concept of cointegration applies to a wide variety of economic models. Any equilibrium relationship among a set of nonstationary variables implies that their stochastic trends must be linked. After all, the equilibrium relationship means that the variables cannot move independently of each other. This linkage among the stochastic trends necessitates that the variables be cointegrated. Since the trends of cointegrated variables are linked, the dynamic paths of such variables must bear some relation to the current deviation from the equilibrium relationship. Thus, the conventional wisdom of differencing all nonstationary variables used in a regression analysis was incorrect. After all, if the linear relationship is already stationary, differencing the relationship entails a misspecification error.

Theoretical Background

1. Cointegrated variables: Engle and Granger's (1987) formal analysis of cointegration begins by considering a set of economic variables in long-run equilibrium when:

$$\beta_1 x_{1t} + \beta_2 x_{2t} + \dots + \beta_n x_{nt} = 0$$

If we let β and x_t denote the vectors $(\beta_1, \beta_2, \dots, \beta_n)$ and $(x_{1t}, x_{2t}, \dots, x_{nt})'$, the system is in long-run equilibrium when $\beta x_t = 0$. The deviation from long-run equilibrium-called the **equilibrium error**-is e_t, so that:

$$e_t = \beta x_t$$

If the equilibrium is meaningful, it must be the case that the equilibrium error process is stationary. Engle and Granger (1987) provide the following definition of cointegration.

The components of the vector $x_t = (x_{1t}, x_{2t}, \ldots, x_{nt})'$ are said to be *cointegrated of order d, b*, denoted by $x_t \sim CI(d, b)$ if:

1. All components of x_t are integrated of order d

2. There exists a vector $\beta = (\beta_1, \beta_2, \ldots, \beta_n)$ such that linear combination $\beta x_t = \beta_1 x_{1t} + \beta_2 x_{2t} + \ldots + \beta_n x_{nt}$ is integrated of order $(d - b)$, where $b > 0$.

The vector β is called the **cointegrating vector**.[1]

There are four very important points to note about the definition:

1. Cointegration refers to a **linear** combination of nonstationary variables. Theoretically, it is quite possible that nonlinear long-run relationships exist among a set of integrated variables. Also note that the cointegrating vector is not unique. If $(\beta_1, \beta_2, \ldots, \beta_n)$ is a cointegrating vector, then for any nonzero value of λ, $(\lambda\beta_1, \lambda\beta_2, \ldots, \lambda\beta_n)$ is also a cointegrating vector. Typically, one of the variables is used to *normalize* the cointegrating vector by fixing its coefficient at unity. To normalize the cointegrating vector with respect to x_{1t}, simply select $\lambda = 1/\beta_1$.

2. All variables must be integrated of the same order. Of course, this does not imply that all integrated variables are cointegrated; usually, a set of $I(1)$ variables is *not* cointegrated. Such a lack of cointegration implies no long-run equilibrium among the variables so that they can wander arbitrarily far from each other.

3. If x_t has n components, there may be as many as n-1 linearly independent cointegrating vectors. Clearly, if x_t contains only two variables, there can be *at most* one independent cointegrating vector. The number of cointegrating vectors is called the **cointegrating rank** of x_t.

4. Most of the cointegration literature concentrates on the case in which each variable contains a single unit root. The reason is that traditional regression or time series analysis applies when variables are $I(0)$ and few economic variables are integrated of an order higher than unity. When it is unambiguous, many authors use the term "cointegration" to refer to the case in which variables are $CI(1, 1)$. The remainder of the handbook follows this convention.

Figure 6.1 illustrates some of the important properties of cointegration relationships. In case 1, both the $\{y_t\}$ and $\{z_t\}$ sequences were constructed so as to be random walk plus noise processes. Although the 20 realizations shown generally decline, extending the sample would eliminate this tendency. In any event, neither series shows any tendency to return to a long-run level and formal Dickey-Fuller tests are not able to reject the null hypothesis of a unit root in either series. Although each series is nonstationary, you can see that they do move together. In

---

[1] To include an intercept term, simply set all realizations of one $\{x_{it}\}$ sequence equal to unity. In the text, the long-run relationship with an intercept will be denoted by $\beta_0 + \beta_1 x_{1t} + \ldots + \beta_n x_{nt} = 0$.

Figure 6.1

Illustrating Cointegrated Processes

Case 1: The $\{y_t\}$ and $\{z_t\}$ sequences are both random walk plus noise processes. Although each is nonstationary the two sequences have the same stochastic trend; hence they are cointegrated such that the linear combination $(y_t - z_t)$ is stationary. The equilibrium error term is an $I(0)$ process.

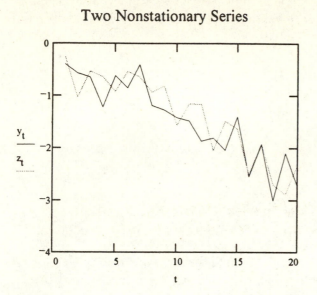

Two Nonstationary Series

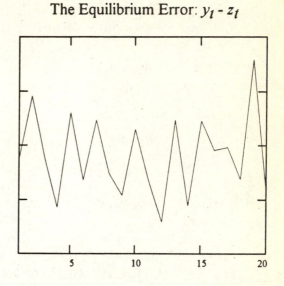

The Equilibrium Error: $y_t - z_t$

Case 2: All three sequences are random walk plus noise processes. As constructed, no two are cointegrated. However, the linear combination $(y_t + z_t - w_t)$ is stationary; hence, the three are cointegrated. The equilibrium error is an $I(0)$ process.

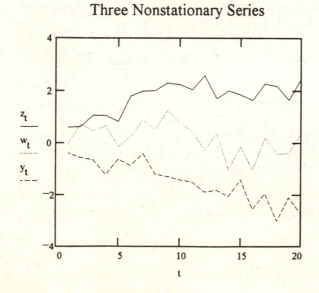

Three Nonstationary Series

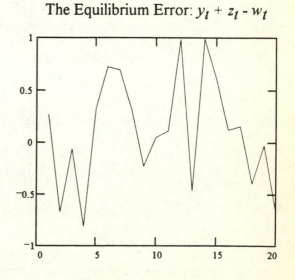

The Equilibrium Error: $y_t + z_t - w_t$

Cointegration and Error Correction 153

fact, the difference between the series $(y_t - z_t)$-shown in the second panel-is stationary; the "equilibrium error" term $e_t = (y_t - z_t)$ has a zero mean and a constant variance.

Case 2 illustrates cointegration among three random walk plus noise processes. As in case 1, no series exhibits a tendency to return to a long-run level and formal Dickey-Fuller tests are not able to reject the null hypothesis of a unit root in any of the three. In contrast to the previous case, no two series are cointegrated; each series seems to "meander" away from the other two. However, as shown in the second panel, there exists a stationary linear combination of the three: $e_t = y_t + z_t - w_t$. Thus, it follows that the dynamic behavior of *at least* one variable must be restricted by the values of the other variables in the system.

2. Cointegration and error correction: A principal feature of cointegrated variables is that their time paths are influenced by the extent of any deviation from long-run equilibrium. Thus, the short-run dynamics must be influenced by the deviation from the long-run relationship.

Formally, the $(n \times 1)$ vector $x_t = (x_{1t}, x_{2t}, \ldots, x_{nt})'$ has an error-correction representation if it can be expressed in the form:

$$\Delta x_t = \pi_0 - \pi x_{t-1} + \pi_1 \Delta x_{t-1} + \pi_2 \Delta x_{t-2} + \ldots + \pi_p \Delta x_{t-p} + \epsilon_t \qquad (6.1)$$

where π_0 is an $(n \times 1)$ vector of intercept terms with elements π_{i0}, the π_i are $(n \times n)$ coefficient matrices with elements $\pi_{jk}(i)$, π is a matrix with elements π_{jk} such that one or more of the $\pi_{jk} \neq 0$; and ϵ_t is an $(n \times 1)$ vector with elements ϵ_{it}. Note that the disturbance terms are such that ϵ_{it} may be correlated with ϵ_{jt}.

Let all variables in x_t be $I(1)$. Now, if there is an error-correction representation of these variables as in (6.1), there is necessarily a linear combination of the $I(1)$ variables that is stationary. Solving (6.1) for πx_{t-1}, we obtain

$$\pi x_{t-1} = \Delta x_t - \pi_0 - \Sigma \pi_i \Delta x_{t-i} - \epsilon_t$$

Since each expression on the right-hand side is stationary, πx_{t-1} must also be stationary. Since π contains only constants, each row of π is a cointegrating vector of x_t. For example, the first row can be written as $(\pi_{11} x_{1t-1} + \pi_{12} x_{2t-1} + \ldots + \pi_{1n} x_{nt-1})$. Since each series x_{it-1} is $I(1)$, $(\pi_{11}, \pi_{12}, \ldots, \pi_{1n})$ must be a cointegrating vector for x_t. Thus, an error-correction model for $I(1)$ variables necessarily implies cointegration. It can also be shown that cointegration implies error correction. This result is called the **Granger representation theorem** stating that for any set of $I(1)$ variables, error correction and cointegration are equivalent representations.

The key feature in (6.1) is the presence of the matrix π. There are three important points to note:

1. If all elements of π equal zero, (6.1) is a traditional VAR in first differences. In such circumstances, there is no error-correction representation since Δx_t does not respond to the previous period's deviation from long-run equilibrium.

2. If one or more of the π_{jk} differs from zero, Δx_t responds to the previous period's deviation from long-run equilibrium. Hence, *estimating x_t as a VAR in first differences is inappropriate if x_t has an error-correction representation*. The omission of the expression πx_{t-1} entails a specification error if x_t has an error-correction representation as in (6.1). In general, all variables in a cointegrated system will respond to a deviation from long-run equilibrium. However, it is possible that some of the adjustment parameters are zero so that only some of the variables do respond to the discrepancy from long-run equilibrium.

3. This result illustrates the very important insights of Johansen (1988) and Stock and Watson (1988) that **we can use the rank of π to determine whether or not the variables in $\{x_t\}$ are cointegrated**. To elaborate, consider the simple case of a first-order VAR:

$$x_t = A_1 x_{t-1} + \epsilon_t \tag{6.2}$$

where x_t is the $(n \times 1)$ vector $(x_{1t}, x_{2t}, \ldots, x_{nt})'$; ϵ_t is the $(n \times 1)$ vector $(\epsilon_{1t}, \epsilon_{2t}, \ldots, \epsilon_{nt})'$; A_1 is an $(n \times n)$ matrix of parameters.

Subtracting x_{t-1} from each side of (6.2) and letting I be an $(n \times n)$ identity matrix, we get

$$\begin{aligned}\Delta x_t &= -(I - A_1)x_{t-1} + \epsilon_t \\ &= \pi x_{t-1} + \epsilon_t\end{aligned} \tag{6.3}$$

where π is the $(n \times n)$ matrix $-(I - A_1)$ and π_{ij} denotes the element in row i and column j of π. As you can see, (6.3) is a special case of (6.1) such that all $\pi_i = 0$.

Again, the crucial issue for cointegration concerns the rank of the $(n \times n)$ matrix π. If the rank of this matrix is zero, each element of π must equal zero. In this instance, (6.3) is equivalent to an n-variable VAR in first differences:

$$\Delta x_t = \epsilon_t$$

Here, each $\Delta x_{it} = \epsilon_{it}$ so that the first difference of each variable in the vector x_t is $I(0)$. Since each $x_{it} = x_{it-1} + \epsilon_{it}$, all the $\{x_{it}\}$ sequences are unit-root processes and there is no linear combination of the variables which is stationary.

At the other extreme, suppose that π is of full rank. The long-run solution to (6.3) is given by the n independent equations:

$$\pi_{11}x_{1t} + \pi_{12}x_{2t} + \pi_{13}x_{3t} + \ldots + \pi_{1n}x_{nt} = 0$$
$$\pi_{21}x_{1t} + \pi_{22}x_{2t} + \pi_{23}x_{3t} + \ldots + \pi_{2n}x_{nt} = 0$$

$$(6.4)$$

$$\pi_{n1}x_{1t} + \pi_{n2}x_{2t} + \pi_{n3}x_{3t} + \ldots + \pi_{nn}x_{nt} = 0$$

Each of these n equations is an independent restriction on the long-run solution of the variables; the n variables in the system face n long-run constraints. In this case, each of the n variables contained in the vector x_t must be stationary with the long-run values given by (6.4). Each row of π is a cointegrating vector so that there are n cointegrating vectors of the n variables in the dynamic system.

In intermediate cases, in which the rank of π is equal to r, there are r cointegrating vectors. If $r = 1$, there is a single cointegrating vector given by any row of the matrix π. Each $\{x_{it}\}$ sequence can be written in error-correction form. For example, if we normalize with respect to x_{1t-1}, set $\alpha_1 = \pi_{11}$, and set $\beta_{ij} = \pi_{ij}/\pi_{11}$, we can write Δx_{1t} as:

$$\Delta x_{1t} = \alpha_1(x_{1t-1} + \beta_{12}x_{2t-1} + \ldots + \beta_{1n}x_{nt-1}) + \epsilon_{1t} \qquad (6.5)$$

In the long run, the $\{x_{it}\}$ will satisfy the relationship:

$$x_{1t} + \beta_{12}x_{2t} + \ldots + \beta_{1n}x_{nt} = 0$$

Hence, the normalized cointegrating vector is $(1, \beta_{12}, \beta_{13}, \ldots, \beta_{1n})$ and the speed of adjustment parameter is α_1. In the same way, with two cointegration vectors the long-run values of the variables will satisfy the two relationships:

$$\pi_{11}x_{1t} + \pi_{12}x_{2t} + \ldots + \pi_{1n}x_{nt} = 0$$
$$\pi_{21}x_{1t} + \pi_{22}x_{2t} + \ldots + \pi_{2n}x_{nt} = 0$$

which can be appropriately normalized.

The main point here is that there are two important ways to test for cointegration. The Engle-Granger methodology seeks to determine whether the residuals of the equilibrium relationship are stationary. The Johansen (1988) and Stock-Watson (1988) methodologies determine how many of the characteristic roots of π are less than unity.

3. Testing for cointegration: The Engle-Granger methodology: To explain the Engle-Granger testing procedure, suppose that two variables-say y_t and z_t-are believed to be integrated of order one and you want to determine whether there exists an equilibrium relationship between the two. Engle and Granger (1987) propose a straightforward test to determine whether two $I(1)$ variables are $CI(1, 1)$.

Step 1: Pretest the variables for their order of integration.

By definition, cointegration necessitates that the variables be integrated of the same order. Thus, the first step in the analysis is to pretest each variable to determine its order of integration. The Dickey-Fuller, augmented Dickey-Fuller, and/or Phillips-Perron tests discussed in Chapter 4 can be used to infer the number of unit roots (if any) in each of the variables. If all variables are stationary, it is not necessary to proceed since standard time-series methods apply to stationary variables. If the variables are integrated of different orders, it is possible to conclude they are **not** cointegrated.[1]

Step 2: Estimate the long-run equilibrium relationship.

If the results of Step 1 indicate that both $\{y_t\}$ and $\{z_t\}$ are $I(1)$, the next step is to estimate the long-run equilibrium relationship in the form:

$$y_t = \beta_0 + \beta_1 z_t + e_t \qquad (6.6)$$

If the variables are cointegrated, an OLS regression yields a "super-consistent" estimator of the cointegrating parameters β_0 and β_1. Stock (1988) proves that the OLS estimates of β_0 and β_1 converge faster than in OLS models using stationary variables. In order to determine if the variables are actually cointegrated, denote the residual sequence from (6.6) by $\{\hat{e}_t\}$. Thus, $\{\hat{e}_t\}$ is the series of the estimated residuals of the long-run relationship. If these deviations from long-run equilibrium are found to be stationary, the $\{y_t\}$ and $\{z_t\}$ sequences are cointegrated of order (1, 1). It would be convenient if we could perform a Dickey-Fuller test on these residuals to determine their order of integration. Consider the autoregression of the residuals:

$$\Delta \hat{e}_t = a_1 \hat{e}_{t-1} + \epsilon_t \qquad (6.7)$$

Since the $\{\hat{e}_t\}$ sequence is a residual from a regression equation, there is no need to include an intercept term. The parameter of interest in (6.7) is a_1; if we cannot reject the null hypothesis $a_1 = 0$, we can conclude that the residual series contains a unit root. Hence, we conclude that the $\{y_t\}$ and $\{z_t\}$ sequences are **not** cointegrated. The more precise wording is awkward because of a triple negative, but to be technically correct: *if it is not possible to reject the null hypothesis $a_1 = 0$, we cannot reject the hypothesis that the variables are not cointegrated*. Instead, the rejection of the null hypothesis implies that the residual sequence is stationary. Given that both $\{y_t\}$ and $\{z_t\}$ were found to be $I(1)$ and that the residuals are stationary, we can conclude that the series are cointegrated of order (1, 1).

In most applied studies it is not possible to use the Dickey-Fuller tables themselves. The problem is that the $\{\hat{e}_t\}$ sequence is generated from a regression equation; the researcher does not

---

[1] With three or more variables, various subsets may be cointegrated. For example, a group of $I(2)$ variables may be $CI(2, 1)$ and this group may be cointegrated with a set of $I(1)$ variables.

know the actual error e_t only the estimate of the error $\hat{e}_t$. Only if β_0 and β_1 were known in advance and used to construct the true $\{e_t\}$ sequence would an ordinary Dickey-Fuller table be appropriate. Fortunately, Engle and Granger provide test statistics that can be used to test the hypothesis $a_1 = 0$. If more than two variables appear in the equilibrium relationship, the appropriate tables are provided by Engle and Yoo (1987). If you use n variables and a sample size of 100, the Engle and Yoo (1987) critical values for two through five variables at the 1%, 5% and 10% significance levels are:

The Engle-Yoo Critical Values

n	1%	5%	10%
2	-4.07	-3.37	-3.03
3	-4.45	-3.93	-3.59
4	-4.75	-4.22	-3.89
5	-5.18	-4.58	-4.26

If the residuals of (6.7) do not appear to be white-noise, an augmented Dickey-Fuller test can be used instead of (6.7). Suppose that diagnostic checks indicate that the $\{\epsilon_t\}$ sequence of (6.7) exhibits serial correlation. Instead of using the results from (6.7), estimate the autoregression:

$$\Delta\hat{e}_t = a_1\hat{e}_{t-1} + \sum_i a_{i+1}\Delta\hat{e}_{t-i} + \epsilon_t \tag{6.8}$$

Again, if $a_1 = 0$, we can conclude that the residual sequence is nonstationary and that $\{y_t\}$ and $\{z_t\}$ are not $CI(1, 1)$.

Step 3: Estimate the error-correction model.

If the variables are cointegrated (i.e., if the null hypothesis of no cointegration is rejected) the residuals from the equilibrium regression can be used to estimate the error-correction model. If $\{y_t\}$ and $\{z_t\}$ are $CI(1, 1)$, the variables have the error-correction form:

$$\Delta y_t = \alpha_1 + \alpha_y(y_{t-1} - \beta_1 z_{t-1}) + \sum_i \alpha_{11}(i)\Delta y_{t-i} + \sum_{i=1} \alpha_{12}(i)\Delta z_{t-i} + \epsilon_{yt} \tag{6.9}$$

$$\Delta z_t = \alpha_2 + \alpha_z(y_{t-1} - \beta_1 z_{t-1}) + \sum_i \alpha_{21}(i)\Delta y_{t-i} + \sum_{i=1} \alpha_{22}(i)\Delta z_{t-i} + \epsilon_{zt} \tag{6.10}$$

where β_1 is the parameter of the normalized cointegrating vector; ϵ_{yt} and ϵ_{zt} are white-noise disturbances (which may be correlated with each other); and α_1, α_2, α_y, α_z, $\alpha_{11}(i)$, $\alpha_{12}(i)$, $\alpha_{21}(i)$, $\alpha_{22}(i)$ are all parameters.

Engle and Granger (1987) propose a clever way to circumvent the cross-equation restrictions involved in the direct estimation of (6.9) and (6.10). The value of the residual $\hat{e}_{t-1}$ estimates the deviation from long-run equilibrium in period $(t\text{-}1)$. Hence, it is possible to use the saved residuals $\{\hat{e}_{t-1}\}$ obtained in Step 2 as an instrument for the expression $y_{t-1} - \beta_1 z_{t-1}$ in (6.9) and (6.10). Thus, using the saved residuals from the estimation of the long-run equilibrium relationship, we can estimate the error-correction model as:

$$\Delta y_t = \alpha_1 + \alpha_y \hat{e}_{t-1} + \sum_{i=1} \alpha_{11}(i)\Delta y_{t-i} + \sum_{i=1} \alpha_{12}(i)\Delta z_{t-i} + \epsilon_{yt} \qquad (6.11)$$

$$\Delta z_t = \alpha_2 + \alpha_z \hat{e}_{t-1} + \sum_{i=1} \alpha_{21}(i)\Delta y_{t-i} + \sum_{i=1} \alpha_{22}(i)\Delta z_{t-i} + \epsilon_{zt} \qquad (6.12)$$

Other than the error-correction term $\hat{e}_{t-1}$, (6.11) and (6.12) constitute VAR in first differences. Thus, the error-correction model can be estimated using the VAR methodology developed in Chapter 5. Notably:

1. OLS is an efficient estimation strategy since each equation contains the same set of regressors.

2. Since all terms in (6.11) and (6.12) are stationary [i.e., Δy_t and its lags, Δz_t and its lags, and $\hat{e}_{t-1}$ are $I(0)$] the test statistics used in traditional VAR analysis are appropriate. For example, lag-lengths can be determined using a χ^2-test and the restriction that all $\alpha_{jk}(i) = 0$ can be checked using an F-test.

Step 4: Assess model adequacy.

There are several procedures that can help determine whether the estimated error-correction model is appropriate:

1. You should be careful to assess the adequacy of the model by performing diagnostic checks to determine whether the residuals of the error-correction model approximate white-noise. If the residuals are serially correlated, lag lengths may be too short. Reestimate the model using lag lengths that yield serially uncorrelated errors. An example is provided in the sample program COINT3.PGM below.

2. The *speed of adjustment* coefficients α_y and α_z are of particular interest in that they have important implications for the dynamics of the system. If we focus on (6.12) it is

clear that for any given value of $\hat{e}_{t-1}$, a large value of α_z is associated with a large value of Δz_t. If α_z is zero, the change in z_t does not at all respond to the deviation from long-run equilibrium in period $(t-1)$. If α_z is zero and if all $\alpha_{21}(i) = 0$, then it can be said that $\{\Delta y_t\}$ does not Granger-cause $\{\Delta z_t\}$. We know that α_y and/or α_z must be significantly different from zero if the variables are cointegrated. After all, if both α_y and α_z are zero, there is no error correction and (6.11) and (6.12) comprise nothing more than a VAR in first differences. Moreover, the absolute values of these speed of adjustment coefficients must not be too large. The point estimates should imply that Δy_t and Δz_t converge to the long-run equilibrium relationship.

3. Innovation accounting can help determine whether or not you have estimated a reasonable model. As shown in sample program 1, a simple method is to obtain the impulse responses using the VAR estimated in levels. Exercise 4 shows you how to perform innovation accounting on the error-correction model.

Illustrating the Engle-Granger Methodology

The file labeled COINT1.PRN contains 100 values of three simulated variables. The three variables y, z, and w were constructed so as to be $CI(1, 1)$. Suppose you do not know the true data-generating process and want to use the Engle-Granger methodology to test for cointegration. Sample program 1 (found on the file COINT1.PRG and discussed in detail in the next section) illustrates the essential steps.

The first step is to pretest the variables in order to determine their order of integration. If the data happened to be quarterly, it would be natural to perform the augmented Dickey-Fuller tests using lag lengths that are multiples of 4 (i.e., $p = 4, 8, ...$). For each series, the results of the Dickey-Fuller test and the augmented test using four lags are reported in Table 6.1. Sample program 1 (COINT1.PRG) uses the DFUNIT.SRC procedure to perform these unit-root tests.

Table 6.1
Estimates of α_1 and the Associated t-statistics

	no lags	4 lags
Δy_t	-0.01995 (-0.74157)	-0.02691 (-1.0465)
Δz_t	-0.02069 (-0.99213)	-0.25841 (-1.1437)
Δw_t	-0.03501 (-1.9078)	-0.03747 (-1.9335)

The 95% critical value of the Dickey-Fuller test is -2.89. Since all t-statistics are well below this critical value, we cannot reject the null hypothesis of a unit root in any of the series. Of course, if the data were not simulated, it would be important to perform the various diagnostics checks involved with unit root tests.

Since all three variables are presumed to be jointly determined, the long-run equilibrium regression can be estimated using either y_t, z_t or w_t as the left-hand-side variable. The next step is to use LINREG to estimate the long-run relationship and save the residuals; these residuals are the equilibrium errors. The three estimated long-run relationship (with t-values in parentheses) are:

$$y_t = -0.4843 - 0.9273z_t + 0.97687w_t + e_{yt} \qquad (6.13)$$
$$(-0.5751)\ (-38.095)\ \ (53.462)$$

$$z_t = -0.0589 - 1.0108y_t + 1.02549w_t + e_{zt} \qquad (6.14)$$
$$(-0.6709)\ (-38.095)\ \ (65.323)$$

$$w_t = -0.0852 + 0.9901y_t + 0.95347z_t + e_{wt} \qquad (6.15)$$
$$(-1.0089)\ (52.462)\ \ (65.462)$$

The essence of the test is to determine whether the residuals from the equilibrium regression are stationary. Again, in performing the test, there is no presumption that any one of the three residual series is preferable to any of the others. By using each of the three series to test for a unit root in the equilibrium errors, the estimated values of a_1 are reported in Table 6.2.

Table 6.2
Estimated a_1 and the Associated t-statistic

	no lags	4 lags
Δe_{yt}	-0.44301	-0.59525
	(-5.17489)	(-4.0741)
Δe_{zt}	-0.45195	-0.59344
	(-5.37882)	(-4.2263)
Δe_{wt}	-0.45525	-0.60711
	(-5.3896)	(-4.2247)

Engle and Yoo (1987) report the critical value of the t-statistic as -3.93. Hence, using any one of the three equilibrium regressions, we can conclude that the series are cointegrated of order (1, 1). Fortunately, all three equilibrium regressions yield this same conclusion.

Step 3 entails estimating the error-correction model. Consider the first-order system shown with t-statistics in parentheses:

$$\Delta y_t = 0.0055 - 0.4196\hat{e}_{yt\text{-}1} + 0.186\Delta y_{t\text{-}1} + 0.317\Delta z_{t\text{-}1} - 0.366\Delta w_{t\text{-}1} + \epsilon_{yt}$$
$$\quad\quad (0.172)\quad (\text{-}2.73)\quad\quad (1.12)\quad\quad\quad (1.949)\quad\quad\quad (\text{-}2.255)$$

$$\Delta z_t = \text{-}0.0423 + 0.0087\hat{e}_{yt\text{-}1} + 0.120\Delta y_{t\text{-}1} + 0.227\Delta z_{t\text{-}1} - 0.284\Delta w_{t\text{-}1} + \epsilon_{zt}$$
$$\quad\quad (\text{-}1.118)\quad (0.048)\quad\quad (0.617)\quad\quad\quad (1.188)\quad\quad\quad (\text{-}1.485)$$

$$\Delta w_t = \text{-}0.0397 + 0.1225\hat{e}_{yt\text{-}1} + 0.133\Delta y_{t\text{-}1} + 0.272\Delta z_{t\text{-}1} - 0.397\Delta w_{t\text{-}1} + \epsilon_{wt}$$
$$\quad\quad (\text{-}0.897)\quad (\text{-}0.580)\quad\quad (0.581)\quad\quad\quad (1.212)\quad\quad\quad (\text{-}1.773)$$

where $\hat{e}_{yt\text{-}1}$ is the lagged value of the residual from (6.13).

These three equations comprise a first-order VAR augmented with the single error-correction term $\hat{e}_{yt\text{-}1}$. As shown in sample program 1, the estimation is easily performed by using a SYSTEM-END(SYSTEM) block of instructions. Again, there is an area of ambiguity since the residuals from any of the "equilibrium" relationships could have been used in the estimation. The signs of the speed of adjustment coefficients are in accord with convergence towards the long-run equilibrium. In response to a positive discrepancy in $e_{yt\text{-}1}$ both z_t and w_t tend to increase while y_t tends to decrease. The error-correction term, however, is significant only in the first equation.

Sample Programs

1. **The Engle-Granger method for three simulated series**: The following program uses the 100 observations of three simulated variables found on the file COINT1.PRN. The three variables y, z, and w were constructed so as to be $CI(1,1)$. As discussed in the last section, the Engle-Granger methodology is used to (1) check each variable for a unit root, (2) decompose the forecast error variances, (3) determine whether the variables are cointegrated, and (iv) estimate the error-correction model. The complete program is on the file labeled COINT1.PRG and all of the output can be found on the file labeled COINT1.OUT:

```
cal 1971 1 4                ;*  Allocate space for 100 observations using
all 4 1995:4                ;*     artificial dates 1971:Q1 through 1995:Q4.
open data a:coint1.prn      ;* Modify this line if the data disk is not in drive a:\ .
data(format=prn,org=obs) / y z w
table / y z w               ;* Produce summary statistics for y, z and w.
```

Series	Obs	Mean	Std Error	Minimum	Maximum
Y	100	-4.2810734000	1.4148611864	-6.3307000000	-1.2512500000
Z	100	-2.1437338400	1.7951178291	-5.7040600000	0.6257030000
W	100	-6.3677950000	2.3914378059	-9.6848400000	-1.4460500000

* Next create a graph of the three series using:
graph(key=upright,style=symbols,patterns) 3
 # y
 # z
 # w

Figure 6.2: Three Cointegrated Series

/*The graph gives
the strong
impression that
each series is non-
stationary. The
mean of each
series seems to
meander. Next,
test each series for
a unit root using
DFUNIT.SRC.
Use no lags and
four lags. Compile
the procedure
using:
*/

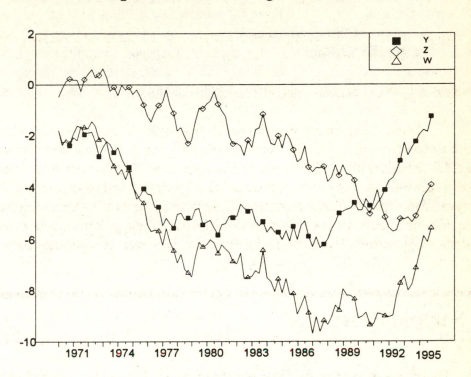

source(noecho) c:\rats\dfunit.src   ;* Modify this line if DFUNIT.SRC is not on c:\rats.

@dfunit(ttest) y
```
        Dickey-Fuller Test with  0 Lags = -0.83249
```
@dfunit(ttest) z
```
        Dickey-Fuller Test with  0 Lags = -0.99213
```
@dfunit(ttest) w
```
        Dickey-Fuller Test with  0 Lags = -1.90781
```
@dfunit(ttest,lags=4) y
```
        Dickey-Fuller Test with  4 Lags = -1.04650
```
@dfunit(ttest,lags=4) z
```
        Dickey-Fuller Test with  4 Lags = -1.14373
```
@dfunit(ttest,lags=4) w
```
        Dickey-Fuller Test with  4 Lags = -1.93350
```

/* The *t*-statistics are all less than the Dickey-Fuller critical values; conclude that all three series
have unit roots. Based on the plots of the series, there is no need to include a trend in the Dickey-
Fuller tests. Tests with other lag lengths yield the identical conclusion. Conclude that all are $I(1)$
and take first differences:
*/

```
diff y / dy                        ;* Take first differences of each variable.
diff z / dz
diff w / dw
```

/*   Exercise 4 at the end of this chapter shows you how to perform innovation accounting on
an error-correction model. The next portion of COINT1.PRG obtains the variance
decompositions of the variables estimated in levels (not first differences). If the variables are
cointegrated, the VAR in first differences in misspecified since the error-correction term is absent.
Towards this end, the next portion of COINT1.PRG determines lag length using the AIC, SBC,
and likelihood ratio tests. Be aware that the likelihood ratio tests are being conducted on
nonstationary variables.
*/

```
system 1 to 3              ;* Set up a VAR of y, z, and w using four lags of each variable.
variables y z w
lags 1 to 4
det constant              ;* Include a constant.
end(system)
estimate(noprint,noftests,outsigma=v) / 1
```

/*   The ESTIMATE instruction saves the residuals in series 1 through 3. Note that v is the
variance/covariance matrix. There are three equations with four lags of each variable plus a
constant in each. Hence, $N = 39$. The multivariate AIC and SBC are calculated using:
*/

```
compute aic = %nobs * %logdet + 2*39
compute sbc = %nobs * %logdet + 39*log(%nobs)
display 'aic = ' aic 'sbc = ' sbc
        aic = -701.57949  sbc = -601.56991
```

* Next set up the model using only two lags of each variable:

```
system 1 to 3
variables y z w
lags 1 to 2
det constant
end(system)
estimate(noprint,noftests,outsigma=v) 72:1 95:4 4
```

/*   The ESTIMATE instruction estimates the model over the same sample period using only
two lags of each variable. The residuals are saved in series 4 through 6. Again, v is the
variance/covariance matrix. Next, compute the AIC and SBC. Now there are only 21 parameters
estimated in the system.
*/

```
compute aic = %nobs * %logdet + 2*21
compute sbc = %nobs * %logdet + 21*log(%nobs)
display 'aic = ' aic 'sbc = ' sbc
        aic = -722.39152 sbc = -668.54020
```

/* Both the AIC and SBC select the model using only two lags. The likelihood ratio test has 18
degrees of freedom (two lags of each of the three variables are omitted from each equation). The
small sample correction is 13 since the unrestricted equations have 13 parameters. Perform the
likelihood ratio test using:
*/

ratio(degrees=18,mcorr=13) 72:1 95:4
 # 1 2 3
 # 4 5 6

```
Log Determinants are  -8.120620e+000  -7.962412e+000
Chi-Squared(18)=       13.131270 with Significance Level 0.78371628
```

* You can safely conclude that lags 3 and 4 can be eliminated. Now, reestimate the model over
* the longest sample period possible and obtain the *F*-statistics for the Granger-causality tests:

```
system 1 to 3
variables y z w
lags 1 to 2
det constant
end(system)
estimate(noprint,outsigma=v) / 1
```

/* To conserve space, the Granger causality tests are shown only on the file COINT1.OUT. If
you examine this file, you can verify that z and w Granger-cause y. However, at conventional
significance levels, both z and w are not Granger-caused by the other variables in the system.
Next, the variance decompositions are obtained as in a standard VAR. The ordering of the
variables is such that y_t contemporaneously affects z_t and w_t, and z_t contemporaneously affects w_t.
Notice that the proportion of the forecast error variance of the $\{y_t\}$ sequence explained by the
$\{z_t\}$ sequence strongly increases as the forecast horizon increases.
*/

errors 3 24 v ;* Obtain the variance decompositions. Note that the IMPULSES option is
 # 1   ;*   not needed here.
 # 2
 # 3

```
Decomposition of Variance for Series Y
Step  Std Error        Y          Z          W
 1    0.283216979  100.00000    0.00000    0.00000
 4    0.497755006   85.72609    6.60884    7.66507
 8    0.759654546   70.25862   16.58693   13.15445
24    1.440049218   47.24319   41.73571   11.02110

Decomposition of Variance for Series Z
Step  Std Error        Y          Z          W
 1    0.350457694    0.34351   99.65649    0.00000
 4    0.665910673    1.81894   97.51729    0.66377
 8    0.854995380    1.19835   98.33293    0.46873
24    1.102383281   11.53004   84.24114    4.22881

Decomposition of Variance for Series W
Step  Std Error        Y          Z          W
 1    0.393402712   33.19136   44.93660   21.87204
 4    0.639216880   32.66358   51.80057   15.53585
 8    0.843777670   43.64620   38.91563   17.43817
24    1.563889805   58.93104   22.15978   18.90917
```

*/   Next, perform the Engle-Granger test for cointegration using the *y* as the left-hand-side
variable. Save the residuals as *residy*. There is an ambiguity since any of the three variables can
be the so-called dependent variable in the equilibrium regression.
*/

linreg y / residy   ;* Estimate the long-run equilibrium relationship.
 # constant z w

Coefficient	Estimate	Standard Error	t-statistic	Significance Level
Constant	−0.048430908	0.084219816	−0.57505	0.56658652
Z	−0.927310591	0.024341969	−38.09513	0.00000000
W	0.976876546	0.018272147	53.46260	0.00000000

* Now check the residuals for the presence of a unit root. If the results are ambiguous, it would
* be desirable to reestimate the long-run relationship without the constant (since the intercept is
* insignificant) and to use other left-hand-side variables.

diff residy / dresidy   ;* Obtain the first difference of the *residy*.

linreg dresidy   ;* Perform the Dickey-Fuller test of the residuals. DO NOT USE
 # residy{1}   ;* DFUNIT.SRC since it necessarily includes a constant.

Coefficient	Estimate	Standard Error	t-statistic	Significance Level
RESIDY{1}	−0.443011608	0.085607716	−5.17490	0.00000121

* Now perform an augmented Dickey-Fuller test of the residuals using four lags:
linreg dresidy
 # residy{1} dresidy{1 to 4}

Coefficient	Estimate	Standard Error	t-statistic	Significance Level
RESIDY{1}	-0.595254462	0.146104532	-4.07417	0.00009927
DRESIDY{1}	0.286121321	0.138733429	2.06238	0.04205390
DRESIDY{2}	0.054085456	0.128136543	0.42209	0.67396420
DRESIDY{3}	0.077239732	0.114310862	0.67570	0.50096432
DRESIDY{4}	0.041108447	0.106308490	0.38669	0.69989837

/* The Dickey-Fuller and augmented Dickey-Fuller tests yield t-statistics of -5.17490 and -4.07417, respectively. The critical values at the 5% and 1% significance levels (see page 158) are -3.93 and -4.45, respectively. (*Note*: You should repeat the augmented test using only one lag.) Conclude that the residuals do not contain a unit root so that the three variables are cointegrated of order (1, 1). As an exercise, you should repeat the analysis using z_t and/or w_t as the "dependent" variable in the equilibrium relationship. Next, set up the error-correction model. */

```
system 1 to 3
variables dy dz dw
lags 1                        ;* Use only one lag of dy, dz, and dw.
det constant residy{1}        ;* Include a constant and the error-correction term.  You can
end(system)                   ;*    use the residuals from the other two equilibrium relations.
estimate(outsigma=v) / 1      ;* Estimate the model and call v the variance/covariance matrix.
```

Dependent Variable DY - Estimation by Least Squares

Coefficient	Estimate	Standard Error	t-statistic	Significance Level
DY{1}	0.186130579	0.166298222	1.11926	0.26591266
DZ{1}	0.317153335	0.162753909	1.94867	0.05434920
DW{1}	-0.366281309	0.162416586	-2.25520	0.02646647
Constant	0.005509065	0.032121776	0.17151	0.86419883
RESIDY{1}	-0.419601220	0.153361286	-2.73603	0.00744857

Dependent Variable DZ - Estimation by Least Squares

Coefficient	Estimate	Standard Error	t-statistic	Significance Level
DY{1}	0.120899631	0.195891283	0.61718	0.53862600
DZ{1}	0.227766848	0.191716254	1.18804	0.23784231
DW{1}	-0.284176102	0.191318902	-1.48535	0.14083230
Constant	-0.042299565	0.037837902	-1.11792	0.26648274
RESIDY{1}	-0.008659560	0.180652196	-0.04793	0.96187085

Dependent Variable DW - Estimation by Least Squares

Coefficient	Estimate	Standard Error	t-statistic	Significance Level
DY{1}	0.133078997	0.229176160	0.58068	0.56285775
DZ{1}	0.271860147	0.224291731	1.21208	0.22855110
DW{1}	-0.396952119	0.223826864	-1.77348	0.07942294
Constant	-0.039697834	0.044267132	-0.89678	0.37215242
RESIDY{1}	0.122531715	0.211347723	0.57976	0.56347596

If we use only one lagged change, the *t*-statistics are equivalent to the displayed *F*-tests for Granger-causality. Again, $\{z_t\}$ and $\{w_t\}$ are not significantly affected by lagged values of the other variables in the system. Note that *residy{1}* is significant only in the dy_t equation. The implication is that only the $\{y_t\}$ series adjusts to deviations from long-run equilibrium.

2. Cointegtation and the term structure: The theory of the term structure of interest rates implies that short-term and long-term interest rates bear an equilibrium relationship. After all, short-term rates cannot continually drift away from long-term rates. The file labeled US.PRN contains the three month T-bill rate (*tbill*), and the 3-year and 10-year rates on government bonds (*r3* and *r10*). The data runs from 1960:1 through 1991:4. The first four lines of COINT2.PRG read these rates from the file US.PRN:

```
cal 60 1 4
all 10 91:4
open data a:\us.prn                    ;* Modify this line if the data is not in drive a:\ .
data(format=prn,org=obs) / tbill r3 r10
```

* Figure 6.3 was created using the following GRAPH instruction:
graph(key=upright,style=symbols,patterns) 3
 # tbill
 # r3
 # r10

Figure 6.3: Three Interest Rates

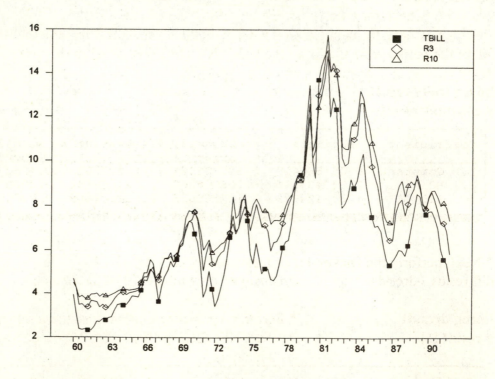

/* Notice that each series bears a strong relationship to the other two. It may be that each bilateral pair is cointegrated. If so, there will be multiple cointegrating vectors. Suppose that in the long run:

$$tbill_t + \beta_1 r3_t = 0$$
$$tbill_t + \beta_2 r10_t = 0$$
and:
$$r3_t + \beta_3 r10_t = 0.$$

As such, there will be multiple linear combinations of *tbill, r3*, and *r10* that are stationary. Next, check each series for a unit root using DFUNIT.SRC. The first set of tests use no lags and the next set assumes four lags.
*/

```
source(noecho) c:\rats\dfunit.src      ;* Modify this line if DFUNIT.SRC is not in drive c:\rats
@dfunit(ttest) tbill
        Dickey-Fuller Test with  0 Lags =  -1.84935
@dfunit(ttest) r3
        Dickey-Fuller Test with  0 Lags =  -1.55412
@dfunit(ttest) r10
        Dickey-Fuller Test with  0 Lags =  -1.38446


* Now use four lags
@dfunit(ttest,lags=4) tbill
        Dickey-Fuller Test with  4 Lags =  -2.21122
@dfunit(ttest,lags=4)  r3
        Dickey-Fuller Test with  4 Lags =  -1.99020
@dfunit(ttest,lags=4)  r10
        Dickey-Fuller Test with  4 Lags =  -1.90275
```

/* The *t*-statistics are all less than the Dickey-Fuller critical values. Conclude that all have unit roots. Next, estimate the long-run equilibrium relationship among the three rates treating *tbill* as the left-hand-side variable and saving the residuals as *resids1*. As an exercise, you should:

   1. Check for cointegration among the bilateral pairs.
   2. Check for cointegration among the three variables using other left-hand-side variables.
All of the output from the following LINREG instruction is contained in the file COINT2.OUT.
*/

linreg tbill / resid1
 # constant r3 r10

Coefficient		Estimate	Standard Error	t-statistic	Significance Level
1.	Constant	0.050882429	0.145308521	0.35017	0.72680178
2.	R3	2.253485316	0.105706307	21.31836	0.00000000
3.	R10	-1.344124039	0.107563623	-12.49608	0.00000000

```
* Next, perform the Dickey-Fuller test on the resid1 series:
diff resid1 / dresid1               ;* Obtain the first difference of the residuals.


linreg dresid1                      ;* Perform the Dickey-Fuller test of the residuals.  Do not use
# resid1{1}                         ;*    DFUNIT.SRC or PPUNIT.SRC since they necessarily include
                                    ;*    an intercept.
```

Coefficient	Estimate	Standard Error	t-statistic	Significance Level
1. RESID1{1}	-0.317528430	0.067137334	-4.72954	0.00000593

* Now, use four lagged changes:
linreg dresid1   ;* Perform the augmented Dickey-Fuller test using four lags.
 # resid1{1} dresid1{1 to 4}

Coefficient	Estimate	Standard Error	t-statistic	Significance Level
1. RESID1{1}	-0.418691045	0.091680121	-4.56687	0.00001224
2. DRESID1{1}	0.271754711	0.102834263	2.64265	0.00934231
3. DRESID1{2}	-0.094825790	0.103189750	-0.91895	0.35999855
4. DRESID1{3}	0.168750323	0.091585715	1.84254	0.06790649
5. DRESID1{4}	0.193131566	0.092316265	2.09206	0.03857693

* The *t*-values from the two tests (-4.72954 and -4.56687) are such that the null hypothesis of a
* unit root can be rejected. Conclude that the three series are cointegrated. Prepare to estimate
* the error-correction model by taking the first difference of each series using:

diff tbill / dtbill
diff r3 / dr3
diff r10 / dr10

/* Set up a three-variable VAR including the error-correction term. Use four lags of each
variable. At this stage, the output from the ESTIMATE instruction is unnecessary. Use the
NOPRINT and NOFTESTS options to suppress the printing. Use the OUTSIGMA= option to
calculate the variance/covariance matrix and save the residuals in series 1 through 3.
*/
system 1 to 3
variables dtbill dr3 dr10
lags 1 to 4
det constant resid1{1}
end(system)
estimate(noprint,noftests,outsigma=v) / 1

* Compute the AIC and SBC noting that 42 parameters are estimated in the model:
compute aic = %nobs * %logdet + 2*42
compute sbc = %nobs * %logdet + 42*log(%nobs)
display 'aic = ' aic 'sbc = ' sbc
       aic = -764.05363 sbc = -645.94188

* To determine whether two lags are sufficient, estimate the model over the same sample period.
system 1 to 3
variables dtbill dr3 dr10
lags 1 to 2
det constant resid1{1}
end(system)
estimate(noprint,noftests,outsigma=v) 61:2 91:4 4

* With only 24 coefficient estimates, the AIC and SBC strongly select the model with two lags:
compute aic = %nobs * %logdet + 2*24
compute sbc = %nobs * %logdet + 24*log(%nobs)
display 'aic = ' aic 'sbc = ' sbc
```
        aic = -774.62345 sbc = -707.13103
```

* The likelihood ratio test has 18 degrees of freedom and a small sample correction of 14 (the
* equations in the unrestricted model contain 14 parameters):
ratio(degrees=18,mcorr=14) 61:2 91:4
 # 1 2 3
 # 4 5 6

```
Log Determinants are -6.894745e+000 -6.687996e+000
Chi-Squared(18)=      22.535680 with Significance Level 0.20906809
```

* Conclude that lags 3 and 4 can be eliminated. To determine whether one lag is sufficient, use:
system 1 to 3
variables dtbill dr3 dr10
lags 1
det constant resid1{1}
end(system)
estimate(noprint,noftests,outsigma=v) 61:2 91:4 1

* Since the model contains 15 parameters, the AIC and SBC are calculated as:
compute aic = %nobs * %logdet + 2*15
compute sbc = %nobs * %logdet + 15*log(%nobs)
display 'aic = ' aic 'sbc = ' sbc
```
        aic = -759.71467 sbc = -717.53191
```

/* The AIC selects the model with two lags and the SBC selects the model with one lag. To
perform the likelihood ratio test, note that there are nine degrees of freedom (one lag of each
variable in each equation) and a small sample correction of 8:
*/

ratio(degrees=9,mcorr=8) 61:2 91:4
 # 1 2 3
 # 4 5 6

```
Log Determinants are -6.420444e+000 -6.687996e+000
Chi-Squared(9)=      30.768374 with Significance Level 0.00032437
```

/* Reject the null hypothesis of one lag. Although the SBC is in conflict with the AIC and
likelihood ratio test, it seems wise to proceed with the two-lag model. To estimate the model
over the full sample period, use:
*/

```
system 1 to 3
variables dtbill dr3 dr10
lags 1 to 2
det constant resid1{1}
end(system)
```
estimate /

Coefficient	Estimate	Standard Error	t-statistic	Significance Level
1. DTBILL{1}	-0.003851440	0.224642498	-0.01714	0.98635034
2. DTBILL{2}	-0.157634727	0.221785118	-0.71075	0.47865095
3. DR3{1}	0.360325356	0.573140279	0.62869	0.53078000
4. DR3{2}	-0.279476717	0.563538519	-0.49593	0.62087279
5. DR10{1}	-0.078770214	0.558558159	-0.14102	0.88809335
6. DR10{2}	0.060787189	0.547364680	0.11105	0.91176359
7. Constant	0.018041247	0.076130035	0.23698	0.81308723
8. RESID1{1}	0.258267992	0.183923583	1.40421	0.16290426

F-Tests, Dependent Variable DTBILL

Variable	F-Statistic	Signif
DTBILL	0.2602	0.7713333
DR3	0.3863	0.6804094
DR10	0.0162	0.9839073

Coefficient	Estimate	Standard Error	t-statistic	Significance Level
1. DTBILL{1}	-0.149375025	0.176995366	-0.84395	0.40042027
2. DTBILL{2}	0.014137228	0.174744042	0.08090	0.93565773
3. DR3{1}	0.362100609	0.451576057	0.80186	0.42425978
4. DR3{2}	-0.605750444	0.444010850	-1.36427	0.17510127
5. DR10{1}	0.025149431	0.440086834	0.05715	0.95452596
6. DR10{2}	0.508717693	0.431267515	1.17959	0.24055736
7. Constant	0.010065258	0.059982699	0.16780	0.86702821
8. RESID1{1}	0.474512172	0.144913015	3.27446	0.00139267

F-Tests, Dependent Variable DR3

Variable	F-Statistic	Signif
DTBILL	0.3873	0.6797253
DR3	1.4867	0.2303594
DR10	0.6969	0.5001875

Coefficient	Estimate	Standard Error	t-statistic	Significance Level
1. DTBILL{1}	-0.086195823	0.130802872	-0.65898	0.51120665
2. DTBILL{2}	-0.049313563	0.129139102	-0.38186	0.70325498
3. DR3{1}	0.202209369	0.333723117	0.60592	0.54574186
4. DR3{2}	-0.343834711	0.328132288	-1.04785	0.29686572
5. DR10{1}	0.108340117	0.325232367	0.33312	0.73964288
6. DR10{2}	0.427008294	0.318714726	1.33978	0.18291262
7. Constant	0.017109094	0.044328332	0.38596	0.70022503
8. RESID1{1}	0.384645371	0.107093418	3.59168	0.00048161

F-Tests, Dependent Variable DR10

Variable	F-Statistic	Signif
DTBILL	0.2506	0.7787812
DR3	0.8689	0.4221008
DR10	0.9498	0.3897883

/* Notice that the *F*-tests suggest that no variable is affected by lagged changes in the others. However, the error-correction term is significant in the *dr3$_t$* and *dr10$_t$* equations. Each of these variables adjusts to a deviation from long-run equilibrium. Innovation accounting can be performed using the method shown in Exercise 4 at the end of this chapter.
*/

The Johansen Methodology

Although the Engle and Granger (1987) procedure is easily implemented, it does have several important limitations. The estimation of the long-run equilibrium regression requires that the researcher place one variable on the left-hand side and use the others as regressors. In practice, it is possible to find that one regression indicates the variables are cointegrated whereas reversing the order indicates no cointegration. This is a very undesirable feature of the procedure since the test for cointegration should be invariant to the choice of the variable selected for normalization. Moreover, in tests using three or more variables, we know that there may be more than one cointegrating vector. The method has no systematic procedure for the separate estimation of the multiple cointegrating vectors.

Another limitation of the Engle-Granger procedure is that it relies on a **two-step** estimator. The first-step is to generate the error-series $\{\hat{e}_t\}$ and the second-step uses these generated errors to estimate a regression of the form $\Delta\hat{e}_t = a_1\hat{e}_{t-1} + \dots$. Thus, the coefficient a_1 is obtained by estimating a regression using the residuals from another regression. Hence, any error introduced by the researcher in Step 1 is carried into Step 2. Fortunately, the Johansen (1988) maximum likelihood estimators circumvent the use of two-step estimators *and* can estimate and test for the presence of multiple cointegrating vectors. Moreover, the tests allows the researcher to test restricted versions of the cointegrating vector(s) and the speed of adjustment parameters.

Reconsider the *n*-variable first-order VAR given by (6.3): $x_t = A_1 x_{t-1} + \epsilon_t$. Subtract x_{t-1} from each side to obtain:

$$\Delta x_t = A_1 x_{t-1} - x_{t-1} + \epsilon_t$$
$$= (A_1 - I)x_{t-1} + \epsilon_t$$
$$= \pi x_{t-1} + \epsilon_t$$

where x_t and ϵ_t are ($n \times 1$) vectors; A_1 is an ($n \times n$) matrix of parameters; I is an ($n \times n$) identity matrix; and π is defined to be ($A_1 - I$).

The rank of π equals the number of cointegrating vectors. There are several ways to generalize the model:

1. The equation is easily modified to allow for the presence of a drift term; simply let:

$$\Delta x_t = A_0 + \pi x_{t-1} + \epsilon_t$$

where A_0 is a $(n \times 1)$ vector of constants $(a_{01}, a_{02}, \dots, a_{0n})'$.

The effect of including the various a_{0i} is to allow for a linear time trend in the data-generating process. You would want to include the drift term if the variables exhibited a decided tendency to increase or decrease. Here, the rank of π can be viewed as the number of cointegrating relationships existing in the "detrended" data. Suppose that the rank of $\pi = 1$ so there is exactly one cointegrating vector. In this case, each $\{\Delta x_{it}\}$ sequence has an expected value of a_{i0} if $\pi_{11}x_{1t-1} + \pi_{12}x_{2t-1} + \dots + \pi_{1n}x_{nt-1} = 0$.

Additionally, seasonal dummy variables can be appended to the model such that:

$$\Delta x_t = A_0 + \pi x_{t-1} + \Psi D_t + \epsilon_t$$

where Ψ is an $(n \times (f\text{-}1))$ matrix of parameters, D_t is an $((f\text{-}1) \times 1)$ matrix of seasonal dummy variables, and f is the declared *frequency* on the CALENDAR statement. Thus, there are three seasonal dummy variables and an intercept using quarterly data. **Note: This is the only form of model that the JOHANSEN.400 procedure can estimate**.

2. An intercept can be included in the cointegrating vector. Consider an $n+1$ variable system but let all values of x_{n+1} equal unity (i.e., $x_{n+1,1} = 1$, $x_{n+1,2} = 1$, ...) so that:

$$\Delta x_t = \pi^* x_{t-1}^* + \epsilon_t$$

where $x_t = (x_t, x_{2t}, \dots, x_{nt})'$, $x_{t-1}^* = (x_{1t-1}, x_{2t-1}, \dots, x_{nt-1}, 1)'$,

and
$$\pi^* = \begin{bmatrix} \pi_{11} & \pi_{12} & \cdots & \pi_{1n} & \pi_{10} \\ \pi_{21} & \pi_{22} & \cdots & \pi_{2n} & \pi_{20} \\ . & . & \cdots & . & . \\ \pi_{n1} & \pi_{n2} & \cdots & \pi_{nn} & \pi_{n0} \end{bmatrix}$$

Here the cointegrating vectors have the form:

$$\pi_{11}x_{1t} + \pi_{12}x_{2t} + \pi_{13}x_{3t} + \dots + \pi_{1n}x_{1n} + \pi_{10} = 0$$
$$\pi_{21}x_{1t} + \pi_{22}x_{2t} + \pi_{23}x_{3t} + \dots + \pi_{2n}x_{1n} + \pi_{20} = 0$$
...

3. The multivariate model can also be generalized to allow for a higher-order autoregressive process. Consider:

$$\Delta x_t = \sum_{i=1}^{p-1} \pi_i \Delta x_{t-i} + \pi x_{t-p} + \epsilon_t$$

Again, the key feature is rank of the matrix π; the rank of π is equal to the number of independent cointegrating vectors.

The number of distinct cointegrating vectors can be obtained by checking the significance of the characteristic roots of π. We know that the rank of a matrix is equal to the number of its characteristic roots that differ from zero. Suppose we obtained the matrix π and ordered the n characteristic roots such that $\lambda_1 > \lambda_2 > ... > \lambda_n$. If the variables in x_t are *not* cointegrated, the rank of π is zero and all of these characteristic roots will equal unity. Since $\ln(1) = 0$, each of the expressions $\ln(1 - \lambda_i)$ will equal zero if the variables are not cointegrated. Similarly, if the rank of π is to unity, the first expression $\ln(1 - \lambda_1)$ will be negative and all the other expressions are such that $\ln(1 - \lambda_2) = \ln(1 - \lambda_3) = ... = \ln(1 - \lambda_n) = 0$.

In practice, we can obtain only estimates of π and its characteristic roots. The test for the number of characteristic roots that are insignificantly different from unity can be conducted using the following test two statistics:

$$\lambda_{\text{trace}}(r) = -T \sum_{i=r+1}^{n} \ln(1 - \hat{\lambda}_i)$$

$$\lambda_{\text{max}}(r, r+1) = -T \ln(1 - \hat{\lambda}_{r+1})$$

where $\hat{\lambda}_i$ are the estimated values of the characteristic roots (also called eigenvalues) obtained from the estimated π matrix; and T is the number of usable observations. When the appropriate values of r are clear, these statistics are simply referred to as λ_{trace} and λ_{max}.

The first statistic tests the null hypothesis that the number of distinct cointegrating vectors is less than or equal to r against a general alternative. From the previous discussion, it should be clear that λ_{trace} equals zero when all $\lambda_i = 0$. The further the estimated characteristic roots are from zero, the larger the λ_{trace} statistic. The second statistic tests the null that the number of cointegrating vectors is r against the alternative of $r+1$ cointegrating vectors. Again, if the estimated value of the characteristic root is close to zero, λ_{max} will be small.

Osterwald-Lenum (1992) refines the critical values of the λ_{trace} and λ_{max} statistics originally calculated by Johansen and Juselius (1990) in their Monte Carlo analysis. The distribution of these statistics depends on:

1. The number of nonstationary components under the null hypothesis (i.e., $n - r$)

2. The form of the vector A_0. There are separate critical values for models with a drift term, a constant in the cointegrating vector, intervention dummy variables, and models without any deterministic elements.

One of the most interesting aspects of the Johansen procedure is that it allows for testing restricted forms of the cointegrating vector(s). The key insight to all such hypothesis tests is that *if there are r cointegrating vectors, only these r linear combinations of the variables are stationary*. All other linear combinations are nonstationary. Thus, suppose you reestimate the model restricting the parameters of π. If the restrictions are not binding, you should find that the number of cointegrating vectors has *not* diminished.

To test for the presence of an intercept in the cointegrating vector as opposed to the unrestricted drift A_0, estimate the two forms of the model. Denote the ordered characteristic roots of unrestricted π matrix by $\hat{\lambda}_1, \hat{\lambda}_2, \ldots, \hat{\lambda}_n$ and the characteristic roots of the model with the intercept(s) in the cointegrating vector(s) by $\hat{\lambda}_1^*, \ldots, \hat{\lambda}_n^*$. Suppose that the unrestricted form of the model has r nonzero characteristic roots. Asymptotically, the statistic:

$$-T \sum_{i=r+1}^{n} [\ln(1 - \hat{\lambda}_i^*) - \ln(1 - \hat{\lambda}_i)]$$

has a χ^2 distribution with $(n - r)$ degrees of freedom.

The intuition behind the test is that all values of $\ln(1 - \hat{\lambda}_i^*)$ and $\ln(1 - \hat{\lambda}_i)$ should be equivalent if the restriction is not binding. Hence, small values for the test statistic imply that it is permissible to include the intercept in the cointegrating vector. However, the likelihood of finding a stationary linear combination of the n variables is greater with the intercept in the cointegrating vector than if the intercept is absent from the cointegrating vector. Thus, a large value of $\hat{\lambda}_{r+1}^*$ [and a corresponding large value of $-T \ln(1 - \hat{\lambda}_{r+1}^*)$] implies that the restriction artificially inflates the number of cointegrating vectors. Thus, as proven by Johansen (1991), if the test statistic is sufficiently large, it is possible to reject the null hypothesis of an intercept in the cointegrating vector(s) and conclude that there is a linear trend in the variables.

In order to test other restrictions on the cointegrating vector, Johansen defines the two matrices α and β both of dimension $(n \times r)$ where r is the rank of π. The properties of α and β are such that:

$$\pi = \alpha \beta'$$

The matrix β is the matrix of cointegrating parameters and the matrix α is the matrix of weights with which each cointegrating vector enters the n equations of the VAR. In a sense, α can be viewed as the matrix of the speed of adjustment parameters. Due to the cross-equation restrictions, it is not possible to estimate α and β using OLS. However, if you use maximum likelihood estimation, it is possible to (1) estimate the error-correction model; (2) determine the rank of π; (3) use the r most significant cointegrating vectors to form β'; and (4) select α such that $\pi = \alpha\beta'$.

Once α and β' are determined, testing various restrictions on α and β' is straightforward if you remember the fundamental point: if there are r cointegrating vectors, only these r linear combinations of the variables are stationary. Thus, the test statistics involve comparing the number of cointegrating vectors under the null and alternative hypotheses. Again, let $\hat{\lambda}_1, \hat{\lambda}_2, \dots ,$ $\hat{\lambda}_n$ and $\hat{\lambda}_1^*, \dots , \hat{\lambda}_n^*$ denote the ordered characteristic roots of the unrestricted and restricted models, respectively. To test restrictions on β, form the test statistic:

$$T \sum_{i=1}^{r} [\, \ln(1 - \hat{\lambda}_i^*) - \ln(1 - \hat{\lambda}_i) \,]$$

Asymptotically, this statistic has a χ^2 distribution with degrees of freedom equal to the number of restrictions placed on β. Large values of $\hat{\lambda}_i^*$ relative to $\hat{\lambda}_i$ (for $i \le r$) imply a reduced number of cointegrating vectors. Hence, the restriction embedded in the null hypothesis is binding if the calculated value of the test statistic exceeds that in a χ^2 table. Restrictions on α can be tested in the same way.

Tests for the number of cointegrating vectors, restrictions on β, and restrictions on α can all be performed using the JOHANSEN.400, and CATS in RATS procedures. CATS in RATS can also test for the presence of the intercept term. You need to download the JOHANSEN.400 procedure from the RATS bulletin board. The phone number is 1-708-864-8816. If you have a new version of RATS (version 4.0) or later, use JOHANSEN.400. JOHANSEN.400 will not work with RATS 3.0; the older JOHANSEN.SRC procedure may still be available for RATS 3.0 users. CATS in RATS is available for purchase directly from Estima.

Although the next section is designed primarily for JOHANSEN.400 users, CATS in RATS users should also read through the section (especially Part 2 concerning hypothesis testing).

Using the Johansen.400 Procedure

An interesting way to illustrate the Johansen methodology is to use exactly the same data as in the Engle-Granger section. Although sample program 1 found that the simulated variables y, z, and w are cointegrated, a comparison of the two procedures is useful.

You compile the JOHANSEN.400 procedure using:

    source(noecho) c:\rats\johansen.400

After compiling, you invoke the procedure using:[1]

@johansen(options) *start end*
 # list of dependent variables

where: *start end*   The range of data to use. The procedure automatically adjusts for
                         lag lengths. Do **not** use the slash (/) to allow RATS to
                         select the default range. (Should you use the slash, RATS
                         can produce errors if you invoke the procedure more than
                         once within the same program.)

list of dependent variables   The variables to include in the cointegration tests.

    The main option is:

LAGS =   The number of lags to use in the VAR. The default is two. Note that you must
            use at least one lag.

    JOHANSEN.400 does not give you any flexibility concerning the form of the deterministic
elements to include in the model. The procedure will automatically include seasonal dummy
variables in the model and will include a drift term. For example, if you use quarterly data, the
procedure will automatically include three seasonal dummy variables and an intercept. *There is
no way to include a constant in the cointegrating relationship.* However, as shown in Enders
(1995, pp. 387-389), appropriately constraining the drift terms is equivalent to including a
constant in the cointegrating vector. As such, the JOHANSEN.400 procedure will yield
reasonable results if, in fact, the constant belongs in the cointegrating vector. As explained on
page 174 above, the form of the estimated model is:

$$\Delta x_t = A_0 + \pi x_{t-1} + \Psi D_t + \epsilon_t$$

where A_0 are the drift terms, and D_t are the seasonal dummy variables.

    The data for this section is found on the file labeled COINT3.PRN; note that the variables

---

[1]   Note that users of JOHANSEN.400 may experience an error message indicating that the 4(5F9.3)
format is not supported. To correct this problem, use a wordprocessor to edit the procedure. Use "SEARCH
and REPLACE" to replace all occurrences of '4(5F9.3)' (including the single quotation marks) with `free`.
All resulting statements in JOHANSEN.400 will read `format=free`. Be sure to save the appropriately
modified procedure as an ASCII text file.

have been renamed y, z, and x. The variable name w is reserved for the JOHANSEN.400 procedure; hence, the third variable is now called x. All program statements and some of the associated output are on the file labeled COINT3.PRG. The first four program statements read the three variables into memory. The fifth line is used to compile JOHANSEN.400:

```
cal 1971 1 4                            ;*  Allocate space for 100 observations using the
all 4 1995:4                            ;*     artificial dates 1971:Q1 through 1995:Q4.
open data a:coint3.prn                   ;* Modify this line if the data set is not on drive a:\.
data(format=prn,org=obs) / y z x
source(noecho) c:\rats\johansen.400  ;* Modify this line if you use JOHANSEN.SRC or if
                                        ;*     the procedure is not on the c:\rats directory.
```

/* It is good practice to pretest all variables to assess their order of integration. Plot the data to see if a linear time trend is likely to be present in the data-generating process. Although forms of the Johansen tests can detect differing orders of integration, it is wise not to mix variables with different orders of integration. As in sample program 1, compile DFUNIT.SRC and perform the univariate unit-root tests. The program statements and output are not reported here since they are precisely those reported in sample program 1.

The results of the Johansen tests can be quite sensitive to the lag length and on the appropriateness of the normality assumption concerning the error terms. The most common procedure to test for lag length is to use the RATIO instruction illustrated in sample program 1. Letting $\sum_r$ and $\sum_u$ denote the covariance matrices from the model with a restricted and unrestricted lag lengths, use:

$$(T\text{-}c)(\log|\textstyle\sum_r| - \log|\textstyle\sum_u|)$$

where: T = number of observations; c = number of parameters in the unrestricted system; and $\log|\sum_i|$ = natural logarithm of the determinant of $\sum_i$. Asymptotically, this statistic has a χ^2 distribution with degrees of freedom equal to the number of coefficient restrictions. Alternately, you can select lag length using the multivariate generalizations of the AIC or SBC.

In sample program 1, a VAR using two lags of the undifferenced data was found to be adequate. Since JOHANSEN.400 procedure uses differenced data, select a lag length of one for the LAGS= option. As you will see shortly, you should be careful about the results of such tests since the estimated residuals may still be correlated.

Next, invoke the procedure using:[1]
*/

---

[1] At this point, the JOHANSEN.400 procedure is menu-driven. As such, the commentary below is not set off by asterisks.

```
@johansen(lags=1) 71:1 95:4
# y z x
```

```
Statistics on Series No Label(8)
Quarterly Data From 1971:02 To 1995:04
Observations    99
Sample Mean     0.00555868687        Variance                0.108170
Standard Error 0.32889230782         SE of Sample Mean       0.033055
t-Statistic         0.16817          Signif Level (Mean=0) 0.86679990
Skewness           -0.20617          Signif Level (Sk=0)   0.40949521
Kurtosis           -0.72382          Signif Level (Ku=0)   0.15603543
```

RATS displays the summary statistics of the *first difference* of each variable; note that the sereis are named only by number. To conserve space, the output is shown here only for the first difference of y; all output can be found on the file COINT3.OUT. The result is identical to that if you were to enter:

diff y / dy
statistics dy

1. Determining the rank of π: Next, RATS reports the estimated values of the characteristic roots. Here the ordered characteristic roots are $\lambda_1 = 0.26247$, $\lambda_2 = 0.10703$, and $\lambda_3 = 0.03573$. The λ_{max} and λ_{trace} statistics are displayed on the next two lines. The form of the output is:

```
Solving the eigenvalue problem and calculating the LR-tests

lambda, lambda-max- and tracetest
   0.26247    0.10703    0.03573
  30.14032   11.20663    3.60231
   3.60231   14.80894   44.94926
```

Table 6.3 shows how to interpret this output. Since 44.94926 exceeds the 95% critical value of the λ_{trace} statistic (in the first panel of Table C, the critical value is 29.68), it is possible to reject the null hypothesis of no cointegrating vectors and accept the alternative of one or more cointegrating vectors. Next, we can use the $\lambda_{trace}(1)$ statistic to test the null of $r \leq 1$ against the alternative of two or three cointegrating vectors. Since the $\lambda_{trace}(1)$ statistic of 14.80894 is less than the 95% critical value of 15.41, conclude that there is a single cointegrating vector. However, at the 90% level, $\lambda_{trace}(1)$ statistic of 14.80894 exceeds the critical value of 13.33.

If we use the λ_{max} statistic, the null hypothesis of no cointegrating vectors ($r = 0$) against the specific alternative $r = 1$ is clearly rejected. The calculated value $\lambda_{max}(0, 1) = 30.14032$ exceeds the 95% and 90% critical values. Reject the null of no cointegration. To test $r = 1$ against the alternative of $r = 1$, note that the calculated value of $\lambda_{max}(1, 2)$ is 11.20663 whereas the critical values at the 95% and 90% significance levels are 14.07 and 12.07, respectively. Thus, conclude there is a single cointegrating vector.

Table 6.3
The λ_{max} and λ_{trace} Tests

Null Hypothesis	Alternative Hypothesis		95% Critical Value	90% Critical Value
λ_{trace} tests:		λ_{trace} value		
$r = 0$	$r > 0$	44.94926	29.68	26.79
$r \leq 1$	$r > 1$	14.80894	15.41	13.33
$r \leq 2$	$r > 2$	3.60231	3.76	2.69
λ_{max} tests:		λ_{max} value		
$r = 0$	$r = 1$	30.14032	20.97	18.60
$r = 1$	$r = 2$	11.2066	14.07	12.07
$r = 2$	$r = 3$	3.60231	3.76	2.69

Next, RATS prompts you for the variable to use for normalization in each of the vectors.[1] Since there is no particular reason to choose one variable over the others, enter 1 at each prompt (i.e, normalize each vector with respect to y). At this point, the JOHANSEN.400 procedure requests that you enter a filename. RATS uses this file to create a hardcopy of your output. Enter a name such as COINT.OUT. If you now halt execution of the program, you can verify that file contains the following information:

```
Autocorrelations in the error-process
Lag 1        2        3        4        5        6        7        8
-0.257    0.006    0.043    0.053   -0.216    0.111   -0.147    0.075
 0.046    0.006   -0.084   -0.079   -0.081   -0.129   -0.011    0.015
-0.198    0.035   -0.050    0.094   -0.072    0.068   -0.026   -0.012
```

The first-order autocorrelations in the error process in the Δy_t and Δx_t equations of -0.257 and -0.198 are distressingly large. It is best to reestimate the model using a lag length of two. Consider:

@johansen(lags=2) 71:1 95:4
 # y z x

As in the case of a single lag, normalize each vector with respect to variable 1 (i.e., y). The statistics on the dy, dz, and dw series are not presented here. In addition to the statistics concerning the first differences of each variable, RATS also displays:

---

[1] At this point, you may also choose to create graphs of the data and output.

```
Solving the eigenvalue problem and calculating the LR-tests

lambda, lambda-max- and tracetest
   0.32496    0.13401    0.02536
  38.51272   14.10061    2.51767
   2.51767   16.61829   55.13101
```

Now the ordered characteristic roots are $\lambda_1 = 0.32496$, $\lambda_2 = 0.13401$, and $\lambda_3 = 0.02536$. These are new value RATS uses to calculate the λ_{trace} and λ_{max} statistics. For example:

$$\lambda_{trace}(0) = -T \left[\ln(1 - \lambda_1) + \ln(1 - \lambda_2) + \ln(1 - \lambda_3) \right]$$
$$= -98 \left[\ln(1 - 0.32498) + \ln(1 - 0.13401) + \ln(1 - 0.02536) \right]$$
$$= 55.13101$$

The appropriate use of these statistics can be illustrated using Table 6.4. Consider the hypothesis that the variables are not cointegrated (so that the rank $\pi = 0$). Depending on the alternative hypothesis, there are two possible test statistics to use. If we are simply interested in the hypothesis that the variables are not cointegrated ($r = 0$) against the alternative of one or more cointegrating vectors ($r > 0$), use the $\lambda_{trace}(0)$ statistic. Since 55.13101 exceeds the 95% critical value of the λ_{trace} statistic, it is possible to reject the null hypothesis of no cointegrating vectors and accept the alternative of one or more cointegrating vectors. Next, we can use the $\lambda_{trace}(1)$ statistic to test the null of $r \leq 1$ against the alternative of two or three cointegrating vectors. In this case, the $\lambda_{trace}(1)$ statistic is 16.61829. Since 16.61829 exceeds the 95% critical value of 15.41, we can reject the null hypothesis at standard significance levels. At this point, conclude that there are two cointegrating vectors.

Table 6.4
The λ_{max} and λ_{trace} Tests

Null Hypothesis	Alternative Hypothesis		95% Critical Value	90% Critical Value
λ_{trace} tests:		λ_{trace} value		
$r = 0$	$r > 0$	55.13101	29.68	26.79
$r \leq 1$	$r > 1$	16.61829	15.41	13.33
$r \leq 2$	$r > 2$	2.51767	3.76	2.69
λ_{max} tests:		λ_{max} value		
$r = 0$	$r = 1$	38.51272	20.97	18.60
$r = 1$	$r = 2$	14.10061	14.07	12.07
$r = 2$	$r = 3$	2.51767	3.76	2.69

If you use the λ_{max} statistic, the null hypothesis of no cointegrating vectors ($r = 0$) against the specific alternative $r = 1$ is clearly rejected. The calculated value $\lambda_{max}(0, 1) = 38.51272$ exceeds the 95% critical value of 20.97. Note that the test of the null hypothesis $r = 1$ against the specific alternative $r = 2$ can be rejected at the 95% level. The calculated value of $\lambda_{max}(1, 2)$ is 14.10061 whereas the critical value at the 95% significance level is 14.07. Even though the actual data-generating process contains only one cointegrating vector, the realizations are such that researchers willing to use the 95% significance level would incorrectly conclude that there are two cointegrating vectors. Here, the 97.5% significance level (the critical value is 16.05) selects the correct number of cointegrating vectors. Of course, part of the problem is due to the fact that the model is estimated with a drift, when no drift is present in the data generating process.

Opening the output file to check for autocorrelation in the residuals reveals:

```
Autocorrelations in the error-process
Lag  1        2        3        4        5        6        7        8
   -0.003   -0.041    0.063   -0.010   -0.140   -0.029   -0.126    0.051
   -0.017    0.053   -0.075   -0.070   -0.054   -0.090   -0.043    0.054
   -0.020    0.002   -0.025    0.073   -0.005    0.040   -0.010   -0.046
```

Since the autocorrelations are all small, the model with two lags is satisfactory. At the prompt, a normalization was chosen with respect to variable y. RATS displays the β matrix with all variables normalized with respect to y, the associated speed of adjustment martix α, and the π matrix. At this point, all matrices are of order 3 x 3 since you have not specified the number of cointegrating vectors:

```
beta
  1.000    1.000    1.000
  1.042    0.662   -0.080
 -1.019   -0.911    0.199

alpha
 -0.546    0.144   -0.014
 -0.192    0.148    0.029
 -0.256    0.358    0.006

pi
 -0.416   -0.472    0.422
 -0.016   -0.105    0.067
  0.107   -0.031   -0.064
```

Next, RATS displays the menu:

choice H2: $\pi = \alpha\beta'$
choice H3: $\beta = H\Phi$
choice H4: $\alpha = A\Theta$
choice H5: $\beta = H\Phi$ & $\alpha=A\Theta'$

Choice H2 allows you to select the number of cointegrating vectors, choice H3 allows you to test restrictions on β, choice H4 allows you to test restrictions on α, and choice H5 allows you to test restrictions on both α and β. RATS informs you that choice H2 must be selected before performing any of the others. The reason is that the number of cointegrating vectors must be specified prior to imposing the restrictions.

Select choice H2 and at the prompt INPUT THE NUMBER OF COINTEGRATING VECTORS, enter the appropriate number. Since we know there is a single cointegrating vector, enter 1. RATS now displays the single normalized cointegrating vector β and associated speed of adjustment vector α:

```
beta
   1.000
   1.042
  -1.019

alpha
  -0.546
  -0.192
  -0.256
```

The estimated values of the β_i are close to their theoretical values (recall that the data was constructed imposing the long-run relationship $w_t = y_t + z_t$). The constant in the cointegrating vector (β_0) is not displayed; the long-run equilibrium relationship is:

$$\beta_0 + y_t + 1.042z_t - 1.019x_t = 0$$

The values of α are such that the coefficients on the error-correction term in the dy, dz, and dx equations are -0.546, -0.192, and -0.256, respectively.

2. Testing coefficient restrictions: Once you select the number of cointegrating vectors, you can impose restrictions on the values of β and/or α. At first, the way to input the restrictions into RATS may not seem straightforward. Consider the long-run equilibrium relationship:

$$\beta_1 y_t + \beta_2 z_t + \beta_3 x_t = 0$$

Now suppose you want to test the restriction that $\beta_1 = \beta_2$. From the menu, you select *choice H3: $\beta = H\Phi$*. In matrix form, the restriction can be written as:

$$\begin{bmatrix} \beta_1 \\ \beta_2 \\ \beta_3 \end{bmatrix} = \begin{bmatrix} 1 & 0 \\ 1 & 0 \\ 0 & 1 \end{bmatrix} \begin{bmatrix} \Phi_{11} \\ \Phi_{21} \end{bmatrix}$$

where Φ_{11} and Φ_{21} are arbitrary constants, and the matrix H is called the design matrix.

Thus, the restriction is equivalent to $\beta_1 = \Phi_{11}$, $\beta_2 = \Phi_{11}$, and $\beta_3 = \Phi_{21}$, so that $\beta_1 = \beta_2$ and β_3 is the arbitrary value Φ_{21}. Instead, suppose you want to test the restriction $\beta_1 = \beta_2 = -\beta_3$. In essence, there are **two** separate restrictions here: $\beta_1 = \beta_2$ *and* $\beta_1 = -\beta_3$. From the menu, select *choice H3: $\beta = H\Phi$*. In matrix form, this set of restrictions can be written as:

$$
\begin{bmatrix} \beta_1 \\ \beta_2 \\ \beta_3 \end{bmatrix} = \begin{bmatrix} 1 \\ 1 \\ -1 \end{bmatrix} \begin{bmatrix} \Phi_{11} \end{bmatrix}
$$

so that $\beta_1 = \Phi_{11}$, $\beta_2 = \Phi_{11}$, and $\beta_3 = -\Phi_{11}$ or $\beta_1 = \beta_2 = -\beta_3$. To generalize, suppose you find a single cointegrating vector for n variables and want to impose m restrictions on β. Form the matrix H with dimensions n x $(n-m)$ and the matrix of free parameters Φ with dimensions $(n-m)$ x 1. You must find the elements of H such that $\beta = H\Phi$. After you select *choice H3: $\beta = H\Phi$*, RATS will prompt you for the number of restrictions you want to impose. Enter the number and RATS will display the H matrix with the appropriate dimensions.[1] You then enter each element of H such that: $\beta = H\Phi$. RATS then reestimates the model with the restrictions imposed. Consider the output on the file COINT3.OUT:

Restriction 1: $\beta_1 = \beta_2$. After you select *choice H3: $\beta = H\Phi$*, RATS displays:

```
The Design-matrix
0.00   0.00
0.00   0.00
0.00   0.00
```

At the prompt *ENTER row, column, value*, enter 1, 1, 1. RATS now displays:
```
The Design-matrix
1.00   0.00
0.00   0.00
0.00   0.00
```

Now, at the prompt *ENTER row, column, value*, enter 2, 1, 1. RATS displays:
```
The Design-matrix
1.00   0.00
1.00   0.00
0.00   0.00
```

At the prompt *ENTER row, column, value*, enter 3, 2, 1. RATS displays:
```
The Design-matrix
1.00   0.00
1.00   0.00
0.00   1.00
```

---

[1] In some versions of the procedure, RATS will prompt you for each element of H.

Since the H matrix is in the appropriate form, at the prompt *ENTER row, column, value* simply press the ENTER key. RATS displays:[1]

```
The likelihood ratio test (CHI²(r*( 1 )))
   0.7615
```

With one degree of freedom, the marginal significance level of $\chi^2 = 0.7615$ is 0.38. If you normalize the restricted matrix with respect to y, the procedure also displays:

```
The restricted beta matrix
     1.0000            1.0000
     1.0000            1.0000
    -0.9989           -1.4825

The restricted alpha matrix
    -0.5574            0.0521
    -0.1555           -1.9242e-003
    -0.1839            0.0720
```

The restricted cointegrating vector is such that $y_t + z_t - 0.9989 x_t = 0$. The speed of adjustment terms in dy_t, dz_t, and dx_t equations are -0.5574, -0.1555, and -0.1839, respectively.

To test the restriction $\beta_1 = \beta_2 = -\beta_3$, again select *choice H3: $\beta = H\Phi$* from the displayed menu. RATS will prompt you for the number of restrictions you want to impose; enter 2 since you want to test two restrictions. RATS displays:

```
The Design-matrix
0.00
0.00
0.00
```

At the next three prompts, enter 1, 1, 1; 2, 1, 1; and 3, 2, -1, respectively. RATS displays:

```
The Design-matrix
 1.00
 1.00
-1.00
```

Press the ENTER key and RATS displays:

```
* Solving the eigenvalue problem *
The restricted eigenvectors
      4.4222

The likelihood ratio test (CHI²(r*( 2 )))
      0.7661
```

---

[1] In some version of JOHANSEN.400, the value 8.3048 is also displayed. This value should be ignored.

```
The restricted beta matrix
      1.0000
      1.0000
     -1.0000

The restricted alpha matrix
     -0.5558
     -0.1560
     -0.1804
```

With two degrees of freedom, $\chi^2 = 0.7661$ is less than the critical value for any conventional significance level. Do not reject the null hypothesis. Conclude the cointegrating vector is $y_t + z_t - x_t = 0$ and that the three speed of adjustment terms are -0.5558, -0.1560, and -0.1804.

Restrictions with multiple cointegrating vectors: JOHANSEN.400 does not allow you to separately restrict the cointegrating vectors. Any restriction must be imposed on all vectors. To make a point, suppose we used the results of the $\lambda_{max}(1, 2)$ test at the 90% level and concluded that there were two cointegrating vectors among the three variables. In this situation, β has a rank of two and the two cointegrating vectors can be written as:

$$\beta = \begin{bmatrix} \beta_{11} & \beta_{12} \\ \beta_{21} & \beta_{22} \\ \beta_{31} & \beta_{32} \end{bmatrix}$$

Now suppose you want to impose the restriction $\beta_{11} = \beta_{21}$ and $\beta_{12} = \beta_{22}$. Again, select *choice H3: $\beta = H\Phi$* and indicate that you want to impose one restriction (i.e., there is one restriction per cointegrating vector). RATS now displays the H matrix and you must enter each element of H such that $\beta = H\Phi$. Consider:

$$\begin{bmatrix} \beta_{11} & \beta_{12} \\ \beta_{21} & \beta_{22} \\ \beta_{31} & \beta_{32} \end{bmatrix} = \begin{bmatrix} 1 & 0 \\ 1 & 0 \\ 0 & 1 \end{bmatrix} \begin{bmatrix} \Phi_{11} & \Phi_{12} \\ \Phi_{21} & \Phi_{22} \end{bmatrix}$$

The restriction is such that $\beta_{11} = \beta_{21} = \Phi_{11}$, $\beta_{12} = \beta_{22} = \Phi_{12}$, and β_{31} and β_{31} are arbitrary constants. Now suppose you want to impose two restrictions on each cointegrating vector. Specifically, to test the restrictions $\beta_{11} = \beta_{21}$, $\beta_{11} = -\beta_{31}$, $\beta_{12} = \beta_{22}$, and $\beta_{12} = -\beta_{32}$, use:

$$\begin{bmatrix} \beta_{11} & \beta_{12} \\ \beta_{21} & \beta_{22} \\ \beta_{31} & \beta_{32} \end{bmatrix} = \begin{bmatrix} 1 \\ 1 \\ -1 \end{bmatrix} \begin{bmatrix} \Phi_{11} & \Phi_{12} \end{bmatrix}$$

Hence, the restriction is such that $\beta_{11} = \beta_{21} = -\beta_{31} = \Phi_{11}$ and $\beta_{12} = \beta_{22} = -\beta_{32} = \Phi_{12}$. The output from restricting the multiple cointegrating vectors is contained on the file COINT3.PRG. To generalize, suppose you find r cointegrating vectors for n variables and want to impose the same m restrictions on each column of β. Form the matrix H with dimensions (n x $(n-m)$) and the matrix of free parameters Φ with dimensions ($(n-m)$ x r). You must find the elements of H such that $\beta = H\Phi$. Testing restrictions on α employ the identical methodology. The α matrix has dimensions n x r. Form the (n x $(n-m)$) matrix A and the ($(n-m)$ x r) matrix Θ and select the elements of A such that $\alpha = A\Theta$. Additional details are provided in the next section.

Introduction to CATS in RATS

This section illustrates the Johansen methodology for CATS in RATS (or simply CATS) users by utilizing exactly the same data as in the Engle-Granger section. In sample program 1, the simulated variables y, z, and w are found to be cointegrated. All program statements are on the file labeled CATS.PRG. CATS writes some of the key output to a file you designate; in CATS.PRG, this file is called CATS.OUT. You can find both of these files of the data disk. If you installed CATS on the c:\cats directory, the procedure is compiled as follows:

```
source(noecho) c\cats\catsmain.src
```

After compiling, the standard way to invoke CATS is:

```
@cats(options) start end
# list of dependent variables
```

where: *start end*   The range of data to use. The procedure automatically adjusts for lag lengths.

list of dependent variables   The variables to include in the cointegration analysis.

The main options are:[1]

LAGS =   The number of lags to use in the VAR. The default is 2. Note that you must use
              at least one lag.
DETTREND= The type of deterministic components to include in the model. Use:
              NONE for a model without any deterministic components.
              CIMEAN for a model with a constant in the cointegrating vector(s).
              DRIFT for a model with a drift.
              CIDRIFT for a model with a time trend in the cointegration vector(s) and
              in the VAR portion of the model.
SEASON=   The number of seasonal dummy variables to include (the default is none). CATS
              includes s-1 seasonal dummy variables. For example, with quarterly data,
              season=4 includes three seasonal dummies.
BATCH   This option allows you to use CATS in batch mode. It is usually easier to use
              CATS in batch mode.

Example: You can obtain all of the results of the JOHANSEN.400 section using:
@cats(lags=2,detrend=drift,season=4,batch) 71:1 95:4
y z w

This specification calls for a model with two lags of dy, dz, and dw, a drift term, and three
seasonal dummy variables. Recall that this is the only form of the model that can be
estimated by JOHANSEN.400.

The first four program statements of CATS.PRG read the three variables into memory.
(*Note*: As opposed to JOHANSEN.400, CATS does not reserve the variable name w for its own
use. Hence, the program below can use the data file COINT1.PRN.) The fifth line is used to
compile the procedure.

```
cal 1971 1 4                         ;* Allocate space for 100 observations using the
all 4 1995:4                         ;*   artificial dates 1971:Q1 through 1995:Q4.
open data a:coint1.prn               ;* Modify this line if the data set is not on drive a:\.
source(noecho) c:\cats\catsmain.src  ;* Modify this line if CATSMAIN.SRC is not in the c:\cats
                                     ;*   directory.
open copy a:\cats.out                ;* Designate the output file as a:\cats.out.
```

The next two lines of CATS.PRG begin CATS. Given the results of the previous sections,
the model is estimated over the complete sample period using two lags of each variable. As
opposed to the results of the previous section, the option DETTREND=CIMEAN includes the
constant in the cointegrating vector.

---

[1] In addition to seasonal variables, CATS in RATS also allows you to work with weakly exogenous
variables and dummy variables. See the *CATS in RATS Manual* for additional details.

```
@cats(lags=2,dettrend=cimean,batch)  71:1 95:4
# y z w
```

Eigenv.	L-max	Trace	H0:r	p-r	L-max90	Trace90
0.3260	38.66	56.79	0	3	14.09	31.88
0.1403	14.82	18.12	1	2	10.29	17.79
0.0332	3.31	3.31	2	1	7.50	7.50

The λ_{max} and λ_{trace} statistics are displayed for the null hypotheses $r = 0$, 1, and 2 along with the critical values for the 90% significance level.[1] Moreover, CATS displays the β, α, and π matrices:

```
BETA (transposed)
    Y        Z        W        CONSTANT
  4.112    4.256   -4.178      0.055
 -2.314   -1.461    2.077      0.422
 -0.039    0.409   -0.560     -2.401

ALPHA
 -0.133   -0.059    0.028
 -0.040   -0.074   -0.054
 -0.053   -0.155   -0.008

PI
    Y        Z        W        CONSTANT
 -0.410   -0.468    0.417     -0.099
  0.008   -0.086    0.045      0.097
  0.140   -0.004   -0.095     -0.049
```

Note that the β matrix is such that the estimated system is:

$$4.112y_t + 4.256z_t - 4.178w_t + 0.055$$
$$-2.314y_t - 1.461z_t + 2.077w_t + 0.422$$
$$-0.039y_t + 0.409z_t - 0.560w_t - 2.401$$

1. **Determining the rank of π**: CATS reports the estimated values of the characteristic roots as $\lambda_1 = 0.3260$, $\lambda_2 = 0.1403$, and $\lambda_3 = 0.0332$. The λ_{max} and λ_{trace} statistics are displayed in the next columns and the 90% critical values are displayed in the last two columns. As in the previous section, these statistics are calculated such that:

$$\lambda_{trace}(0) = -T\,[\,\ln(1 - \lambda_1) + \ln(1 - \lambda_2) + \ln(1 - \lambda_3)\,]$$
$$= -98\,[\,\ln(1 - 0.3260) + \ln(1 - 0.1403) + \ln(1 - 0.0332)\,] = 56.79$$

---

[1] Note that CATS displays the Johansen and Nielson (1993) critical values instead of the familiar Osterwald-Lenum (1992) critical values reported Table C of this text. Use Table B.1 if there are no deterministic components in the model, Table B.2 if you include a constant in the cointegrating vector, and Table B.3 if you include a drift term. Note that only the λ_{trace} values are reported in the tables.

Consider the hypothesis that the variables are not cointegrated (so that the rank $\pi = 0$). Depending on the alternative hypothesis, there are two possible test statistics to use. If we are simply interested in the hypothesis that the variables are not cointegrated ($r = 0$) against the alternative of one or more cointegrating vectors ($r > 0$), use the $\lambda_{trace}(0)$ statistic. Since 56.79 exceeds the 90% critical value of the λ_{trace} statistic, it is possible to reject the null hypothesis of no cointegrating vectors and accept the alternative of one or more cointegrating vectors.

Next, we can use the $\lambda_{trace}(1)$ statistic to test the null of $r \leq 1$ against the alternative of two or three cointegrating vectors. In this case, the $\lambda_{trace}(1)$ statistic is 18.12. Since 18.12 exceeds the 90% critical value of 17.79 we can reject again the null hypothesis. Failing to reject an incorrect null hypothesis is always a danger of using wide confidence intervals. CATS does not display the 95% critical values. If you use the Osterwald-Lenum (1992) critical values shown in Table C, the 95% critical values for $r = 0$, $r = 1$, and $r = 2$ are 31.52, 17.95, and 8.18, respectively. With these critical values, it is possible to reject the null $r = 0$ (since 56.79 > 31.52), and the null $r \leq 1$ (since 18.12 > 17.75). At the 97.5% significance level, reject the null $r = 0$ (since 56.79 > 34.48) but do not reject the null $r = 1$ (since 18.12 < 20.08).

If you use the λ_{max} statistic, the null hypothesis of no cointegrating vectors ($r = 0$) against the specific alternative $r = 1$ is clearly rejected. The calculated value $\lambda_{max}(0, 1) = 38.66$ exceeds the 90% critical value of 14.09. Note that the test of the null hypothesis $r = 1$ against the specific alternative $r = 2$ can also be rejected at the 90%. The calculated value of $\lambda_{max}(1, 2)$ is 14.82 whereas the critical values at the 90% significance level is 10.29. Even though the actual data generating process contains only one cointegrating vector, the realizations are such that researchers willing to use the 90% significance level would incorrectly conclude that there are two cointegrating vectors. If you use the Osterwald-Lenum (1992) critical values shown in Table C, the 95% critical values for $r = 0$, $r = 1$, and $r = 2$ are 21.07, 14.90, and 8.18, respectively. With these critical values, it is possible to reject the null $r = 0$ (since 38.66 > 21.07), but not the null $r = 1$ (since 14.82 < 14.90).

Based on these tests, you should set the rank of π equal to 1. Select *RANK of pi* from the main menu and enter 1. RATS now displays:

```
EIGENVECTOR(S)  (transposed)
   Y         Z         W       CONSTANT
 4.1115    4.2556    -4.1783    0.0547
```

so that the cointegration relationship is $4.1115y_t + 4.2566z_t - 4.1783w_t + 0.0547 = 0$.

Next, CATS prompts you for the variable to use for normalization in each of the vectors. Since there is no particular reason to choose one variable over the others, enter 1 at each prompt (i.e., normalize each vector with respect to y). CATS displays the normalized cointegrating vector, the associated values of α_y, α_z, and α_w, and the *t*-statistics for the null hypotheses $\alpha_i = 0$:

```
BETA (transposed)
Y            Z            W            CONSTANT
1.000        1.035        -1.016       0.013

ALPHA                                  T-VALUES FOR ALPHA
DY                        -0.546       -4.526
DZ                        -0.166       -1.102
DW                        -0.219       -1.247
```

The estimated values of the β_i are close to their theoretical values (recall that the data was constructed imposing the long-run relationship $w_t = y_t + z_t$):

$$y_t + 1.035z_t - 1.016w_t + 0.013 = 0$$

The values of α are such that the coefficients on the error-correction term in the dy_t, dz_t, and dw_t equations are -0.546, -0.166, and -0.219, respectively. At conventional significance levels, only dy_t adjusts to a deviation from the long-run equilibrium relationship.

2. Testing coefficient restrictions: As in the previous section, once you select the number of cointegrating vectors, you can test restrictions on the resulting values of β and/or α. Suppose you want to test the restriction that the intercept is zero. From the menu, you select *Restrictions on subsets of β*. You are prompted for the number of groups: enter 1 since there is a single cointegrating vector. At the prompt *Input the Number of Restrictions*, enter 1 (since $\beta_0 = 0$ is a single restriction). In matrix form, the restriction can be written as:

$$\begin{bmatrix} \beta_1 \\ \beta_2 \\ \beta_3 \\ \beta_0 \end{bmatrix} = \begin{bmatrix} 1 & 0 & 0 \\ 0 & 1 & 0 \\ 0 & 0 & 1 \\ 0 & 0 & 0 \end{bmatrix} \begin{bmatrix} \Phi_{11} \\ \Phi_{21} \\ \Phi_{31} \end{bmatrix}$$

where Φ_{11}, Φ_{21} and Φ_{31} are arbitrary constants.

Thus, the restriction is equivalent to $\beta_1 = \Phi_{11}$, $\beta_2 = \Phi_{21}$, and $\beta_3 = \Phi_{31}$ and $\beta_0 = 0$. CATS displays:

```
beta'=H'*fi'

     Y          Z          W       CONSTANT
   0.00       0.00       0.00        0.00
   0.00       0.00       0.00        0.00
   0.00       0.00       0.00        0.00
```

The method of inputting the restrictions differs slightly from that of the previous section. First, the design matrix is transposed. As such, you must keep inputting restrictions until CATS displays:

```
Y        Z        W       CONSTANT
1.00     0.00     0.00     0.00
0.00     1.00     0.00     0.00
0.00     0.00     1.00     0.00
```

Second, the design matrix is filled row by row. Thus, at the prompt *ENTER ROW ELEMENT*, enter 1 (for the first element of row 1). At the prompt *INPUT VALUE*, enter the value of 1. Now at the new prompt *ENTER ROW ELEMENT*, just press the ENTER key to move to row 2. At the prompt *ENTER ROW ELEMENT*, enter 2 (for the second element of row 2) and at the prompt *INPUT VALUE*, enter the value of 1. Continue in this fashion until you complete row 3. CATS will display the restricted cointegrating vector and the χ^2 test results:

```
EIGENVECTOR(S) (transposed)
   Y          Z         W       CONSTANT
-4.1078    -4.2595    4.1850    0.0000

The LR test, CHISQ(1) =   0.01 , p-value = 0.92
```

At the next prompt, normalizing this vector with respect to *y* yields the restricted normalized cointegrating vector and the associated α values:

```
BETA (transposed)
Y          Z          W        CONSTANT
1.000      1.037     -1.019      0.000

ALPHA                     T-VALUES FOR ALPHA
DY               -0.544        -4.504
DZ               -0.167        -1.112
DW               -0.217        -1.237
```

Instead, suppose you want to test the **three** restrictions: $\beta_1 = \beta_2$, $\beta_1 = -\beta_3$, and $\beta_3 = 0$ (so that the normalized cointegrating vector has the form $y_t + z_t - w_t = 0$). In matrix form, the restrictions can be written as:

$$\begin{bmatrix} \beta_1 \\ \beta_2 \\ \beta_3 \\ \beta_4 \end{bmatrix} = \begin{bmatrix} 1 \\ 1 \\ -1 \\ 0 \end{bmatrix} [\Phi_{11}]$$

From the menu, you select *Restrictions on subsets of β.* You are prompted for the number of groups: enter 1. At the prompt *Input the Number of Restrictions*, enter 3. CATS displays:

```
beta'=H'*fi'
Y          Z          W        CONSTANT
0.00       0.00       0.00       0.00
```

As before, continue to input restrictions until the design matrix is:

```
Y       Z       W        CONSTANT
1.00    1.00    -1.00    0.00
```

CATS will display the restricted cointegrating vector and the Chi-square test results:

```
EIGENVECTOR(S) (transposed)
Y        Z        W        CONSTANT
4.2898   4.2898   -4.2898  0.0000
```

The LR test, CHISQ(3) =   1.81 , p-value = 0.61

At the next prompt, normalizing this vector with respect to y yields the restricted normalized cointegrating vector and the associated α values:

```
BETA (transposed)
Y        Z        W        CONSTANT
1.000    1.000    -1.000   0.000


ALPHA                     T-VALUES FOR ALPHA
DY            -0.526      -4.118
DZ            -0.089      -0.565
DW            -0.108      -0.587
```

Accept the null hypothesis that the cointegrating vector is $y_t + z_t - w_t = 0$ (the marginal significance level is 0.61). Again, the error-correction term is significant only in the dy_t equation.

Although the model appears to perform adequately, an analysis of the residuals should be performed before being content with the results. From the main CATS menu, select *RESIDUAL ANALYSIS*; some of the displayed diagnostic statistics include:

```
TEST FOR AUTOCORRELATION
L-B(24), CHISQ(204)  = 198.189, p-val = 0.60
LM(1),   CHISQ(9)    =   4.437, p-val = 0.88
LM(4),   CHISQ(9)    =  13.809, p-val = 0.13

TEST FOR NORMALITY
CHISQ(6)             =   2.673, p-val = 0.85
```

The Ljung-Box test suggests that the first 24 residuals are serially uncorrelated and the residuals appear normal. You can obtain a high resolution plot of some key diagnostic statistics from the *RESIDUALS* option (choice 3) from the *GRAPHICS MENU*. Figure 6.4 shows the output for the dy series (CATS produces a similar set of diagrams for each of the series). The actual and fitted values of dy do not indicate any periods in which the model fits poorly and the standardized residuals seem to be normally distributed. The standardized residuals do not show any periods of extreme volatility and the ACF of the residuals does not show evidence of autocorrelation. The model appears to be satisfactory.

Restrictions with Multiple Cointegrating Vectors: To illustrate process of restricting multiple cointegrating, suppose we used the results of the $\lambda_{max}(1, 2)$ test at the 90% level and

Figure 6.4: Output from the RESIDUALS Option of the GRAPHICS Menu

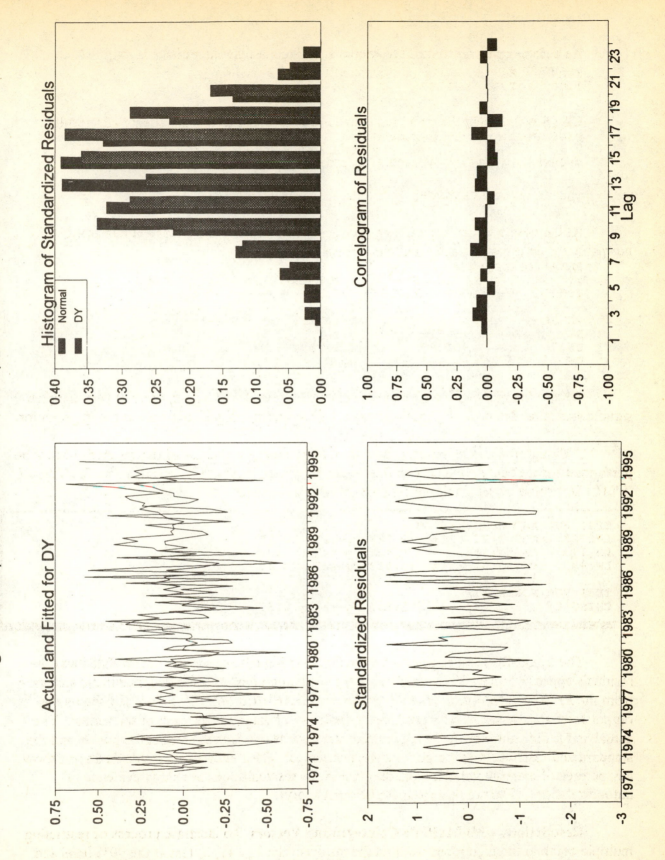

concluded that there were two cointegrating vectors among the three variables. In this situation, β has a rank of 2 and the two cointegrating vectors can be written as:

$$\beta = \begin{bmatrix} \beta_{11} & \beta_{12} \\ \beta_{21} & \beta_{22} \\ \beta_{31} & \beta_{32} \\ \beta_{01} & \beta_{02} \end{bmatrix}$$

Now suppose you want to impose the restriction $\beta_{11} = \beta_{21}$ and $\beta_{11} = -\beta_{31}$ on the first cointegrating vector and $\beta_{12} = \beta_{22}$ and $\beta_{12} = -\beta_{32}$ on the second. Return to the choice *RANK of pi* from the main CATS menu and enter 2. RATS now displays the two vectors:

```
Re-normalisation of the eigenvectors

EIGENVECTOR(S) (transposed)
Y            Z            W            CONSTANT
   4.1115       4.2556      -4.1783       0.0547
  -2.3145      -1.4608       2.0773       0.4224
```

At the prompt, normalize with respect to variable 1 to obtain the two most significant vectors, and the associated values of α:

```
The matrices based on 2 cointegration vectors

BETA (transposed)
      Y            Z            W            CONSTANT
   1.000        1.035       -1.016        0.013
   1.000        0.631       -0.898       -0.182

ALPHA                                     T-VALUES FOR ALPHA
DY               -0.546      0.137        -4.622      2.058
DZ               -0.166      0.171        -1.126      2.068
DW               -0.219      0.358        -1.340      3.897
```

Again, select *choice H3: $\beta = H\Phi$* and indicate that you want to impose *2* restriction (i.e., there are 2 restrictions per cointegrating vector). RATS now displays the *H* matrix and you must input each element of *H* such that $\beta = H\Phi$. Consider:

$$\begin{bmatrix} \beta_{11} & \beta_{12} \\ \beta_{21} & \beta_{22} \\ \beta_{31} & \beta_{32} \\ \beta_{01} & \beta_{02} \end{bmatrix} = \begin{bmatrix} 1 & 0 \\ 1 & 0 \\ -1 & 0 \\ 0 & 1 \end{bmatrix} \begin{bmatrix} \Phi_{11} & \Phi_{12} \\ \Phi_{21} & \Phi_{22} \end{bmatrix}$$

As such $\beta_{11} = \beta_{21} = -\beta_{31} = \Phi_{11}$, $\beta_{12} = \beta_{22} = -\beta_{32} = \Phi_{12}$, and β_{31} and β_{31} are arbitrary constants. CATS displays:

```
beta'=H'*fi'
   Y         Z         W       CONSTANT
 0.00      0.00      0.00       0.00
 0.00      0.00      0.00       0.00
```

You must input the restrictions row by row until CATS displays:

```
   Y         Z         W       CONSTANT
 1.00      1.00     -1.00       0.00
 0.00      0.00      0.00       1.00
```

CATS displays the restricted cointegrating vector and χ^2 test results:

```
EIGENVECTOR(S) (transposed)
   Y         Z         W           CONSTANT
4.4047    4.4047    -4.4047       0.1754
0.3043    0.3043    -0.3043       1.0222
```

```
The LR test, CHISQ(4) =   13.83 , p-value = 0.01
```

Reject the restriction at the 0.01 level; the two cointegrating vectors cannot be written as:

$$y_t + z_t - w_t + \beta_{01} = 0$$
$$y_t + z_t - w_t + \beta_{02} = 0$$

Additional Exercises

1. The Engle-Granger methodology has a degree of ambiguity since any of the variables can be the "left-hand-side" variable. Modify COINT1.PRG such that you:

   (a) Estimate the long-run equilibrium relationship using dz as the dependent variable and check the residuals for stationarity.

   (b) Estimate the error-correction model using the residuals from the dz equation as the error-correction term.

2. Sample program 2 demonstrated that the interest rates *tbill*, *r3*, and *r10* are cointegrated. However, Figure 6.3 suggests that bilateral pairs may be cointegrated (e.g., *tbill* may be cointegrated with *r3* and *r3* may be cointegrated with *r10*).

   (a) Use the Engle-Granger methodology to check for cointegrating relationships between the bilateral pairs of interest rates.

(b) How may cointegrating vectors should you find if each bilateral pair of interest rates is $CI(1, 1)$? Use the Johansen methodology to determine the number of cointegrating vectors for the three rates.

3. CATS users should reproduce the results of the JOHANSEN.400 section. JOHANSEN.400 necessarily estimated a model with a drift term and seasonal dummy variables. Open COINT3.PGM, compile CATSMAIN.SRC, and replace the line:

```
@johansen(lags=2) 71:1 95:4 with @cats(lags=2,detrend=drift,season=4,batch).
```

4. This advanced exercise will enable you perform innovation accounting on an error-correction model. If you need help, the file labeled ECM.PRG contains the necessary program steps.[1] Follow the steps in COINT1.PRG so as to read y, z, and w into memory. Take the first difference of each variable.

(a) Use LINREG to estimate the long run equilibrium relationship between y, z, and w. Use y_t as the dependent variable and do not include a constant. Store the residuals as the variable ec.

(b) Use the following instructions to estimate the system of equations:
    system 1 to 3
    variables dy dz dw
    lags 1 to 2
    det constant ec{1}
    equation(identity) 4 ec
    # y{1} z{1} w{1}
    associate 4
    # 1 -%beta(1) -%beta(2)
    end(system)
    estimate(noftests,outsigma=v) / 1

(c) Use the following instructions to obtain the variance decompositions:
    errors 4 8 v
    # 1
    # 2
    # 3
    # 4

(d) Modify the program so as to:
    (i)   use a lag length of one
    (ii) include a constant in the cointegrating vector, and
    (iii) obtain the impulse responses.

---

[1] I would like to thank Richard Clarida (Columbia University) for suggesting this method.

Statistical Tables

Table A   Empirical Cumulative Distribution of τ

	Probability of a Smaller Value							
	0.01	0.025	0.05	0.10	0.90	0.95	0.975	0.99
Sample Size								
No Constant or Time ($a_0 = a_2 = 0$)				τ				
25	-2.66	-2.26	-1.95	-1.60	0.92	1.33	1.70	2.16
50	-2.62	-2.25	-1.95	-1.61	0.91	1.31	1.66	2.08
100	-2.60	-2.24	-1.95	-1.61	0.90	1.29	1.64	2.03
250	-2.58	-2.23	-1.95	-1.62	0.89	1.29	1.63	2.01
300	-2.58	-2.23	-1.95	-1.62	0.89	1.28	1.62	2.00
∞	-2.58	-2.23	-1.95	-1.62	0.89	1.28	1.62	2.00
Constant ($a_2 = 0$)				τ_μ				
25	-3.75	-3.33	-3.00	-2.62	-0.37	0.00	0.34	0.72
50	-3.58	-3.22	-2.93	-2.60	-0.40	-0.03	0.29	0.66
100	-3.51	-3.17	-2.89	-2.58	-0.42	-0.05	0.26	0.63
250	-3.46	-3.14	-2.88	-2.57	-0.42	-0.06	0.24	0.62
500	-3.44	-3.13	-2.87	-2.57	-0.43	-0.07	0.24	0.61
∞	-3.43	-3.12	-2.86	-2.57	-0.44	-0.07	0.23	0.60
Constant + Time				τ_τ				
25	-4.38	-3.95	-3.60	-3.24	-1.14	-0.80	-0.50	-0.15
50	-4.15	-3.80	-3.50	-3.18	-1.19	-0.87	-0.58	-0.24
100	-4.04	-3.73	-3.45	-3.15	-1.22	-0.90	-0.62	-0.28
250	-3.99	-3.69	-3.43	-3.13	-1.23	-0.92	-0.64	-0.31
500	-3.98	-3.68	-3.42	-3.13	-1.24	-0.93	-0.65	-0.32
∞	-3.96	-3.66	-3.41	-3.12	-1.25	-0.94	-0.66	-0.33

Table B   Empirical Distribution of Φ

Probability of a Smaller Value

Sample size n	0.90	0.95	0.975	0.99
		Φ_1		
25	4.12	5.18	6.30	7.88
50	3.94	4.86	5.80	7.06
100	3.86	4.71	5.57	6.70
250	3.81	4.63	5.45	6.52
500	3.79	4.61	5.41	6.47
∞	3.78	4.59	5.38	6.43
		Φ_2		
25	4.67	5.68	6.75	8.21
50	4.31	5.13	5.94	7.02
100	4.16	4.88	5.59	6.50
250	4.07	4.75	5.40	6.22
500	4.05	4.71	5.35	6.15
∞	4.03	4.68	5.31	6.09
		Φ_3		
25	5.91	7.24	8.65	10.61
50	5.61	6.73	7.81	9.31
100	5.47	6.49	7.44	8.73
250	5.39	6.34	7.25	8.43
500	5.36	6.30	7.20	8.34
∞	5.34	6.25	7.16	8.27

TABLE C Empirical Distributions of the λ_{max} and λ_{trace} Statistics

n-r	90%	95%	97.5%	99%	90%	95%	97.5%	99%

λ_{max} and λ_{trace} statistics with drift

n-r			λ_{max}				λ_{trace}	
1	2.69	3.76	4.95	6.65	2.69	3.76	4.95	6.65
2	12.07	14.07	16.05	18.63	13.33	15.41	17.52	20.04
3	18.60	20.97	23.09	25.52	26.79	29.68	32.56	35.65
4	24.73	27.07	28.98	32.24	43.95	47.21	50.35	54.46
5	30.90	33.46	35.71	38.77	64.84	68.52	71.80	76.07

λ_{max} and λ_{trace} statistics with a constant in the cointegrating vector

n-r			λ_{max}				λ_{trace}	
1	6.50	8.18	9.72	11.65	6.50	8.18	9.72	11.65
2	12.91	14.90	17.07	19.19	15.66	17.95	20.08	23.52
3	18.90	21.07	22.89	25.75	28.71	31.52	34.48	37.22
4	24.78	27.14	29.16	32.14	45.23	48.28	51.54	55.43
5	30.84	33.32	35.80	38.78	66.49	70.60	74.04	78.87

Source: Osterwald-Lenum (1992).

References

Bell, W. and S. Hilmer. "Issues Involved with the Seasonal Adjustment of Economic Time Series." *Journal of Business and Economic Statistics* 2, (1984), 291-320.

Bernanke, Ben. "Alternative Explanations of Money-Income Correlation." *Carnegie-Rochester Conference Series on Public Policy* 25 (1986), 49 - 100.

Beverage, Stephen and Charles Nelson. "A New Approach to Decomposition of Economic Time Series into Permanent and Transitory Components with Particular Attention to Measurement of the Business Cycle." *Journal of Monetary Economics* 7 (1981), 151-74.

Bollerslev, Tim. "Generalized Autoregressive Conditional Heteroscedasticity." *Journal of Econometrics* 31 (1986), 307-27.

Box, George and Gwilym Jenkins. *Time Series Analysis, Forecasting, and Control.* (Holden Day: San Francisco) 1976.

Campbell, John Y. and Pierre Perron. "Pitfalls and Opportunities: What Macroeconomists Should Know About Unit Roots." *NBER Working Paper Series: Technical Working Paper 100.* (April 1991).

Dickey, David and Wayne A. Fuller. "Distribution of the Estimates for Autoregressive time Series With a Unit Root." *Journal of the American Statistical Association* 74 (1979), 427-431.

_____, "Likelihood Ratio Statistics for Autoregressive Time Series with a Unit Root." *Econometrica* 49 (1981), 1057-1072.

Dickey, David, W. Bell and R. Miller. "Unit Roots in Time Series Models: Tests and Implications." *American Statistician* 40 (1986), 12-26.

Dickey, David and S. Pantula. "Determining the Order of Differencing in Autoregressive Processes." *Journal of Business and Economic Statistics* 15 (1987), 455-61.

Doan, Thomas. *RATS User's Manual.* (Estima: Evanston, Il.) 1992.

Enders, Walter. *Applied Econometric Time Series.* (John Wiley and Sons: New York) 1995.

_____, "ARIMA and Cointegration Tests of Purchasing Power Parity." *Review of Economics and Statistics* 70 (1988), 504-08.

Engle, Robert F. "Autoregressive Conditional Heteroscedasticity with Estimates of the Variance of United Kingdom Inflation." *Econometrica* 50 (1982), 987-1007.

_____, and Tim Bollerslev. "Modelling the Persistence of Conditional Variances." *Econometric Reviews* 5 (1986), 1 - 50.

_____, and Clive W. J. Granger. "Cointegration and Error-Correction: Representation, Estimation, and Testing." *Econometrica* 55 (1987), 251-276.

_____, and David Kraft. "Multiperiod Forecast Error Variances of Inflation Based on the ARCH Model." in A. Zellner, ed., *Applied Time Series Analysis of Economic Data.* (Bureau of the Census: Washington, D.C.) 1983. pp. 293-302.

_____, David Lilien and Russell Robins. "Estimating Time Varying Risk Premia in the Term Structure: The ARCH-M Model." *Econometrica* 55 (1987), 391-407.

_____, and B. Yoo. "Forecasting and Testing in Cointegrated Systems." *Journal of Econometrics* 35 (1987), 143-59.

Fuller, Wayne. *Introduction to Statistical Time Series.* (John Wiley and Sons: New York). 1976.

Granger, Clive and P. Newbold. "Spurious Regressions in Econometrics." *Journal of Econometrics 2* (1974), 111-20.

Hylleberg, S., R. Engle, C. Granger, and B. Yoo. "Seasonal Integration and Cointegration." *Journal of Econometrics* 44 (1990), 215-38.

Johansen, Soren. "Statistical Analysis of Cointegration Vectors." *Journal of Economic Dynamics and Control* 12 (1988), 231-254.

_____, "Estimation and Hypothesis testing of Cointegrating Vectors in Gaussian Vector Autoregressive Models." *Econometrica* 59 (1991), 1551-80.

Johansen, Soren, and Katerina Juselius. "Maximum Likelihood Estimation and Inference on Cointegration with Application to the Demand For Money." *Oxford Bulletin of Economics and Statistics* 52 (1990), 169-209.

_____, "Testing Structural Hypotheses in a Multivariate Cointegration Analysis of PPP and the UIP for UK." *Journal of Econometrics* 53 (1992), 211-44.

Johansen, Soren, and B. Nielson. *Asymptotics for Cointegration Rank Tests in the Presence of Intervention Dummies.* (University of Copenhagen Institute of Mathematical Statistics: Denmark). 1993.

Ljung, G. and George Box. "On a Measure of Lack of Fit in Time Series Models." *Biometrica* 65 (1978), 297-303.

Osterwald-Lenum, M. "A Note with Fractiles of the Asymptotic Distribution of the Maximum Likelihood Cointegration Rank Test Statistics: Four Cases." *Oxford Bulletin of Economics and Statistics* 54 (1992), 461-72.

Perron, Pierre. "The Great Crash, The Oil Price Shock, and the Unit Root Hypothesis." *Econometrica* 57 (1989), 1361-1401.

Phillips, Peter. "Understanding Spurious Regressions in Econometrics." *Journal of Econometrics* 33 (1986), 311-40.

Phillips, Peter and Pierre Perron. "Testing for a Unit Root in Time Series Regression." *Biometrica* 75 (1988) 335-46.

Said, S. and David Dickey. "Testing for Unit Roots in Autoregressive-Moving Average Models with Unknown Order." *Biometrica* 71 (1984), 599-607.

Sims, Christopher. "Macroeconomics and Reality." *Econometrica* 48 (1980), 1-49.

_____. "Are Forecasting Models Usable for Policy Analysis?" *Federal Reserve Bank of Minneapolis Quarterly Review* (Winter 1986) 3-16.

Stock, James. "Asymptotic Properties of Least-Squares Estimators of Cointegrating Vectors." *Econometrica* 55 (1987), 1035-56.

_____, and Mark Watson. "Testing for Common Trends." *Journal of the American Statistical Association* 83 (Dec. 1988), 1097-1107.

NOTES

NOTES

NOTES

NOTES

NOTES

NOTES

NOTES

NOTES

_____

NOTES

NOTES

NOTES

_____

NOTES